Tourists and Tourism

BERG

Ethnicity and Identity

SERIES

ISSN: 1354-3628

General Editors:
Shirley Ardener, **Founding Director, Centre for Cross-Cultural Research on Women, University of Oxford**

Tamara Dragadze, **School of Slavonic and East European Studies, University of London**

Jonathan Webber, **Institute of Social and Cultural Anthropology, University of Oxford**

Books previously published in the Series
Sharon Macdonald (ed.), *Inside European Identities: Ethnography in Western Europe*

Joanne Eicher (ed.), *Dress and Ethnicity*

Jeremy MacClancy (ed.), *Sport, Identity and Ethnicity*

Tourists and Tourism

Identifying with People and Places

EDITED BY
Simone Abram, Jacqueline Waldren and Donald V.L. Macleod

Oxford • New York

First published in 1997 by
Berg
Editorial offices:
150 Cowley Road, Oxford, OX4 1JJ, UK
70 Washington Square South, New York, NY 10012, USA

Berg is the imprint of Oxford International Publishers Ltd.

Library of Congress Cataloging-in-Publication Data

A catalogue record for this book is available from the Library of Congress.

British Library Cataloguing-in-Publication Data

A catalogue record for this book is available from the British Library.

ISBN   1 85973 900 8 (Cloth)
1 85973 905 9 (Paper)

Typeset by JS Typesetting, Wellingborough, Northants.
Printed in the United Kingdom by WBC Book Manufacturers, Bridgend,
Mid Glamorgan.

Contents

Acknowledgements

The articles in this collection were all presented in the Ethnicity and Identity seminar series entitled 'Tourism: Construction and Deconstruction of Identity' at the Institute of Social and Cultural Anthropology in 1994, with the exception of those by Niels Sampath and Hazel Tucker, who kindly contributed their papers afterwards. We have renamed the book to reflect the emphasis in the papers on the negotiation of feelings of identity by participants in tourist encounters. Thus we consider both tourists as people and tourism as a phenomenon, considering the interaction of notions of identity within tourist encounters.

The editors owe much to the organisers of the Ethnicity and Identity series, Shirley Ardener, Tamara Dragadze and Jonathan Webber for their instigation of the seminars and, hence, this collection.

We should also like to offer our thanks to Tamara Kohn, for her helpful comments, and the attentive audience that offered constructive comments and discussion during the seminar series.

Simone Abram
Jacqueline Waldren
Donald V. L. Macleod

Notes on Contributors

Simone Abram is a Research Fellow at the University of Wales, Cardiff. In 1994 she gained a D.Phil. in Social Anthropology from Oxford University, and her research since has concerned public participation in the English planning system.

Connie Atkinson is a former New Orleans, Louisiana (USA) journalist who is now a researcher at the Institute of Popular Music, University of Liverpool, looking at popular music's role in the urban regeneration strategies of Liverpool and New Orleans.

Sara Cohen is a lecturer at the Institute of Popular Music, University of Liverpool. In 1987 she was awarded a D.Phil. in Social Anthropology from Oxford University, and she has since published a book and numerous articles based on ethnographic research on popular music in Britain.

Michael Hitchcock is Professor of Tourism at the University of North London. He has worked at Liverpool Museum and the Horniman Museum in London, and was Senior Lecturer in South-East Asian Development Sociology at the University of Hull.

Tamara Kohn is a Lecturer in Anthropology at the University of Durham. She has carried out fieldwork in the Scottish Hebrides, east Nepal, and north-east England. Her work has focused on the experiences of incomers, intermarriage, tourism, and the creation of identity. Recent publications include 'Incomers and fieldworkers: a comparative study of social experience', in K. Hastrup and P. Hervik (eds), *Social Experience And Anthropological Knowledge*, Routledge, 1994 and 'She came out of the field and into my home: reflections, dreams and a search for anthropological method', in A. Cohen and N. Rapport (eds), *Questions Of Consciousness*, Routledge, 1995.

Donald V. L. Macleod was Visiting Professor in Cultural Anthropology at Macalaster College, USA in 1995–6, and has tutored at Oxford and London Universities. His D.Phil. (Oxford 1993) looked at change in a Canary Island fishing settlement, and he has since been researching into globalization, political ecology, human identity and alternative tourism.

Mark Nuttall is a Lecturer in the Department of Sociology, University of Aberdeen. He is also Affiliate Assistant Professor of Anthropology at the University of Alaska, Fairbanks. His publications include *Arctic Homeland: kinship, community and development in northwest Greenland* (University of Toronto Press, 1992) and *White Settlers: the impact of rural repopulation in Scotland* with Charles Jedrej (Harwood Academic Publishers, 1996).

Niels M. Sampath is a D.Phil. candidate in Social Anthropology at the University of Oxford. Between 1986 and 1989 he spent 21 months in Trinidad researching rural East Indian masculine identity. His ongoing research interests include economic migration and the anthropology of flight and aviation.

King Chung Siu is an Assistant Professor in the School of Design, Hong Kong Polytechnic University. He teaches and writes about cultural issues related to art and design education in Hong Kong and is now researching into art education in the People's Republic of China.

Nick Stanley is Director of Research at Birmingham Institute of Art and Design, University of Central England. His research has largely been in the anthropology of visual representation in both photography and museology. His publications include *Recording Island Melanesia* (Pacific Arts, 1994), *Creating Vision: photography in education*, with S. Isherwood (Cornerhouse Press, 1994) and *Representing the Past as the Future: the Shenzhen Chinese Folk Culture Villages and the marketing of Chinese identity* with King Chung Siu (Journal of Museum Ethnography, 1995).

Ken Teague is Deputy Keeper of Anthropology at the Horniman Museum in London. His main fieldwork was on Nepalese material culture, but extensive travel in Asia since before the development of mass tourism has led to his interest in tourism studies generally. He has published extensively in the fields of Asian studies and Museum studies.

Hazel Tucker completed an MA in Social Anthropology at the University of Durham in 1995. She is now undertaking doctoral research, also at Durham, and is continuing to investigate the 'tourist site' of Cappadokya in central Turkey.

Jacqueline Waldren is a Tutor and part-time Lecturer at the University of Oxford and Oxford Brookes University, and is Research Associate at the Centre for Cross-Cultural Research on Women at Queen Elizabeth House, University of Oxford. Her latest publication is entitled *Insiders and Outsiders: Paradise and Reality in Mallorca* and her current research concerns the impact of tourism and development on concepts of gender and sexuality in various Spanish-speaking countries.

Introduction: Tourists and Tourism — Identifying with People and Places

Simone Abram and
Jacqueline Waldren

Over the past decade there has been an explosion of interest in tourism from within social anthropology, geography and sociology. More and more students of ethnography are setting out to engage in fieldwork on 'tourism', yet the range of publications available to them is still limited. While the vast majority of published books on tourism concern economic or planning aspects of tourism as a business, only a tiny (although steadily increasing) number of studies consider the meanings of the social relations gathered under the umbrella of 'tourist encounters', despite the general acknowledgement that tourism effects social change. Mass tourism is tainted with the imagery of a totalising modernity that tarnishes all it touches, destroying 'authentic cultures' and polluting earthly 'paradises', so that it has become a truism to state that tourism destroys the very object of its desire. However, the very pervasiveness of tourism, as a way of thinking and of living in a 'post-' modern/structural/colonial world has yet to be related to contemporary discussions of the finer issues in social anthropology. This collection thus aims to address the relationship between issues of cultural, ethnic or national identities and the notions and expectations of tourists and those whom they visit.

Tourism

Many studies of tourism begin by stating the enormous economic growth of the 'tourism industry' in recent years (e.g. Boniface and Fowler 1993:

1

xi, 2). The post-war boom in tourism, and the economic changes this heralded, are offered up to the reader, either to contrast the economic approach with an anthropological approach, or to signal the importance of tourism as a serious subject, one that justifies an academic analysis. Whilst it may still be true that there are academics who refuse to take seriously the study of holidays and adverts, this need hardly concern the growing body of students of tourism, be they economists, sociologists, anthropologists or others, for whom the study of tourism requires no special justification. What is rather more problematic, and may underlie this clinging to economic context, is that there is confusion over the definition of tourism. It may be that we cling to the economic figures to disguise our unease with the all-encompassing category of tourism, which we know to be more highly differentiated than these categorical statements would suggest.

Much of the early research in the anthropology and sociology of tourism was concerned with defining the subject. Smith (1978), for example, or Erik Cohen (1984) attempted to define and typologise tourism and tourists, to delimit the study, grounding it in a practice or an identity. As Kohn notes (this volume, Chapter 1), many authors still begin by trying to define tourism, and these attempts box in the parameters of their studies and presuppose a limited role for tourists. However, each typology of tourism begs questions, and can be challenged. If, as Smith has it, 'in general a tourist is a temporarily leisured person who voluntarily visits a place away from home for the purpose of experiencing a change' (1978), then how do we include visitors who become residents (Kohn, Waldren, Macleod, this volume, Chapters 1, 3, 7) or business tourists in the category? Or if tourism is 'a leisure activity which presupposes its opposite, namely regulated and organised work' (Urry 1990: 2), then is there a semantic confusion in the idea of a working holiday? Picking at the details of typologies in this way might seem small-minded, but it indicates something that we take for granted: that 'tourism' is a word only loosely associated with a phenomenon, and that this phenomenon is not one, but many sets of practices, with few clear boundaries but some central ideas. Rather than posit a new typology of tourism, we might accept that it is one of Needham's 'polythetic classifications' (1975: 36), defined not by neat boundaries but by common features, by 'family resemblances' rather than the fulfilment of prescriptive criteria. In this sense, we resort frequently to the economic data on tourism not only to represent the norms of tourism, which we then reconsider, but to locate tourism as a field of study, to find subjects to compare.

Tourists

The same difficulties arise with the identification of 'tourists'. Each chapter in this volume challenges our assumptions of the dichotomies common in tourism studies. As Abram asks in this volume, 'is it possible to divide tourist from non-tourist, tourist-season from out-of-season, performance from "reality"?' The answer, made explicit by Kohn, is that 'the category of tourist is extremely pliable, and over time visitors to a particular locale may transcend their positions as tourists and make the place a regular haunt or even "home"'. The foundational (structural) division of 'hosts' and 'guests' (Smith 1978), analogous (or, rather, metaphorical) to that between 'locals' and 'tourists', disguises so many further divisions that it is no longer an adequate basis for anthropological enquiry. Knight, for example, explains that '[the] usage of the term hosts joins together people with quite different relationships to the visitors, placing those who have direct contact with, or indeed direct economic benefit from the presence of, tourists, alongside those with no such direct connection' (1996: 166). The term 'hosts' can no longer suffice as an analytical identification, but becomes the starting-point for further enquiry.

The impossibility of identifying a 'host community', even by symbolic boundaries, parallels debates over how any community can be said to 'exist'. Macleod (this volume, Chapter 7) illustrates the difficulty with which a community is identified or a categorisation located, by demonstrating the slipperiness of the term 'alternative traveller' and its lack of material markers. For Tucker, though, it is a commonality of expectations and ideology that 'identifies' tourists, in relation to the residents of a Turkish village (this volume, Chapter 6). Anthony Cohen's redefinition of community as the place 'where one acquires culture' (1985: 15) opposes the identity of those within symbolic community boundaries with the difference of those outside them, but Strathern (1981) had already shown that the identification of those 'inside' was like the desert mirage, disappearing further into the distance as one approached. The symbolism of the boundaries was supposed to allow flexibility, as they could be constantly redrawn according to context, to be more or less inclusive. However, while contributors to this volume do show how 'localness' and 'belonging' are constantly redefined, they go somewhat further in denying that any static notion of community can be sustained over time. In other words, it is not that the boundaries exist, and can be variously expressed; rather, that if community can be said to have 'existence', then it does so only through its expressions. Thus, the 'community' is not a 'thing' with independent existence but, rather, a relational concept that is articulated through actions, discourse and symbols. It is thus constituted by its representations, and, as Sara Cohen shows (this volume, Chapter 4), its performance.

Identity

If this is the case, then the argument about community is a reworking of the question of identity itself: how do people identify with each other, and in opposition to different others? Whilst this notion of 'identity' is often portrayed as something handed down, or acquired at birth, we must differentiate, once again, between emic and etic notions. 'Identity' is not solely an analytical term, and many of the people portrayed in this collection use the term in their own ways. In the spirit Macdonald proposes, this collection explores the 'ways in which identities are defined and experienced by various peoples themselves' (1993: 6); but we cannot do this on the assumption that such peoples have not been exposed to, or even party to, the theoretical discussion of identity that has been so prominent in recent years. In this sense, we can disagree with the 'objects' of our studies, and engage in dialogue with them about the meaning of 'identity'.

For Hall, this question of identifying, with and in opposition to, describes a discursive activity; identity does not consist of some authentic essence, but is a strategic and positional activity (1996). In other words, identities are not the sign of an 'identical, naturally-constituted unity' but are 'the product of the marking of differences and exclusion' (ibid., p. 5). In his view, 'identities can function as points of identification and attachment only *because* of their capacity to exclude, to leave out, to render "outside"', and the unities that identities appear to proclaim are 'constructed within the play of power and exclusion' (ibid.). Thus, identity is not a fixed point from which to make exclusions, but is actually constructed through the demarcation of 'difference from' and 'exclusion of'. For Bhabha, this 'social articulation of difference' thus forms a 'complex, on-going negotiation' (1994: 2). From this perspective, Bauman then asserts that identity has the ontological status of a project and a postulate, and '[h]ence, "identity", though ostensibly a noun, behaves like a verb, albeit a strange one to be sure: it appears only in the future tense' (1996: 19).

However, this demarcation of difference does often appear through expressions of commonality. In other words, while expressions of 'identity' can be understood relationally as demarcations of the difference between 'us' and 'them', the cases in this volume show how these expressions still tend to appear to constitute collections of images, sounds, actions that are related to places and/or peoples. Hence, people continue to represent their 'identity' in terms of folkloric costumes (Abram, this volume, Chapter 2) and practices such as music, dance, cuisine, etc., and assert the authority of their local knowledge by claiming their status in terms of identity (for example the 'last Indians' of Nuttall's Chapter 11 in this volume). In some sense, the focal 'identity' exists as an imaginative notion: 'we' exist through the exclusion of 'them', and 'we' find an expression of our 'identity' in characteristic practices or rituals. Rituals of identity at least appear to be expressions of 'who we are', albeit in opposition to those who are not us. In performances for 'tourists', for example, some grouping of people may perform, say, a song or a dance, that is emblematic of a collectivity (Cohen, Chapter 4 and Atkinson, Chapter 5 in this volume). In many of these performances we can see that, in contrast to Bauman's assertion, 'identity' appears not only in the future, but, emphatically, in the past tense as well. Repeated instances of harking back to idealised (and equally unrealisable) past 'identities' in the form of 'heritage' representations may reflect participants' anxieties about the fragility of the identity they aspire to in the present and future.

The conflict here between emic and etic notions of 'identity' is clear: the performers may feel that they are representing an essential identity, a residual or potential essence where their culture is located (as per Anthony Cohen, cited above); and, for many of the 'tourists' described in this book, identity is the location of 'culture' under threat from modernity (Tucker, this volume, Chapter 6), and thus defines the exotic, different 'other' that they wish to experience (what Selwyn (1996: 6–7) has called the 'authentically social'). However, it is arguable whether the practices attributed to 'identity' represent it, or whether they actually constitute it. Frith argues that 'the issue is not how a particular piece of music or a performance reflects the people, but how it produces them, how it creates and constructs an experience' (Frith 1996: 109). Whilst for Carston, for example, identity is 'intrinsically fluid, moulded and *acquired* through life, and *shaped* by the activities in which individuals engage' (1995: 317, emphasis added), thus taking on the quality of a possession, for Frith, like Sara Cohen (this volume, Chapter 4), groups do not agree on values and then express them in music; rather, they get to know themselves as a group through cultural activity. In the context of tourism, 'tourists', however defined, can become a new audience to whom these activities are presented, thus adding a relational dimension to performances.

The earlier formulations of 'hosts' and 'guests' assumed that 'us' and 'them' were clearly differentiated in tourist encounters; but if the exclusion of 'tourists' from local activities as 'outsiders' is constitutive of the identity of insider, then this volume is concerned with the variability of those inclusions and exclusions. Differences between tourists are played out through discursive constructions of the real and the authentic (Tucker, Nuttall, this volume, Chapters 6 and 11), and residents assert and reassert the differences between visitors, residents, part-time residents, returnees and frequent visitors through discourse and action (Kohn, Abram, Waldren, Tucker, this volume, Chapters 1, 2, 3, 6). If we accept that identity is a process of expression and exclusion, then the importance of the many forms of tourism lies in their dynamic influence on these processes. In this volume, the authors each attempt to question these conflicting notions of what 'identity' is, revealing the various meanings that are shaped and produced by the dynamic interchange that constitutes tourism encounters.

Tourism as Identity

Although tourism is heralded as a new dimension of the movement of people, it is only the latest of many waves of movement to different places and into different 'communities'. For Bauman (1996), it is not the movement that is new, but the change in ideology from modernity to postmodernity that marks contemporary tourism apart from earlier precursors. Indeed, for Bauman, tourism becomes the metaphor for postmodernity, succeeding that of the pilgrim of modernity. The pilgrim's idea of progress, based on self-improvement and the journey 'towards truth', is betrayed in postmodernity, as 'the demand for the skills needed to practice . . . professions seldom lasts as long as the time needed to acquire them' (ibid., p. 24), so that life must be lived as a 'continuous present' (ibid.). Given his view that identity appears only as a postulate, the contemporary unreliability of the future proves catastrophic for the project of identity. Thus, in his apocalyptic view, 'the horror of the new situation is that all diligent work of construction may prove to be in vain; . . . [w]ell constructed and durable identity turns from an asset to a liability' (ibid.). In this scenario, 'life itself turns into an extended tourist escapade, as tourist conduct becomes the mode of life and the tourist stance grows into the character' (ibid., p. 30). Bauman thus agrees with Nuryanti, for whom: 'the concept of tourism . . . is really a form of modern consciousness' (1996: 249). Thus, we can no longer define tourism by the activities engaged in by people we call tourists, as the label 'tourist' has become a marker applicable to many contemporary activities. Whereas early tourism studies relied on structural analyses, we must now acknowledge questions of knowledge and consciousness.

We can claim that consciousness of local distinctiveness, or sense of place, is produced through relations with the outside world rather than as a result of isolation. The presence of 'others' can threaten local relations or strengthen them (as Waldren describes, this volume, Chapter 3). Once we begin to see the difficulties in defining 'locals', the meanings associated with 'tourism' are seen to reflect many conflicts internal to what may previously have been perceived as homogeneous groups. The representation of 'cultures' in the museums described by Hitchcock *et al.* (this volume, Chapter 10), particularly those of the Folk Culture Villages of the Chinese museum, exemplifies the conflict between continuity and change, and between the identity constituted by cultural expressions, and that consisting of residual bodies of knowledge. In these examples, the question of who is representing whom reveals the theoretical notions of identity held by the museum administrators. Teague shows how it is necessary to rethink the place of 'tourist art' in relation to 'collectors' art' (this volume, Chapter 9) in the context of a breakdown in the authority of 'high culture'. In contrast, the Chinese examples of attempts to place people in time as well as place in a 'heritage' representation show no evidence of reflexive enquiry into the nature of representation, nor do they bear much resemblance to critical history. These attempts to confine people to pre-ordained 'cultures' and 'places' confuse notions of time and tradition, and put judgemental evaluations on to 'cultures', with political motivations. The question of who is identifying with whom in these representations becomes a thorny conceptual problem. If the representations produce the identities, then what is being produced in these tableaux? In a semiotic analysis, they can be said to be acting as signs that function in various ways, metaphorically or metonymically; but whereas, for example, Urry's (1990) semiotic approach limits his tourist gaze to visual perception, the contributors to this volume broaden the scope of tourism studies to consider oral/aural and embodied experiences as part of the semiotic relations within tourism.

Beyond the Visual

The limitation of tourist activity to the visual is discussed by Tucker (this volume, Chapter 6). Whereas Adler (1989) traced the development within tourism from an emphasis on interaction and education (in the Grand Tour) through to the emphasis on the visual ('sight-seeing'), Tucker reminds us that holiday-makers may also desire bodily experiences. Even the stereotypical sun-seeking tourist, reviled by the 'alternative' travellers that Macleod seeks to describe (this volume, Chapter 7), searches for the bodily experience of sun-burning, swimming in the waters and, of course, the sexual experiences that Bowman brought to our attention (1989). Thus, the tourist does more than gaze (Urry 1990); tourism is more than simply visual, and also incorporates bodily experience. While the gaze serves as a useful analytical approach to the relations of power in tourism, it is only a small part of those relations. Furthermore, Tucker also shows that the tourist gaze is returned: when the women in Goreme pass judgement on the tourists from behind closed windows, they are challenging the power of the tourist gaze.

If imagery in tourism is not restricted to the visual, then for Sara Cohen and Atkinson, as well as Sampath (Chapter 8), music and dance are also important components of tourist experience. Music tourism, in the case of Liverpool and New Orleans (Cohen and Atkinson, this volume, Chapters 4 and 5 respectively) produces the sense of place, often called 'cultural capital' (Meethan 1996: 323), so highly valued in the marketing of 'destinations'. For Meethan, this process of production of the city involves the visual consumption of signs and, increasingly, simulacra and staged events in which urban townscapes are transformed into aestheticised spaces of entertainment and pleasure (ibid.). Cohen and Atkinson, though, challenge the notion that this aestheticised consumption is limited to the visual, highlighting the role of sound and music in the production of place. Atkinson shows how music has multiple roles, serving not only as an 'attraction', but also as a signal that a place is open for occupation: where music stops, tourists hesitate to venture. In both cases, arts and culture are promoted as major factors in individuals' choices of destinations not only to visit, but to move to and live in, so that music is now explicitly bound up with the politics of place and with the struggle for identity and belonging, power and prestige.

The tourists effectively create the place, as their presence constitutes an audience that can be construed as non-local, thus reconstituting a distinction between those 'of' the place and those merely 'in' it. Thus, Nuttall (this volume, Chapter 11) can argue that Alaskans, faced with tourist demands for 'authentic culture', respond by 'construct[ing] an identity as a people living in areas largely untouched by modernity and change and both hosts and guests conspire together in the production of authenticity'. This contrasts with the projects of the authors in Boissevain's collection *Coping with Tourists* (1996), who discuss the effects of long-term 'mass tourism' or 'the commoditization of culture' on local populations, i.e. the 'impact' of 'tourism' on concepts of kinship, religion, social stratification, residence patterns and inheritance in the light of various forms of social, economic and technological development. The present collection, in contrast, observes the interplay between government interests, the tourism industry and the development of concepts of heritage, local identity and perceptions of belonging. We show how the power relation is more than mutual exploitation, giving examples of 'hosts' biting back, and blurring the distinctions between actors. When so many of the people once thought to be 'hosts' now can be recognised as tourists in their own right (either as holiday-makers or as individuals engaged in the postmodern consciousness of the instability of 'identity'), we must reconcile ourselves to the awareness that we (as travellers, tourists and writers) are part of the changing perspectives that are interacting to delineate new and different identities.

Conclusions

In this volume we consider the meanings behind the phenomena called 'tourism', the interactions between people labelled 'tourists' and the people and places they visit. By focusing on the negotiation of 'identity', the symbolic aspects of tourism rituals can be understood in relation to the discourses of authenticity, exoticism and myth upheld by the 'observers' of tourism (ourselves included) identified by Selwyn (1996). Thus Chapters 1–3 by Kohn, Abram and Waldren respectively begin the volume by opening up categorisations, and shifting the focus from structural analyses of tourism, to the idea of tourism as a process, and from the assumption that tourists act as the motors of change, to the idea that tourist encounters generate change for tourists as well. Thus, Kohn argues that tourist identities are not static. Taking a diachronic perspective the picture changes, allowing categories to become fluid and permeable. Waldren also gives a long-term perspective on the renegotiation of categorisations of tourists and insiders, showing how these have changed, but also how they can be called up instrumentally, and used to promote different interests. Abram relates these issues to the performance of symbols of locality, arguing that in tourism, different audiences are presented with different versions of the past, according to their relationship with it. Thus the past takes on different forms in relation to the present.

The view of the world 'as populated by endangered authenticities' (Clifford 1988: 5) found by Kohn (Chapter 1), Abram (Chapter 2), Tucker (Chapter 6), Nuttall (Chapter 11) and Waldren (Chapter 3) as a constant of tourist representations, is challenged by them and shown to conceal more complex social relations. However, the notion of cultural authenticity is persistent, and is still the object of desire of 'alternative tourists', as is shown by Tucker (Chapter 6) and Macleod (Chapter 7). The paradox of tourism, as old as tourism itself, whereby authenticity must be signalled, but once framed loses its authenticity (Culler 1988), is expanded by Tucker, who questions the attraction of the simulacrum over the real, insisting that these tourists want bodily and social experience, in which the economic is problematised as anti-social and unauthentic.

Whilst Macleod notes the importance of how 'identities' are perceived, the political use of essentialised 'cultures' finds its most explicit expression in the museum representations described by Hitchcock, Stanley and Siu (Chapter 10). These authors also bring out the political contexts and controversies of such representations of 'folk cultures', showing how and why certain representations are favoured. By asking again who represents what and why, Teague (Chapter 9) reconceptualises the notions of tourism, and the motivations of anthropology and museums, showing them all to be 'journeys' undertaken to change perceived images and symbols within historical, economic and political, as well as social, contexts. Cohen and Atkinson (Chapters 4 and 5 respectively) draw our attention to the business of marketing of cities for tourism through the 'sound of the city', and for Sampath (Chapter 8), it is through the marketing of Carnival as Trinidadian 'culture' that an anthropological perspective on international tourism is developed.

Each of the chapters in this collection indicates the historical context of tourism development, and each, also, relates local activity to global processes, to show in detail how global economic and social trends of migration and consumption are played out in local encounters. We thus highlight representations of idealised 'identities' and 'cultures' in tourist attractions, and the adaptation of these by political agents, to show how individuals and collectivities draw on these notions to renegotiate their own approaches to identification and demarcation of difference. Thus, Nuttall (Chapter 11) shows people constructing 'indigenous' views of the environment and representing 'indigenous culture' for tourist consumption, empowering themselves by renegotiating their perceived cultural identities.

Most importantly, this collection challenges received wisdom about the 'commoditisation' of culture assumed in tourism. Rather than arguing that tourism destroys authentic local culture, we show how it can provide the setting for people to reconsider how they identify themselves, and how they relate to the rest of the world. Thus, while we do not propose any overarching theory of society (cf. Selwyn (1996: 6) on MacCannell), we do further the conceptual understanding of tourism processes through detailed ethnographic comparison, thereby raising new questions about the social relations of tourism.

References

Adler, Judith (1989). Origins of Sightseeing. *Annals of Tourism Research* 16: 7–19.

Bhabha, Homi K. (1994). *The Location of Culture*. London: Routledge.

Bauman, Zygmunt (1996). From Pilgrim to Tourist – Or a Short History of Identity. In S. Hall and P. duGay (eds), *Questions of Cultural Identity*. London: Sage.

Boissevain, Jeremy (ed.) (1996). *Coping with Tourists*. Oxford: Berghahn.

Boniface, Priscilla and Peter J. Fowler (1993). *Heritage and Tourism in 'The Global Village'*. London: Routledge.

Bowman, Glen (1989). 'Fucking Tourists: Sexual Relations and Tourists in Jerusalem's Old City'. *Critical Anthropology* IX (2): 77–93.

Carston, Janet (1995). The Politics of Forgetting: Migration, Kinship and Memory on the Periphery of the Southeast Asian State. *Journal of the Royal Anthropological Institute* 1: 317–35.

Clifford, James (1988). *The Predicament of Culture: Twentieth Century Ethnography, Literature and Art*. Cambridge, Mass.: Harvard University Press.

Cohen, Anthony P. (1985). *The Symbolic Construction Of Community*. London: Routledge.

Cohen, Erik (1984). The Sociology Of Tourism: Approaches, Issues And Findings. *Annual Review of Sociology* 10: 373–92.

Culler, Jonathan (1988). *Framing the Sign: Criticism and its Institutions*. London: University of Oklahoma Press.

Frith, Simon (1996). Music and Identity. In S. Hall and P. duGay (eds), *Questions of Cultural Identity*. London: Sage.

Hall, Stuart (1996). Introduction: Who Needs Identity? In S. Hall and P. duGay (eds), *Questions Of Cultural Identity*.

Knight, John (1996). Competing Hospitalities in Japanese Rural Tourism. *Annals of Tourism Research* 23(1): 165–80.

Macdonald, Sharon (1993). Identity Complexes in Western Europe. In S. Macdonald (ed.), *Inside European Identities*. Oxford: Berg.

Meethan, Kevin (1996). *Annals of Tourism Research* 23(2): 322–40.

Needham, Rodney (1975). *Against the Tranquility of Axioms*. Berkeley: University of California Press.

Nuryanti, Wiendu (1996). Heritage and Postmodern Tourism. *Annals of Tourism Research* 23(2): 249–60.

Selwyn, Tom (1996). Introduction. In T. Selwyn (ed.), *The Tourist Image: Myths and Myth Making in Tourism*. Chichester: Wiley.

Smith, Valene (1978). *Hosts and Guests: The Anthropology of Tourism*. Oxford: Basil Blackwell.

Strathern, Marilyn (1981). *Kinship At The Core*. Cambridge: Cambridge University Press.

Urry, John (1990). *The Tourist Gaze: Leisure and Travel In Contemporary Societies*. London: Sage.

1

Island Involvement and the Evolving Tourist

Tamara Kohn

Introduction

This chapter examines tourism as a process, rather than its social and economic structures. Structure, however, has been at the forefront of the anthropology of tourism. In MacCannell's book, *The Tourist* (1976), it is suggested that the structural paradigm in anthropology is best suited to handle the subject of tourism. Following in the footsteps of Durkheim and Levi-Strauss, he suggests that 'tourist attractions are an unplanned typology of structure that provides direct access to the modern consciousness or "world view", . . . tourist attractions are precisely analogous to the religious symbolism of primitive people' (1976: 2). Many other authors, while not ascribing a structuralist paradigm to their work, begin their enquiries by attempting to define 'tourism'. This not only boxes in the parameters of their studies, but also presupposes a very limited role, with minimal flexibility for the tourists themselves. In one article, Cohen warns us of the dangers of stereotyping the tourist. He provides a number of examples in which a tourist might deviate from being a 'voluntary, temporary traveller, travelling in the expectation of pleasure from the novelty and change experienced on a relatively long and non-recurrent round-trip' (1974: 533). By so doing, Cohen allows for a degree of flexibility in our structural, definitional typologies; but they remain with us just the same.

When tourism researchers show an interest in socio-cultural change, it is usually for that of the receiving community, and takes the form of an impact study (cf. Milman and Pizam 1988; Dogan 1989; Wilkinson 1989). The tourists themselves, as Nuñez and many others have suggested, are 'less likely to borrow from their hosts than their hosts are from them' (1978: 208); hence 'etic' definitions of 'tourists' are felt to encompass all tourist identities. Tourists and the industry of 'tourism' that they represent have been seen as contributors to and carriers of a host of changes and 'pressures exerted from the centre' (Cohen 1987: 16) which corrode 'traditional' ways of life in remote areas, and are held responsible for the 'destruction of savagery and nature' (MacCannell 1992: 18). The tourist has not been seen as one who may be more than just briefly changed by his experience, but as one who consistently effects change.

A corollary to the more traditional gaze at tourist impact is represented in the recent attention given to the construction of 'place' through tourism (cf. Gold and Gold 1995; Urry 1995). This, however, is more about the ways in which the past and future of a locale are shaped for an imagined, stereotyped, and sometimes demonized tourist 'clientele' than it is about the felt identity shifts that take place within the 'touring' individuals whose relationships with other people and locales alter through time. Studies of 'space' and 'place' can only benefit from a closer examination of tourist experiences and identities. This chapter sets out to show how these identities are not always so static and impenetrable by beginning, not with an ascribed academic definition of the study group, but with the terms and definitions expressed by residents of a small, rural, island community. In a volume of the *Annals of Tourism Research*, entitled 'The Evolution of Tourism' (Butler and Wall 1985), the authors carefully illustrate the continuity and change of touristic styles and the very structure of the tourist industry through time. This chapter is also concerned with an evolution through time, not at the industry level, but at the level of the individual tourist. It is, therefore, a study of tourist identity.

Issues of structure continue to inform a strong dualistic impulse in the anthropology of tourism. That 'hosts' and 'guests', for instance, always divide themselves into discrete units that are vastly different from one another is questionable, especially in studies of rural tourism in the UK. According to Smith, 'even in complex societies in which economic disparities may be mitigated, the tendency to view visitors as "outsiders" is evident' (1978: 7). And yet, as Urry points out, 'some places *only* exist because of visitors . . . such as the Lake District . . . [and] visitors are in a sense as much local as are "real" locals' (1995: 166). The semantic wrestling that we do with identity categories (for example the visitor-local vs the real-local) shows us that our typologies need further unpacking than we have allowed in our tourism studies thus far. The movement that an individual's body and identity undergoes (from home in Glasgow to summer home in the Hebrides, for instance), as well as the fluidity found within named identity categories (for example 'incomer', 'guest', 'islander', 'local', etc.) are examined in this chapter.

To do this, material is drawn from three years of anthropological fieldwork (1984–7) on a small island in the Inner Hebrides of Scotland, as well as from oral history and written historical accounts about the island. I suggest that, in this small island context at least, tourism may be seen as one modern element in a larger process of shifting identities, whereby incomers may become islanders. This chapter will, therefore, emphasize process over structure, and will begin with individuals rather than with the industry of tourism *per se*. For those interested in how tourists affect the host community, this case study will perhaps provide an example of the ultimate 'impact', for it shows how tourists over time may possibly become part of and thus create the host community. The ethnographic, processual perspective adopted here gives added complexity to recent models of 'the tourist' experience.

Ethnography

I conducted field research on a small Inner Hebridean island off the west coast of Scotland, twelve miles long and three miles wide. From the sea, as the boat approaches from the south-east, all beaches and beauty spots are hidden from view, and the tourist sees only a long, flat, grey and generally uninviting rock. It takes three and a half hours on the Caledonian Macbrayne ferry to get to the island from the nearest mainland port, and during the period of my residence there, this ferry travelled only three times a week in the winter and four times a week in the summer season. Because of the infrequency of transport connections and the crack-of-dawn departure of the ferry, a trip to the island from the London area took around twenty-four hours. To all intents and purposes the island could be seen as a 'remote area' (Ardener 1987). Between 1984 and 1987, its resident winter population averaged 150, sixteen of whom were children between twelve and sixteen years old who attended high school and resided during term in school hostels on the mainland.

The island's economy was, in the mid-1980s, based primarily on stock farming of sheep and cattle, and all the grazing land and fields outside the village were divided between seven owners. Other full-time and part-time occupations included lobster fishing, running basic services (such as the shops and the pier), and tourism. A characteristic of the island economy was that in order to make a living during all seasons, occupational pluralism was extensively practised. A fisherman might also work on the pier on boat days, drive the 'school run', and lead the coastguard. A woman working in the shop might also knit sweaters on commission and take in people for bed and breakfast. Of the winter population, about

75 per cent of the adults of working age were people who were not born on the island.

Relatively few visitors came to the island between October and May. Public places such as the pier on boat days, the two shops, and the one hotel pub were dominated during the winter by small but dedicated gatherings of people who shared local gossip, news about livestock and weather forecasts, and details about a myriad of evening social events in which they were involved. In the pier shed a little semicircle of these residents waited for the boat to bring food supplies and mail; in the shops groups assembled to wait for their bread and milk orders; and in the pub, a single arc of beer and whisky drinkers lined the counter and shared in a large and often quite expensive series of 'rounds'.

The summer season was marked by an explosion of the population and a total shift in the atmosphere and social function of these public places. The groups either dispersed altogether or were divided and then expanded by new faces. Rounds in the pub, for instance, became directed at smaller groups of family and close friends or neighbours. As the population swelled in the summer to at least two or three times its winter size, residents recognised and reached out to include many of the new arrivals. A study of identity which avoids detailed attention to the part-time cast of characters that pass through the place would be only half a study. So: who were these summer visitors? When a summer ferry arrived, a single stream of people carried their bags and cameras down the passenger ramp, and vehicles packed solid with people and supplies drove off the car ramp. An island-born resident once joked that the whole island sinks a few inches during this time. The mass of visitors were carefully distinguished by the resident population as follows:

1. 'Day-trippers' were holiday-makers who took an advertised excursion trip on the Cal-Mac ferry and disembarked with only a light bag and camera to explore. Most of these visitors leisurely walked the quarter mile to the village, stopping at the gift shop. From there they either had a pub lunch in the hotel, or they set off walking on one of the two roads leading out of the village, and then turned back in time to catch the return ferry to the mainland, approximately three hours after their arrival.

2. 'Yachties', as the name implies, arrived not on the ferry but in their own boats. These yachts were moored in the village bay for anything from a few hours to an entire week. If it has been said that the term 'tourist' may in many places be locally imbued with derogatory meaning, the term 'yachtie' was just that much worse. Locals sometimes made snide remarks about these people, who were instantly recognised by their boating attire

and yellow 'wellies'. Perhaps this was a class-related prejudice, for one cannot instantly place a tourist off the ferry in any income bracket, but the yachties always appeared to be in a higher one. Also, people felt that 'yachties' only saw the island as another place where they could comfortably moor for the night, and that most were uninterested in the island *per se*. They also had a reputation for not spending much money on the island except at the hotel pub.

3. The term 'tourist' covered all other holiday-makers who did not own a home on the island, did not have kin there, or were not themselves originally from the island. It included people who stumbled upon the island in their search for remoteness, peace and wilderness, who would stay in either the hotel, the guest-house, rented cottages, bed-and-breakfast houses, tents, dormobiles, or caravans. Sometimes 'tourists' learned of the place through friends, and often stayed as house-guests on the island, although those who stayed with local families were usually just called 'visitors'. 'Tourists' who enjoyed their visit, whether it was for two days or many weeks, often indicated that they appreciated the lack of a strong tourist infrastructure there. Some brought their own cars, others hired bicycles, mopeds or a ride in the guest-house jeep to get to see as much of the island as they could and to visit some of the best sandy beaches. Some travelled by foot or occasionally by hitching rides. Most tourists came from England, Wales, or mainland Scotland; but there were a few international tourists from the Continent, America, and Australia, for example. As the tourists departed on the boat at the end of their stay, many would probably never be seen again, and they would plan their next holiday in Amsterdam, Majorca or another Hebridean island. Urry suggests that 'contemporary tourists are collectors of gazes . . . . The initial gaze is what counts and people appear to have less and less interest in repeat visits' (1995: 138). And yet this is not true for all, and the question of *why* repeat visits are practised by some people in some places needs to be addressed. On the island discussed here, some tourists would find something particularly enchanting about the place and would plan to return, and their faces and names would become well known in time, locally.

4. Another species in the summer population were the 'Summer-home people', also aptly called the 'Summer Swallows'. They came to 'roost' on the island during the summer, in homes they bought or built up from ruins. Most were professionals, such as musicians, writers, teachers, and business people, who could afford to leave their jobs for a considerable part of the year. Some of these had summered on the island for over thirty years. Many summer-home people who had rebuilt ruins did not (as Erik Cohen and others have noted of some tourists) wish to share life as it was

really lived – they were perfectly aware that most islanders lived in council houses with central heating and all the modern amenities – but wished instead to live life as they believed it *should* be lived, or imagined that it once was lived, an example of the 'countryside aesthetic' that Harrison suggests developed in the nineteenth century amongst the professional middle class (Harrison cited in Urry 1995: 213). Hence their tendency to be found living in beautiful rustic stone cottages, with open fireplaces, exposed lintels and beams, neat stone crevices, hanging ancient tools and glass floats, wood-burning stoves, and outside toilets may contribute another material example of the cultural process Trevor-Roper (1983) has described as the invention of Highland culture and tradition. When one realises that more than 20 per cent of all lived-in dwellings on the island were summer homes, it becomes clear how easily their rather similar rustic remains could leave a strong pseudo-tradition behind for future archaeologists.

Of all the categories described so far, the summer-home people were more involved in the local community than the rest. They stopped in the street and talked to residents, or visited some of them in their homes, they sometimes made crafts to sell in the gift-shop, they attended local fund-raising events, such as dances and sales, and they entered their baking and artwork in the annual agricultural show. They sometimes illustrated their emotional commitment to the place by naming their children and/or pets after island characters and place-names. Full-time residents often commented about how Summer Swallows, despite their apparent zeal for the place, did not always contribute as much to the local economy as did day-trippers and short-term tourists, for they often cut costs by arriving with their vehicles laden with large food and fuel supplies, only purchasing perishables like milk and vegetables in the store.

'Summer Swallows' are a commonly found species in indigenous rural tourism in the UK. The sense of continuity and familiarity with places and people is what appeals to such holiday-makers. Consider the following excerpts from an article in *The Scotsman*, called 'Short-changed by the Tourist Trade', about a nameless Scottish island:

> When the ferry arrives in the summer, exotic cars are disgorged, loaded to the roof and beyond with every conceivable requirement for a fortnight's stay, even down to the family deep freeze on a trailer. They drive off to their crumbling holiday homes, bought for a song by London standards, but a fortune by highland ones, and used just two or three weeks in the year, while young islanders scramble for tumbledown caravans and the rare council house . . . .
> In accents of Morningside and Islington, they talk about us as if we were

invisible, telling funny stories to each other of our quaintness and naivety and complaining about the change and decay which they see all around – the ugly electricity poles . . ., or the incomers.

We, however, are deeply thankful for our ghastly power lines . . .. As for the incomers; true, the Gaelic-speaking population is elderly, their children long gone, and it is the younger, fitter newcomers who catch the ropes of the boat, deliver the mail, mend the leaking roof and serve the double malts in the bar. They keep the school population stable, the shop open and the services functioning twelve months of the year, enabling the summer swallows to enjoy their two weeks in comfort and convenience . . ..

Resources, adequate for a couple of hundred souls, become stretched too thinly when numbers treble or quadruple during the summer months, and it is invariably the working islander who suffers the inevitable deprivations . . . (McEachan 1987: 12).

One can see in this a very interesting and telling construction and collapse of identity markers. McEachan describes a place that is peopled and run by 'incomers', and that is threatened, not by some perceived loss of the Gaidhealtachd, but by the seasonal roosting of 'summer swallows'. In creating an opposition between 'us' (locals) and 'them' (summer swallows), she allows the incomer, who keeps all services running, to become the 'working *islander'*. At least in the context of tourist-bashing, the incomer and islander become indistinguishable. In other situations, island identities are formed around other criteria, such as kinship (see Kohn 1988); but for our purposes here, it is enough to recognise the possible collapse of incomer and islander identities in the face of tourism (particularly of the summer swallow variety). The message at the end of the article is basically that 'we may be losing more than we gain from our brightly-coloured migrants' (McEachan 1987: 12). Clearly, the idea that incomers (upon whom the islands rely for survival) have often been introduced to their new homes through tourism had not occurred to McEachan. If it had, then she would have concluded that 'we' have much to gain from tourism – not only because it is an important industry in the Highlands and Islands, but because it introduces future 'islanders' to the place. Here, let us return to the categories of visitor distinguished on the Inner Hebridean island that is the focus of my research.

The four classifications of summer visitor described so far – the Day-trippers, Yachties, Tourists and Summer Swallows – were all very ambiguous categories on the island. They could all be called 'tourists' in some contexts, for instance when a number of them were crowded on the pier or in a shop. In other contexts they were carefully distinguished, for instance when they wandered on their own, identifiable by their faces, or the colour of their 'wellies'. Because the fully resident population of the island were largely 'incomers' from a great range of geographical and social backgrounds, accents were not necessarily valid markers of 'visitor' or 'tourist' status on this island, despite the temptation to stereotype them as such.

5. The final type of summer arrival that locals distinguished were island-born people and their relations who came to holiday on the island. Many of these resided and worked in the Central Lowlands, and were referred to as the 'Glasgow Cousins'. They came to visit the island in dribs and drabs throughout the summer and very occasionally in the winter; but they came *en masse* particularly during the two weeks in the second half of July when working Glaswegians have their holiday – a time known as the 'Glasgow Fair'. Some of these people had homes or caravans on the island, or else they had family they could stay with. They all knew each other and the older local residents very well, and they visited each other a great deal, while also enjoying holiday pleasures such as beaching, trout-fishing and sea-fishing. They formed a lively contingent at dances and other summer social events held during this period.

Glasgow Cousins sometimes retired back to the community, and in their old age they would quietly settle in to full 'islander' status. A familiar vignette witnessed during one tourist season was when some 'day-trippers' saw an old man lovingly painting his boat. 'Have you always lived here?', they asked. 'Aye', he replied. Later in the pub the trippers bemoaned the tragic loss of the Gaidhealtachd – they saw the old 'islanders', the young 'incomers', and no categories in between. In reality, that old man had spent forty working years in Glasgow. One of his sons lived and worked abroad, but planned to retire to the island. You can see how a pattern perpetuates itself. Remote regions of the Hebrides have long been seen as declining under the encroaching power of the outside world, and incomers as well as tourists have tended to be seen as part of that alien world. The evidence from this research attempts to counter the popular and pervasive ideology of cultural and linguistic decline in the Scottish Hebrides with one that sees culture as potentially regenerative and encompassing. Old men, painting their boats and fixing their nets, will continue to provide images of a culture teetering on the brink of extinction, long after we're gone.

The varieties of visitors who flooded over the island in the summer illustrate that rather firm distinctions *can* be drawn between these people at any one moment or during a short period of time. While a study of tour*ism* might be interested in the economic and social experiences relevant to members of the first three or four groups, or 'tourist categories', at any one time, a study of individual tou*rists*, assuming a *diachronic* perspective, changes the picture significantly, for it allows the categories to have fluid borders. The following case studies illustrate this point.

One family of professional musicians who were living in London read an advertisement in the early 1950s for a caravan one could rent on the east end of the island, and decided to plan a holiday there. They had a lovely first visit, and came back year after year. Slowly they got to know all the locals living in the east end of the island, and by the time I was there they could recount tales of times spent with island characters who were long since dead. After a number of years renting the one holiday caravan on the island, they had decided that they wanted to have their own summer home, and bought a plot with a ruin upon which they built a small stone cottage over a number of years. Although these people still expressed tourist *interests* – they still enjoyed walking on the beach or fishing every day, and still sensed a leisured feeling of getting 'away from it all' (Graburn 1983: 11), they became *more* than tourists over the years. Most summer-home owners began their association in this way, becoming introduced to the island as tourists or stumbling across it as day-trippers.

But what was it that made them return year after year? There was no single natural feature that was outstanding on the island. The beaches were beautiful, but one could never rely on the sunny weather needed to enjoy them properly. When the 'summer swallows' and oft-returning tourists were asked what made them come back, the answer often implied that the decision to do so was out of their hands. Some people said they were 'bewitched' by the place. Others said that it was the island's 'magic'. A children's geography textbook about the island cited a regular visitor saying to a first-timer who had complained about the weather, 'It's all right for you. You don't have to come here again . . . we're addicted to the island and *have* to put up with it.'

It is very tempting as an anthropologist to believe that these sentiments and experiences are particularly revealing – that some magical and bewitching force pulled people into the island and that the ritual of the annual visit revitalised this force. This imagery certainly provided a culturally defined initial reason for attachment to a community to which one had no birthright. The imagery and language of bewitchment were available for those tourists who wished to return to the island, and also indicated that the tourists and other summer visitors often became highly affected by the island world they witnessed in the summertime. Schneider's discussion (1993) about how we become 'enchanted' by

cultures that bombard our senses, baffle us, and challenge our understandings of the world around us can be easily applied to these visitors'
experiences. The period spent away from home and on the island was a
repeatable sacred and enchanting experience.

A number of tourists had, over the years, returned to the island to set
up a permanent home there. For example, a Glaswegian electrician and
his wife took a holiday on the island in the early 1970s. They had a great
time, and returned with their young children another year. Then, when
the island was due to receive its first electricity from generators on a
neighbouring island, a job was advertised for an electrician to wire most
of the houses, and the man took it. The whole family migrated to the
island – the children went to the island school and both parents took up a
selection of part-time jobs to make their living. As their tourist identity
dissolved to make way for a new 'incomer' identity, their lifestyle and
behaviour shifted as well. They were no longer on the island to imbibe
the magic of the place; they were there because it had become their home
and workplace. They did not live a rustic myth of a leisured island life,
but their lifestyle adapted to meet the lifestyle experienced by most other
full-time residents. Namely, they drove their car everywhere, they moved
into modern council housing, and they filled most spare moments with
the responsibilities of actively participating in a busy local social scene,
especially in the winter. Thereafter they took their own annual holidays
in Glasgow or even Spain. The flood of summer tourists that arrived each
year saw them as islanders. They, in turn, saw the flood of strangers as
'bloody tourists'.

While the majority of tourists came and went very quickly, some found
semi-permanent or permanent residence on the island. Some married into
the community. The phenomenon of 'tourists' becoming 'locals' through
marriage has been documented elsewhere (Frey Haas 1976; Kousis 1989);
but the potential of this transformation for regenerating culture has not.
'Ex-tourists' constituted the bulk of the incoming population on the island
studied, and had done so for over thirty years. More than one-fifth of the
fully-resident population in 1987 came to the island in this way. These
new residents would be able, in time, to become rooted to the place.

On the island there was no tremendous clash of culture or language
barrier preventing people from reorienting their senses of belonging, as
some researchers have found to be the case abroad, where an 'environmental bubble' (Cohen 1972: 166) may operate. Many elderly islanders
had 'the Gaelic' and grew up with it as their first language. However,
Gaelic was not used as a tool to establish a social boundary between
islanders and incomers or Gaelic-speakers and English-speakers, as it

seems to have been in some other Highland and Island areas. 'Islanders', in fact, were not always Gaelic-speakers, so that the opposition between people who moved in from the outside and those who appeared to have always been there could not have been enforced through the use of Gaelic.

It did become possible for me, in just three years of island residence, to witness newcomers growing 'proto-roots' on the island as expressed through their community involvement and homogenizing lifestyles. Going back a little further with the help of oral history reveals more solid examples. Two women spoke of the rather difficult times they had had when they arrived on the island in the early 1970s. At that time they had joined and enthusiastically made suggestions at an all-women's social event, and were hurt to hear one islander mutter something unkind about 'incomers trying to run the place'. These women, who in the mid-1980s were well-established incomers themselves, were heard making virtually the same excluding remarks to a brand-new member of the community at her first Knitting Bee. At first glance, these comments all served to reinforce boundaries between people on the island, but a second look shows how the 'boundaries' (if one can even call them that) were really only very quickly and sloppily created. In a very short space of time, some incomers found themselves sliding along the incomer–islander continuum, and delighting in whatever advancement in status this brought.

History

The ability of tourists to become 'rooted' had a lot to do with the flexibility of individual identities and growing commitments to the island community. An understanding of this is enriched by a historical perspective. Tourism is only the latest industry that has brought many new people into the Scottish Isles. In the 1850s, a new laird on this particular island set up large dairy farms to replace small crofting townships. Then he brought in farmers and cattle from Ayrshire in the Lowlands. The numbers of new people arriving were minimal compared to the numbers of islanders that could not meet the high rents the laird imposed and had left the island. A population of over 1,400 people in the 1840s was reduced by half by the 1870s, for a variety of reasons. It is this huge emigration that has interested historians, rather than the tiny immigration that accompanied it. Historians writing about the period of the Clearances in the Highlands and Islands generally have all tended to depict the population decline in terms of a simple replacement of men by sheep and other livestock. In Prebble's book, *The Highland Clearances*, he says 'the choice made by their lairds was real, sheep instead of men, and this was the cause of their exile and of their sorrow' (1963: 21). Karl Marx manipulated the same metaphor when he said that 'in the year 1835 the 15,000 Gaels were already replaced by 131,000 sheep' (1954: 683). Even the recent and academic account of this time found in Eric Richards' history of the Clearances records that 'virtually everywhere . . . was conquered by the sheep. The old economy was transformed under the pressure of the sheep empire' (1982: 161). The farmers who came with these animals are invisible in these accounts. On the island in question, however, some of their descendants remained on the same farms they were given in the nineteenth century. A few descendants of dairy farmers who came from the Outer Hebrides to run cheese factories on the island in the 1930s and 1940s still lived on the island in the 1980s. They were all recognised as island-born locals with a history there. Over many years, not only had they become residentially rooted to the island, but their identities and genealogies had become rooted as well.

Anthropologists working in contemporary island communities have been guilty of a bias similar to that of island historians. They have either totally ignored newcomers brought to the islands as workers, entre-preneurs, and tourists, or they have acknowledged them purely as a minority effectively cut off from some perceived 'real' community. They have often spotted the newcomers in their 1970s guises as escapists, 'peaceniks', artists or nature-seekers, but not as people who have appeared in the Scottish islands in different ways and for very different reasons for centuries. In Crick's insightful comparison of tourists and anthropologists, he writes '. . . tourists are awkward and always marginal. Their identities lie in the home culture and interests derive from that culture, not from the one being visited' (1985: 78–9). This Scottish study, however, illustrates how tourists, given the right historical and socio-cultural context, need not always remain marginal, and how their identities, interests and notions of 'home' (as well as those of the field anthropologist) need not be constricted and immobilised in practice and in our analyses.

Identities are always multiple and hard to describe. McCrone's insightful sociological study of Scotland tells us that what 'is on offer in the late twentieth century is what we might call "pick 'n mix" identity, in which we wear our identities lightly, and change them according to circumstances. Those who would argue for the paramountcy or even the exclusivity of a single identity have a hard time of it in the late twentieth century' (1992: 195). He suggests that 'being black, Glaswegian and female can all characterise one person's culture and social inheritance without one aspect of that identity being paramount'; but this is still far too simple a representation of the complexities of identity. It presumes that it is only with a relatively *fixed repertoire* of identities that the individual may present herself. It suggests that fluidity and multiplicity comes from picking and choosing between these, and not from a reorientation of the very meaning of some of these identities. And yet we have seen that a Glaswegian's sense of 'home' and 'belonging' may alter radically over time (while 'being from Glasgow' remains somewhere in the ragbag). We have also seen how some identities (for instance 'tourist', 'visitor', etc.) *vis-à-vis* individuals' experiences in particular places may alter so much in meaning that they become forgotten, drop away altogether, and transform into other spoken and/or embodied identities ('incomer', 'local', etc.).

A Theoretical Comparison

The orientation presented above can add processual depth to extant models of the tourist experience. Jafari (1987) constructs a model of the tourist in which the individual passes through a number of different phases. From the springboard representing everyday working life, the tourist is 'emancipated' both physically and psychologically and is suspended in a period of 'non-ordinary flotation' where new rules of a 'tourist culture' are adhered to. The tourist may ignore the cultural norms of home as well as of those of the 'magnet' or receiving community. The tourist's non-ordinary experience is depicted as temporarily intersecting with the host's ordinary space. Then, the holiday over, the tourist is repatriated back to his or her ordinary 'springboard'.

This model and imagery is very useful for understanding a single tourist experience. If it is expanded to follow a tourist through many holidays and a potentially changing orientation with respect to 'the magnet' or holiday destination, then it may be able to accommodate the individuals that have been the subject of this paper. The magnet may be the locale for repeated visits. While still enjoying the benefits of being in a 'magical', 'sacred', and 'bewitching' space, the visitors lose their anonymity as they form long-term friendships with locals. Their behaviour in the 'magnet' is thus often adapted to meet the requirements of the receiving community. At some stage the individual may decide to migrate and make this holiday-spot a home. As has been previously illustrated, such a person may come to feel he or she belongs in that place. Or, in Jafari's terms, that place would have become imbued with many of the characteristics of the ordinary 'springboard'. The site of 'animation' becomes the site of 'corporation'. The individual is no longer a tourist, but is a host to other newer tourists in that space, and journeys elsewhere for the freedom of the non-ordinary.

It is suggested that even if such a processual extension of the tourist model only applies to a minority of tourists on holiday, it is none the less crucial to acknowledge it. For the small rural island community introduced here as well as other such areas, the success of tourism depends on these sorts of evolving identities and relations, as does the very continuation of the community and local culture.

Conclusion

This chapter has focused on identifying a process whereby identities are reconstructed through time. It is impossible to witness how this happened in the past; but it can be observed in the present. Tourism has introduced new people to become lured and enchanted into being semi-permanently or even permanently attached to the island community. Of the huge wave of tourists and other pleasure-seekers that have washed over the island, a tiny portion has allowed itself to cling to a pool of rapidly evolving identities. There are occasions, therefore, when tourists may 'be moved to action that lies outside of prescribed tourist roles' (Schwartz 1991: 590). For the small Scottish island described here, tourism may be seen as a modern element in a larger process through which islanders are formed. The way in which individuals may transcend visitor categories and allow a holiday spot to become a workplace and home may parallel the first stages of the process by which descendants of incomers of the nineteenth century achieved islander status in the twentieth.

Perhaps there is a case for suggesting that identities in the Scottish island context are peculiarly apt to be negotiable in a way that identities at some other tourist destinations are not. The processual and historical perspective advocated here and applied elsewhere would allow for the testing of such a suggestion. Relatively long-term field research in a single small community allows the anthropologist to see a bit of change in the making. Factors linked with changing associations with place (such as metaphors of 'bewitchment' and 'addiction', and realignments of 'self' and 'other' in examples of everyday interaction) may be used by the ethnographer as place-specific examples; but we have seen how they may also help to shed new light on theoretical models of 'otherness' and the 'tourist experience'.

Studies of tourism on Scottish islands would be likely to focus on the streams of tourists flowing in and out of those places every summer. The experience of these tourists, viewed synchronically, would appear rather standardised and predictable. The world, however, is not always so carefully ordered, for it exhibits great variability and change. A historical, processual approach allows us to account for this complexity and realise potential patterns of change at more than the structural level. The individual tourist does not just face a world that is completely 'other', and people are never completely caught in the dichotomies of hosts vs. guests or incomers vs. islanders as long as identities remain negotiable.

Acknowledgements

Support for this research came from the Philip Bagby Studentship (Institute of Social Anthropology, University of Oxford), and from Linacre College, Oxford. I wish to extend my gratitude to Peter Riviere, Shirley Ardener, Andrew Russell, Bob Simpson, Michael Carrithers, Sandra Bell, Luisa Elvira Belaunde, Susanna Rostas, and Anne de Sales for their suggestions on earlier drafts of this chapter.

References

Ardener, Edwin (1987). 'Remote Areas': some theoretical considerations. In A. Jackson (ed.), *The Anthropologist at Home*. London: Tavistock Publications.

Cohen, Anthony P. (1987). *Whalsay: Symbol, Segment and Boundary in a Shetland Island Community*. Manchester: Manchester University Press.

Cohen, Erik (1972). Towards a Sociology of International Tourism. *Social Research* 39: 164–82.

Cohen, Erik (1974). Who is a Tourist?: A Conceptual Clarification. *The Sociological Review* 22: 527–55.

Crick, Malcolm (1985). 'Tracing' the Anthropological Self: Quizzical Reflections on Field Work, Tourism, and the Ludic. *Social Analysis* 17: 71–92.

Dogan, Hasan Zafer (1989). Forms of Adjustment: Sociocultural Impacts of Tourism. *Annals of Tourism Research* 16: 216–36.

Frey Haas, V. (1976). The Impact of Mass Tourism on a Rural Community in the Swiss Alps. Unpublished Ph.D. dissertation, Department of Anthropology, University of Michigan, Ann Arbor.

Gold, John R. and Margaret M. Gold (1995). *Imagining Scotland: Tradition, Representation and Promotion in Scottish Tourism since 1750*. Aldershot, England: Scolar Press.

Graburn, Nelson (1983). The Anthropology of Tourism. *Annals of Tourism Research* 10(1): 9–33.

Jafari, Jafar (1987). Tourism Models: The Sociocultural Aspects. *Tourism Management* 1987: 151–9.

Kohn, Tamara (1988). Seasonality and Identity in a Changing Hebridean Community. Unpublished D.Phil. thesis, University of Oxford.

Kousis, Maria (1989). Tourism and the Family in a Rural Cretan Community. *Annals of Tourism Research* 16: 318–32.

MacCannell, Dean (1976). *The Tourist: A New Theory of the Leisure Class.* London: Macmillan.

MacCannell, Dean (1992). *Empty Meeting Grounds: The Tourist Papers.* London: Routledge.

McCrone, David (1992). *Understanding Scotland: The Sociology of a Stateless Nation.* London: Routledge.

McEachan, Elizabeth (1987). Short-Changed by the Tourist Trade. *The Scotsman,* 25 May, p. 12.

Marx, Karl (1954). *Capital,* Vol. 1. London: Lawrence and Wishart (first published in English 1887).

Milman, Andy and Abraham Pizam (1988). Social Impacts of Tourism on Central Florida. *Annals of Tourism Research* 15: 191–204.

Nuñez, Theron (1978). Touristic Studies in Anthropological Perspective. In V. Smith (ed.), *Hosts and Guests: The Anthropology of Tourism,* pp. 207–16. Oxford: Blackwell.

Prebble, John (1963). *The Highland Clearances.* Harmondsworth: Penguin.

Richards, Eric (1982). *A History of the Highland Clearances: Agrarian Transformation and the Evictions 1746–1886.* London: Croom Helm.

Schneider, Mark A. (1993). *Culture and Enchantment.* Chicago: University of Chicago Press.

Schwartz, Ronald D. (1991). Travellers Under Fire: Tourists in the Tibetan Uprising. *Annals of Tourism Research* 18: 588–604.

Smith, Valene (1978). *Hosts and Guests: The Anthropology of Tourism.* Oxford: Blackwell.

Trevor-Roper, Hugh (1983). The Invention of Tradition: The Highland Tradition of Scotland. In E. Hobsbawm and T. Ranger (eds), *The Invention of Tradition,* pp. 15–41, Cambridge: Cambridge University Press.

Urry, John (1995). *Consuming Places.* London: Routledge.

Wilkinson, Paul F. (1989). Strategies for Tourism in Island Microstates. *Annals of Tourism Research* 16: 153–77.

2

Performing for Tourists in Rural France

Simone Abram

When considering ethnicity and identity, one cannot avoid considering history as a significant process of expression and identification. If we are to consider how identities and ethnicities are revealed, expressed or exploited through tourism, then the presentation or negation of history must be foremost in our analyses. Taking Davis's definition of history as 'thought about the past' (1992: 14), we can ask how these thoughts are articulated, and how 'people are seen to interpret and use their particular history in the present' (Collard 1989: 92). Thus, pasts lived through or imagined (see Zonabend 1984) are reinterpreted in the present, and can be thought to reflect present understandings, as well as aspirations for the future.

The location of history in a place is one basis to begin to analyse tourism, whether we are considering the confused attempts to deny historical significance in places of mass, or sun-based tourism (in Anglicised beach resorts such as Zante in Greece or in the tourist bubble of international hotel chains), or the 'commoditisation' of cultural histories in so-called cultural tourism. The central question in this chapter is, thus, what do the presentations of histories to tourists tell us, both about the tourists and about those who are presenting the past to those tourists?

This raises methodological questions, however, as we must first recognise these representations and distinguish between presentations to tourists and representations not made directly to tourists. Not all (re)presentations of the past are immediately distinguishable from general statements of identification since, as Hastrup argues, 'culture and history are adjective to one another' (1992: 5). Thus my initial fieldwork experiences in the Auvergne consisted of a struggle to reconcile the rich presence of the past in daily experience with the compartmentalisation of textualised history in forms that might be considered authoritative. The modernist collection of folklore and tales, which saw 'traditions' as residues of some authentic knowledge, is here put into context as one of many ways to make sense of the past, and that rather rigid notion of tradition is contrasted with one that incorporates both continuity and change. In this chapter, although I offer some detail of the content of representations of the past, I do so in order to ask a set of questions about how these representations form and inform the social relations of tourism and locality. Thus I ask: What happens when tourists come to see or 'experience' the past of a place? What kind of a past is represented to tourists, and how does this differ from other representations of the past? How is the past performed for tourists, and what does it mean to those involved? Is this a case of hosts exploiting guests or vice versa, or is another social situation being created that allows other possibilities to develop? And is it possible to divide tourist from non-tourist, tourist-season from out-of-season, performance from 'reality'?

Finding History

I spent much of my fieldwork in the Auvergne[1] trying to find some kind of local history and wondering what I ought to take notes on. I diligently recorded the stories people told me, taking cuttings from local newspapers about local events, mapping a village and drawing a genealogy, but I constantly felt something was missing. What was it that I was trying to record? I was looking for stories: nice clean narratives about the past, quotable phrases or odd recollections; but, to my naïve disappointment, I found that apart from a very few exceptions, the people I knew tended not to go in for telling the sorts of stories collected by folklorists of the late nineteenth century. They did not know any local legends that required more than a few words to tell, nor did they show much interest in them. When I asked for history, I was told to read the schoolbooks. Yet, despite this lack of clear narrative, the past was being evoked every day in all sorts of ways, and being enacted without necessarily having a theatrical narrative commentary that might have made it more easily recognisable. It was only once I recognised that the performance of 'what we used to do' was more than simple nostalgia, and was rather a distinct history, with its own discourse of knowledge and identity, that I began to understand the echoes of the past that resounded through daily conversation.

In the light of this, the differences between performances put on for tourists and those for local benefit became more recognisable, and the interactions between tourists, locals, tourism and identity became more apparent in all their complexities. It was clearly not enough to question the effect of tourism on local people. This implies a one-way process by which tourists disempower the local 'hosts'. When many of the local population were not locally resident, and many houses were periodically occupied by those with links to the village other than straightforward residence, the first problem became one of distinguishing between locals and tourists. Whereas many studies of communities focus on the acceptance of newcomers as insiders or outsiders (Strathern 1981; Strathern 1982; Cohen 1985), studies of tourism have often included the returning *émigré* as problematic (Kohn 1988; Waldren 1988 and this volume, Chapters 1 and 3 respectively). In the Cantal, the distinction between locals, visitors, absent family/friends and tourists is similarly blurred. Although examples of each exist, many people fall between these crude categories and make our discussions of tourism problematic and the process of identification and expression of ethnicity complex and multi-faceted. However, there is a discourse of tourism amongst those concerned with it in local government and in the local agencies such as the national parks and local museums and other 'tourist attractions', and it is worth investigating to what this refers.

Some Background about Tourism

Tourism in the Cantal, in the mountains of central France, is not mass tourism as seen on the South Coast beaches. The Cantal is a region of wild upland moors and valleys radiating from a central volcanic peak after which the *département* is named, having once, more evocatively, been known as the Upper Auvergne. The Auvergne region has no pretensions to separation from France, unlike the Basque or Breton regions, but, with encouragement from folklorists and politicians in the nineteenth century, is more often seen as the most French of French regions, the place of origin of the French national identity (Liethoudt 1991). However, since the mid-nineteenth century, economic migration, especially to Paris, has depleted the Cantal's population from over 250,000 in 1850 to around 150,000 in 1990, and it is often said, with little exaggeration, that there are more Auvergnats in Paris than there are in the Auvergne.[2] This prolonged migration was of profound importance to the development this century of the perception of the Auvergne in greater France. The migrants who lived and worked in Paris tended to retain a nostalgia for their places of origin that developed into a distinct Auvergnat society within Paris. Thus, when they returned 'home',[3] they brought with them ideas of how their homeland should be that inevitably differed from the perceptions of those residents who had remained at home (Girard 1985). The term 'Auvergnat(e)' thus clearly refers to more than simply those people who live in the Auvergne. Although it is linked with place as a mark of social identity, its meaning incorporates a range of historical, linguistic and artistic features. The question of quite who or what is 'Auvergnat(e)' is as slippery as any question of 'cultural' or 'ethnic identity', but is one that is particularly significant within tourism. Although tourism is often seen as a meeting of 'them' and 'us', as a replaying of the colonial encounter, such a simplistic stereotype breaks down on closer inspection of intra-national or intra-European tourism. When the 'tourists' are also the 'hosts' or their kin, and when 'hosts' can also be 'tourists' elsewhere, the more subtle dynamics of the situation come to the fore.

Although there are records of travellers having passed through the Cantal for as long as records have been kept – indeed in many cases it was the travellers who created the records[4] – the present era of tourism can be seen to have developed from the mass migrations of Auvergnats to Paris since the mid-nineteenth century. Many migrant workers returned to their natal villages for holidays or for seasonal work in the summer pastures, retaining family property for the purpose (a practice favoured by French inheritance laws), and this pattern of periodic return continues into the late twentieth century. Hence the majority of visitors to the Cantal are French people,[5] many of whom have some 'ancestral link' (and often an associated ownership of property) to the region, and this has coloured the way tourism has developed according to particular themes. Many of the visitors to the Cantal are still either migrants from the region or their descendants. Thus, while the population of many of the Cantal's villages trebles during the tourist season, many of these visitors are not referred to by the 'hosts' as 'tourists', but are named individuals or families who tend to stay either in family houses or in rented accommodation in villages and hamlets.

'Tourists' in the Cantal, on the other hand, often stay on camp-sites, many of which are external to villages and towns. Many camp-sites have been constructed in the more recent wave of tourist development, which has intensified since the early 1980s, partly in response to the crumbling of the agricultural economies of the mountain regions of the Cantal and its neighbouring counties, a strategy developed by the *Conseils generals* (effectively the county councils) and the farmers' organisations alike. Tourists can stay in hotels as well, either in small local hotels in the larger villages or in large hotels in the towns, and there are long-established tourist resorts such as Vic-sur-Cère, and the spa-town of Chaudes-Aigues (literally 'hot waters'). The Cantal also has a large number of *gîtes ruraux* that get booked early in the year for the following season, and a growing number of *chambres d'hôtes*, or bed and breakfasts. The season itself is concentrated between 14 July and 15 August, the French national holidays, although most facilities, such as swimming pools and camp-sites, are open from June to September.

It is clear that the term 'tourist' cannot be used to describe all visitors to the Auvergne, nor can the structural division into hosts and guests be used to formulate a set of distinctions between residents and visitors, as these are not clearly separate entities. Many of the visitors to the region are not totally unknown 'outsiders'. Using the more qualified categories above, it is possible to indicate some of the ways in which the past is differentially represented in the context of the relations between different groups. However, one dominating paradigm must be considered as the context for the particular representations that follow: that of rusticity and rurality.

One of the Cantal's most attractive features to returnees and French tourists is that it is an area of mainly dairy farming that has not been 'modernised' and mechanised as much as in other French regions. It is also often said to be one of the least polluted parts of Europe, as the prevailing wind from the Atlantic passes no industrial areas on its way to the Auvergne. This fits in extremely well with urban myths of simple and healthy country living, which have abounded from the Vichy regime's propagandising to the 'back to the land' movement of the 1960s.[6] By the early 1990s, arguments about health and the countryside were centred on debates about the levels of chemical residues in farm produce, and there was widespread concern about the use of chemicals such as hormone treatments in the raising of farm animals.[7] Within the discourse of this debate, however, what had once been seen as the old-fashioned and out-dated state of many Auvergnat farms was beginning to be reinterpreted as a wholesome, 'organic' approach, and certain groups of farmers were not slow to pick up on this as a marketing slogan. In 1990, a group of cattle farmers and butchers in the west of the department began an advertising campaign that emphasised this 'organic' nature of the meat from their farms, to persuade people to buy their relatively dearer produce rather than imported or intensively-produced meat of lower quality.

Most of the French tourists I spoke to at the local markets described one of the attractions of a holiday in the Cantal as the availability of locally-produced food that satisfied their expectations of rural France. The availability of these goods symbolised the continuity of a way of life on old-fashioned, small-scale farms, where the quality of the produce took precedence over its profitability.[8] Going to a farm to buy produce, such as cheese, milk, eggs and poultry raised on grain in the farmyard, or at least buying such produce at market, became an intrinsic part of the holiday – possibly one of the defining features – for many tourists.

Given the importance of this paradigm of the old-fashioned wholesomeness of rustic produce, it is clear that continuity with past practices is central to perceptions of the Auvergne. The following accounts of different representations of the past thus raise questions about how various versions of this past are presented in different ways to different people.

Performing the Past

One of the striking themes of tourist entertainment throughout the Cantal in the early 1990s was that encapsulated by the term '*Patrimoine*', which we can loosely translate as 'heritage'. Indeed, this was common ground throughout most western and northern European countries, as a large literature on heritage indicates (cf. e.g. Lowenthal 1985; Hewison 1987; Merriman 1991; Patrick Wright 1991; Susan Wright 1992). Whilst museum presentations may be considered as a particular, formalised representation of '*Patrimoine*' (see Abram 1994, 1996), we can also look at the ways in which the past is *performed* and related to the present. Certain symbols of the past and of locality recurred often enough to be considered widespread, and foremost among these were costume, song and dance.

In 1991, the course of an international cross-country relay race in the Chataîgneraie in the Southern Cantal (in the upper Lot valley) passed through a number of very picturesque villages. In one of these villages, a small band played 'local' music. The photographs illustrate this scene quite clearly. The first photograph (Fig. 2.1) shows a runner (no. 47) looking across to the band of musicians playing accordions and singing. The second photograph (Fig. 2.2) shows four accordion players, two older men wearing 'Auvergnat' black felt hats, black smocks and neckerchiefs and a younger man and a woman wearing 'ordinary' clothes. The third photograph (Fig. 2.3) shows the whole group with costumed dancers dancing a *bourrée* to the musicians' 'traditional' songs. We can also just see a man wearing clogs and holding a rustic pitchfork. He can be seen more clearly in the fourth photograph (Fig. 2.4), which also shows the woman with him, standing with the musicians, posing, and a videocameraman recording them for the local news programme.

The costumes this last couple are wearing are archetypal 'Auvergnat peasant' costumes, although the man's 'best' suit differs slightly from the 'peasant smocks' of the musicians. The man carries a woven basket and a pitchfork and the woman carries a distaff; both wear clogs. These people were part of a growing number of 'folkloric' groups in the Cantal who perform local music and dances. Each group has its own detailed version of local music and dance, and of the costumes considered authentic. They often performed on occasions when tourists were around, and some performed specifically for tourists; but they also sometimes performed for local events, where it might not be expected that tourists would be present. Whilst it might be taken as clear that the musicians were providing entertainment in a local style, what could we say the costumed couple were doing? We could explain them away as also providing entertainment in a local style, or we might say they were just 'being' Auvergnat. Or we might say they were performing their Auvergnatness, displaying their identity through a series of markers (Culler 1988), exemplifying a folklore. The fact that they had dressed up to display themselves leaves us unable to pretend they were doing nothing. Their very presence demonstrates a problematic of folklore unavoidable in representations of the Auvergne.

The tension in the photographs between those in costume and those in ordinary dress reveals a wider debate over the place of 'folk culture' in time. Certain political groups, such as the Institute for Occitan Studies, promote the idea that the local language should be retained as a tool for continuity between the past and the future, as a vital element of local identity. They extend this thesis by arguing that local arts should be continued in a more spontaneous way, and that people should dance local *Bourrées* in ordinary clothes, to feel that they are part of the present. However, the setting of local arts in the framework of authentic relations with the past, through the use of old-fashioned costume as illustrated by this set of photographs, points to their relevance being as referents to the past. This process was particularly marked amongst nineteenth-century folklorists, who recorded what they perceived as 'authentic' folklore and fixed evolving traditions at one moment, thereby rendering any further change 'inauthentic' (what Chapman (1989) has called the 'freezing of the frame' with reference to Breton costume). It is clear that if local activities and products are not allowed to change as part of a developing tradition, but become signifiers of the past, fixed at a certain moment in time, then they can be opposed to modernity, and thus perceived as inappropriate to the present. Indeed, it must be said that the majority of artefacts and images marketed to tourists by all manner of enterprises in the Auvergne tend to mark their 'Auvergnat-ness' through the sorts of identifying markers seen in old postcards. Those old postcards themselves are also being reproduced and resold, particularly those folkloric images showing musicians and dancers outside bars, or old women spinning with

Figure 2.1.

Figure 2.2.

Figure 2.3.

Figure 2.4.

distaffs, and men in smocks making clogs or using old tools such as long-saws to chop logs.

It appears that for the nineteenth-century moneyed traveller, these were the identifying features of a people 'tarnished by numerous vices but rich in energetic virtues' (Durif 1990 [1860]: 62), so it is easy to see how tourists might expect to see such marks as the 'real' Auvergne. Even as Durif wrote, though, he described how

> village dress is currently undergoing a noticeable change and seems to be disappearing. The clothes worn by men in the fields are more and more like those worn by workers in the towns; the women, for their part, are abandoning their long *coiffes* in favour of fashionable hats, as if they were no longer pretty. Before 1789, in the countryside, one could count those who wore shoes or the farmers' wives who had umbrellas. Today the most meagre peasant, the poorest shepherd owns such objects, which one can no longer call luxuries . . . Is this a good thing? Maybe. But what is dispiriting is that the picturesque, the spicy and tasty grace of their dress, the simplicity of their customs and their local manufacture are gone, alas, never to reappear (Durif 1990 [1860]: 83–4).

I quote Durif at length in order to illustrate that it was ever thus. In Durif's nostalgia for a real, authentic peasant with bare feet and home-made skirts, today's nostalgia for the 'disappearing world' of authentic, 'real' country people, farmers uncontaminated by the modern, the worldly or the technical, resounds as a fundamental misconstruction of the 'isolated peasant'. If they appeared to Durif to be different and quaint, cruelly corrupted by the influence of urban France, his assumption that they once were unconnected to those towns and that their costume and customs were fixed reflected the Modern view of urbanisation and civilisation.[9]

In fact, the tourist presentation does not capture the peasant quite at the point Durif describes, but at the image captured by late-nineteenth- and early-twentieth-century photographs, and at the point of memory that has replaced the mid-nineteenth-century image, although, on close inspection, even this is constantly being revised. The variations in costumes adopted by folkloric groups show not only the local spatial variation in costume, but also the interpretation that the groups have chosen to place on the past. The past and its costumes and customs are recalled in the childhood memories of today's eldest generation, and these memories locate the authenticity of current representations (the 'problem of perspective' for historians noted by Williams – cited in Burke 1989). In particular, those who left for Paris can remember an Auvergne fixed in the time of their youth, or in their parents' descriptions. If, as Durif suggests, Auvergnats away from home spent a great deal of time recalling the virtues of their truly green and pleasant homeland, then the Auvergnats of Paris instilled in their descendants an idea of the Auvergne as it was when they left it (Burke 1989). Although this by no means covers all versions of the representation of the Auvergne from outside, it would seem to be a significant element in the expectations of visitors to the Cantal that it should retain a clear continuity with that past.

This close association between past, image, locality and identity is common both to many forms of tourism and to many strands of folklore. The 'International Folklore Festivals' held in the Cantal, mainly during the summer holiday season, include groups of dancers and musicians from around the world who appear to share an understanding of local folklore's being distinctive through the use of what might be perceived as 'old-fashioned' costume. This is usually understood in opposition to 'modern, Western fashion'; which leads us to another conceptual conundrum. Edwin Ardener, in particular, opened up the question of centres and peripheries by showing that every periphery appeared to its inhabitants as quite central to their world, and that the centre appeared to be central to those ensconced there (Ardener 1987). Similarly, where it may be said that peripheries seem to be old-fashioned if the direction of change is from the centre (Chapman 1989), it is equally possible that these 'peripheries' have their own developments of fashion and trend that may be influenced by the so-called centre, but can also have a life independent of it. The life of rural folklore groups can be seen almost in opposition to urban fashions, and, indeed, is often explicitly described as such, just as urban modernity is defined in opposition to rural backwardness.

Staged, formalised performances of songs and dance and the international exchange in 'folklore' thus confound the realms of locality and history, by creatively interpreting 'local tradition'. The distinct versions of 'local traditions' can be differentiated in terms of the meaning of tradition. While some performances, advertised specifically for tourists and put on to raise money and provide entertainment during the height of the season, present themselves with the commentary 'this tune/dance dates from such-and-such a time, and comes from such-and-such a valley' in an attempt to authenticate themselves, others, which are less formal, and whose commentary says 'this is a bourrée like we used to dance in our youth', retain the more creative elements of a tradition that can incorporate innovation within a certain musical or performance vocabulary. The more formal presentations, whilst attempting to recreate an 'authentic' performance from another era, actually incorporate developments of their own, often 'tidying up' a performance so that it is more accessible in the form of a staged performance to those who may be used to seeing performances of other kinds, using a more theatrical presentation, with a clear distinction between performers and audience, between those with knowledge and those who are outsiders. However, it could be argued that this formal presentation has more in common with urban experiences of theatre, or with 'public' entertainment and spectacles *per se*, than with local 'traditions'.

In contrast, at a village *bal*, or dance, where local musicians play musette-style for people to dance a medley of dances, including some local versions of ballroom dancing as well as the *bourrée* and *gigue* of the Auvergne, those few individuals who get up and dance the *bourrée* with enthusiasm and vitality are enjoying dance for the sake of dance, but are also confirming their Auvergnat-ness to those local spectators who claim the dance is too difficult for them (and these can be the majority in some areas in the Cantal). These are not tourist events; but if a visitor is present, comments may be made, such as those made to me that 'The *bourrée* is only danced in the Auvergne'; 'In Auvergne folklore is king'; 'We've had this music for centuries.' Here the separation between performer and audience became much more informal. There was no stage, but this does not mean that there were not some people with more knowledge than others; rather, it meant that this distinction was not so rigid, and that the potential was there for anyone to join in and learn. Even when the people who dance at a local *bal* are the same people who have learned the dance, or practised it at a rehearsal for a folkloric group performance for tourists, the informal dance, received by a more scrutinising, but perhaps less judgemental, participating audience, is danced in a less studious spirit than is that which purports to inform 'strangers' about 'our' identity. When dancing for themselves, dancers can simply enjoy the dance; whereas, when performing for others, they are more conscious of their audience.

For musicians, the situation is slightly different, as there are formal schools for learning local music (which I will not consider here), whereas learning to dance is still something that can be learned through local *bals* from generation to generation in the older sense of a tradition. Although some younger people said the musette was old people's music, others joined in, and the most popular musicians in the area were a trio of teenagers who had learned to play Auvergnat tunes on their accordions and pipes at the nearby music school in St Flour. Clear generational divisions cannot be definitively drawn, as there were also older people who did not attend *bals*, and it seems that the range of participants was dependent on interest and inclination rather than age.

If we consider the formal folkloric presentations, we can see that the audience is not just 'there', waiting to be entertained, but is also constructed by the performers. In presenting themselves as authentic, knowledgeable and authoritative, the performers define the audience as ignorant of local folkloric identity. At a village dance, the performers of dances are not so distinct from the audience, but can be interchangeable and have more individual social identities, and so the question of authority is less distinct. However, if the markers of identity are still fairly explicit at these kinds of events, in the music in particular, how can we understand the representations encapsulated in apparently unfolkloric events?

Local Events

The sort of events organised for local village fêtes are also often directed towards tourists, at least in name; but they put forward quite a different presentation of local life from those considered above. We might consider a fête in a village called Ferrières, which usually takes the form of a three-day combination of various events, with the patron saint's day falling on the middle day. The structure of the fête can be summarised into the events held on each day, as shown in Table 2.1.

There is clearly a rounded structure to the timetable, beginning and ending with a boules match and a disco; but it is the context and content, as well as the structure of the fête, that are of interest here.

The fête is advertised by the distribution of posters in the bars of surrounding villages, and occasionally even on roadside placards, and the timetable for the fête is also advertised. The main feature in the advertising is the entertainers brought in for the 'showbiz spectacular', who are usually television entertainers in a music hall or variety style, such as an impressionist, a magician, and a musical group. The entertainment is set on a stage built outdoors in the village square, and is thus free for anyone to attend. The only entry fees are for the evening dances, and exemptions from paying go to those who were on the organising committee or took part in the preparations for the fête in some way. (These exemptions were not limited to people living in the village, as several of the helpers were friends or partners of members of the organising committee from other villages or towns, and most of the members of the organising committee lived in the village only at weekends, working elsewhere during the week.)

The social distance between participants and spectators varied throughout the fête, from minimal, during the boules matches or the discos, to a wider separation during the performances of the entertainers (although

Table 2.1. Calendar of Events for the Three Days of the Fête at Ferrières

	Eve of the Fête	Day of the Fête	Last day of the Fête
Early morning		Dawn call of trumpets and firecrackers	
Late morning		Mass for Saint Mary; Laying of wreath at war memorial; Aperitifs and music in the village square	
Afternoon	Open game of boules	Parade of flowered floats through the village; 'Showbiz spectacular'	League game of boules
Early evening	Torchlight procession through village	Tea dance to musette music	
Night	Disco with guest DJ	Main dance in the village hall	Disco with local DJ

some of them invited members of the audience up on stage as part of their act). The 'traditionality' of this event was quite different to that of the tourist performances of folklore, since this was a fête not purporting to represent history or locality. This was 'just what a fête was like'. However, several of the entertainers commented that it was good to see villages putting on fêtes like this, when in so many villages in France the village fête was a thing of the past, and they encouraged the organisers to carry on this great tradition. When asked why the fête was run to this timetable, all the organisers gave the response that this was the way it was done and always had been, some of them going on to explain how it had been improved since previous fêtes. Similarly, although people said the fête had always happened for as long as they could remember, so that it had a past but no beginning, it was not until the third annual fête I went to that I happened to find out that for several years the fête had fallen into desuetude. During these years there was a mass held for the saint, but nobody organised a fête as such, until a new, young and enthusiastic group of villagers revived it in the late 1970s; and this group continued to build the fête into the main event of the summer bank holiday in that area.

Fêtes rise and fall in popularity, with fêtes like this one taking over from those in other villages that had formerly been the most attractive. As the organising committee began to disperse again during the 1990s, as a result of emigration and different personal obligations and priorities, there was no guarantee that this fête would continue; but while it did, it remained the 'life' of the village and the highlight of the village calendar. For those villages that had fêtes, the timetables were nearly always similar to that of this one, with variations in the amount of activity or the performances. For instance, two nearby fêtes held goat-races through the village as the main event of the fête, rather than the float parade at Ferrières; and one had a trapeze artist as the main entertainment. However, all followed at least the structure shown in the timetable, no matter what entertainments were laid on.

Difference

Is there a difference, then, between the performances for tourists and those not for tourists? I would argue that there is, if only in the meaning of the performances to their participants and in relation to their audiences. A tourist performance could be defined by the identification of its audience as outsiders, people who lack local knowledge, but whose requirements for knowledge remain relatively superficial and should remain within the arena of entertainment. These kinds of tourist performances are distractions, to impress upon the tourists the local distinctiveness of the place (see Cohen, this volume, Chapter 4); but the motivations of the performers and the benefits they expect vary widely. However, as we can see that there is a whole spectrum of tourists and tourisms, we can also recognise a parallel, if not a directly corresponding, range of entertainments. What varies most strikingly is how implicit the local knowledge included in the entertainment is. Tourists are assumed to require, and are thus offered, explicit labelling and framing of events and performances by signs and symbols of authenticity, such as the 'Auvergnat' costumes and local music played on 'authentic' instruments, as an array of signifiers of 'Auvergnat-ness' (see Culler 1988). In contrast, these symbols of local knowledge can be expected to be implicit in local events, where they are symbolic of shared knowledge and experience.

Conclusions

The way in which the past is presented in these different contexts gives us an idea of the variety of modes in which the past can be understood and expressed, and this also ensures that we cannot assume that the 'commoditisation of culture' is a straightforward form of commercial de-socialisation. Although there may be clearer cases elsewhere where commoditisation is enacted through a set of exploitative power relations, in this case the representation of local culture can be seen to lead to a revival of interest in local activities and a revalidation of local practices. The way in which the past is 'sold' to tourists need not necessarily be exploitative; it may be an opportunity for the expression of identity. Selling an idea of the past and an idea of the Auvergne, through performance and through the sale of local produce and the images on postcards, has become a means for people to maintain valued practices. More importantly, it enables people to define and express a continuity that they wish to maintain between the past and the future.

But what can this tell us about tourism, identity and ethnicity? For one thing, it tells us that interactions between local residents, ethnically-identifying groups, external audiences, and internal audiences are multivalent and complex. The layers of reflexivity involved in the interaction between locals and visitors, of whatever type, cannot be simply surmised nor summarised. Nor is there a simple 'effect of tourism'. I have suggested that reflexivity with relation to local identity may be provoked or directed by the gaze of tourists as an 'Other', but that, as the tourist-as-outsider is only one of the range of visitors, each with different views on local social life, and the local-as-guest is only one incarnation, defined in relation to the outside tourist, the idea of tourism's 'spoiling local culture' is misleading; it arises from a static, modernist notion of culture and authenticity. On the contrary, tourism of some sorts may enhance local social activity by providing the audience required to frame a performance, and a background against which local identity can be reflected upon. I have also briefly indicated the possible expectations of some tourists about the region and its people and the kinds of benefits they expect from their visit. This is particularly difficult to summarise, though, since each tourist has a different social context for their understanding of the visit. We can say that there is a wide expectation of rurality, in contrast to urban visitors' everyday experience, and that the experience of the returnees is often a conflict between the idealised, often nostalgic 'home' and their experiences of the Auvergne 'now'.

The main argument here, however, is that in order to understand the relation between tourism and identity, we must embrace the diversity of tourists and not attempt to understand them as a homogenous group, ignoring the differences between them, just as we have to acknowledge that there are differences within groups that we call 'hosts'.

It is possible, though, to see tourists experiencing and negotiating the social environment they visit, and this can provide a rich ground for research on tourism.

Acknowledgements

I should like to express my thanks to Richard Cowell, for his constructive (and complimentary) comments on an earlier draft of this chapter.

Notes

1. Fieldwork between July 1990 and September 1991 was funded by the ESRC, to whom I am grateful.
2. An account of the Auvergnats of Paris can be found in Girard (1985). For an account of migrations to and from Spain, see Poitrineau (1985).
3. Auvergnats in Paris, known as 'Bougnats', visited the Auvergne more frequently after 1904, when a special vacation train service was commissioned for them by the creator of the newspaper *l'Auvergnat de Paris*.
4. See d'Aussy an III; Hugo 1835; Malte-Brun 1882; Verne 1991 [1879].
5. According to the statistical surveys of the Conseil General.
6. For an account of this see McDonald (1982).
7. The demonstrations of 1990 in which French farmers hijacked British sheep-trucks, and on one occasion burnt a sheep alive, were intended to raise awareness amongst consumers that these animals had been treated with hormones that leave residues in the meat, rendering it unhealthy for consumption. These actions were part of a widespread range of demonstrations which reached their most vociferous leading up to the European Union and then the 'GATT' negotiations on common agricultural and trade policies. There was, also, already a great deal of resistance to the importation of British cows because of so-called 'mad-cow disease', a full six years before the British–European crisis of May and June 1996 that saw a European Union ban on the sale of British cattle.
8. This provides an interesting reflection on the expectations of other tourists, notably British, for whom the apparent quality of life of the animals took precedence. For French visitors, it seemed that the quality of life of the animals meant that the produce would be of good quality, whereas for the British the quality of life of the

animals was a concern in its own right – a subtle but perhaps revealing difference.
9. France's isolated peasants were the 'savages' of early French sociology, the 'other' to Parisian intellectuals who wrote about them. Today's tourist who looks for an uncorrupted tradition and berates what MacCannell calls the 'staging' of 'traditions and customs' (MacCannell 1976) is following in this philosophical perception that the Capital City is the essence of Modernity and the rural backwater its opposite.

References

Abram, Simone A. (1994). Recollections and Recreations: Tourism, Heritage and History in the French Auvergne. Unpublished D.Phil. thesis, Oxford University.
Abram, Simone A. (1996). Reactions to the Tourist Gaze: A View from the Deep Green Heart of France. In Jeremy Boissevain (ed.), *Coping with Tourists*. Oxford: Berghahn Books.
Ardener, Edwin. (1987). 'Remote areas': Some Theoretical Considerations. In Anthony Jackson (ed.), *Anthropology at Home*, pp. 38–54. London: A.S.A.
Burke, Peter (1989). French Historians and their Cultural Identities. In E. Tonkin, M. McDonald and M. Chapman (eds), *History and Ethnicity*. London: Routledge.
Chapman, Malcolm (1989). *The Freezing of Breton Costume, Then and Now*. Oxford: Institute of Social Anthropology. (Identity and Ethnicity Seminar, 1989.)
Cohen, A. P. (1985). *The Symbolic Construction of Community*. London: Routledge.
Collard, Anna (1989). Investigating Social Memory in a Greek Context. In E. Tonkin, M. McDonald and M. Chapman (eds), *History and Ethnicity*, pp. 89–103. London: Routledge.
Culler, Jonathan (1988). *Framing the Sign: Criticism and its Institutions*. Oxford: Basil Blackwell.
d'Aussy, Legrand (An III). *Voyage fait en 1787 et 1788, dans la ci-devant Haute et Basse- Auvergne . . ..* Paris: le Directeur de l'Imprimerie des Sciences et Arts.
Davis, John (1992). History and the People Without Europe. In K. Hastrup (ed.), *Other Histories*, pp. 14–28. London: Routledge.
Durif, Henri. (1990 [1860]). *Guide historique, archéologique et pittoresque du Voyager dans le Département du Cantal (ancienne Haute Auvergne)*. Aurillac: Editions de la Butte-aux-Cailles.
Girard, Roger (1985). *Quand les Auvergnats partaient conquerir Paris*, ed. Pierre Miquel. Paris: Fayard.
Hastrup, Kirsten (1992). Introduction. In K. Hastrup (ed.), *Other Histories*, pp. 1–13. London: Routledge.

Hewison, Robert (1987). *The Heritage Industry: Britain in a Climate of Decline.* London: Methuen.

Hugo, Abel (1835). *La France Pittoresque ou description pittoresque, topographie et statistique des départements et colonies de la France.* Paris: Delloye. (Editions du Bastion edition, Aurillac 1991, Vol. 1.)

Kohn, Tamara (1988). Seasonality and Identity in a Changing Hebridean Community. Unpublished D.Phil. thesis, Oxford University.

Liethoudt, Catherine (1991). *La bourrée*, Vol. 2. Collection Escapade, ed. Institut d'Etudes Occitanes. Aurillac: Ostal del Libre.

Lowenthal, David (1985). *The Past is a Foreign Country.* Cambridge: Cambridge University Press.

MacCannell, Dean (1976). Staged Authenticity. In idem (ed.), *The Tourist: A New Theory of the Leisure Class*, pp. 91–107. (Originally published in *American Journal of Sociology*, 79 (3), 1973.) London: Macmillan.

McDonald, Maryon E. (1982). Social Aspects of Language and Education in Brittany, France. Unpublished D.Phil. thesis, Oxford University.

Malte-Brun, V. A. (1882). *Le Cantal.* (Editions du Bastion edition, Aurillac, 1988.)

Merriman, Nick (1991). *Beyond the Glass Case: The Past, the Heritage and the Public in Britain.* Leicester: Leicester University Press.

Poitrineau, Abel (1985). *Les Espagnols de l'Auvergne et du Limousin du XVIIème au XIXème siècle.* Aurillac: Malroux-Mazel.

Strathern, Marilyn (1981). *Kinship at the Core: An Anthropology of Elmdon, a Village in North-west Essex in the 1960s.* Cambridge: Cambridge University Press.

Strathern, Marilyn (1982). The Village as an Idea: Constructs of Village-Ness in Elmdon, Essex. In A. P. Cohen (ed.), *Belonging: Identity and Social Organisation in British Rural Cultures.* Manchester: Manchester University Press.

Verne, Jules (1991[1879]). *Géographie illustrée de la France.* Aurillac: Editions du Bastion.

Waldren, Jacqueline (1988). Insiders and Outsiders in a Mallorquin village community. Unpublished D.Phil. thesis, Oxford University.

Wright, Patrick (1991). *On Living in an Old Country: The National Past in Contemporary Britain.* London: Verso.

Wright, Susan (1992). 'Heritage' and Critical History in the Reinvention of Mining Festivals in North-East England. In Jeremy Boissevain (ed.), *Revitalizing European Rituals.* London: Routledge.

Zonabend, Françoise (1984). *The Enduring Memory: Time and History in a French Village.* Manchester: Manchester University Press.

3

We Are Not Tourists — We Live Here

Jacqueline Waldren

This chapter is about identity-creation and a village population's responses to a period of accelerated socio-economic change. The people in the village of Deià on the island of Mallorca have lived side by side with increasing numbers of visitors and resident foreigners for more than a century. During this period their self-identification as *Deianencs* and the way they perceived 'others' as *outsiders, individuals, travellers, tourists, or residents* has changed many times in relation to events in local, national, and international politics and economics.

Deià has been my home for the past thirty-six years, and I believe that what has occurred there over this period offers an example of how this particular community learned to gain full advantage from the social and economic opportunities opened up by foreigners without losing the fabric of social relations, the meanings and values of their culture (Waldren 1996). In fact, I am suggesting that the village has been able to identify itself as 'a community' with its own symbolic boundaries and identity, not despite outsiders, but because of their presence. Against a clear 'other' the local identity of Deianenc could be asserted. The 'other' was never beyond, but linked to the very life and people that were identifying them. The articulation of others in their midst can be documented from the Catalan–Aragonese conquest in 1229 and through the centuries of domination by outside forces, whether city landlords, tax collectors, or the Church, or as subjects of the neighbouring village of Valldemossa until 1583. The conflicts and resulting compromises that have occurred between Deianencs and 'others' have provided a sense of history that allowed various groups within the village to define, develop, adapt and sustain differing ideas of belonging to the village, where different cultures, values and aspirations have been a constant threat to any shared concept of 'local life' or 'community'. Opposition has provided a purpose to those who have formed the village over time, and aided them in constituting relationships and formulating a sense of 'village' identity. However, 'the village' means very different things to different people.

Deià is a relatively small village for Mallorca. It is the fifth smallest of the fifty-two villages on the island. If one looks at the population statistics for 1900 (900) and those of 1988 (566) one would assume that, like other rural villages on Mallorca and throughout western Europe, Deià was a dying village. Actually, Deià's population has been increasing since 1960, when it was at its lowest (450). There are now over 600 permanent residents, of whom 234 are foreign nationals. From April to October there are an additional 500–1,000 'tourists', including first-time visitors, returning Deianencs, family from abroad and holiday residents in the three hotels and *pensions* or in rented houses.

Unlike so many other parts of the island that have been completely transformed by tourism, Deià appears to have remained an 'idyllic' village in the mountains, untouched by the ravages of time. Its stone houses perched on olive-tree-covered terraces, which descend from the church on the top of the hill to the Mediterranean sea below, give little indication of the separate interests of the individuals or family members that reside within, or of the discordances in economic, political, and social relations that often occur. The village projects an ethos of related people, houses and families, of shared space and familiar activities carried on within ancient walls. The landscape and architectural image of the village belie the transformations inside, for behind this façade of 'timelessness' they have integrated new and different relationships, morals, beliefs and values into their lives. The manner in which this village has dealt with change over the past century reveals a subtle, creative, manipulative reordering of old and new conditions while maintaining the image of a 'traditional' village.

What has occurred in Deià is being repeated in one form or another in many parts of the world today; but unlike these other areas that seem to be losing any semblance of local identity, Deianencs have learned to interact with foreign residents and create an identity over time that allows them to bring in the outside world in their own terms without losing the fabric of social life or local values. The manner in which the local people of Deià have reanimated their 'traditional' values and customs, and reinterpreted their identity in terms of the changing conditions of their lives, while gaining the advantages of participating in the modern world, can be useful to other areas that are or will be experiencing similar 'tourist development'.

Drawing on selected aspects of their past, the locals, known as Deianencs, are living and practising what they consider a 'traditional lifestyle' in the midst of the bohemian, chaotic, and often disruptive life of those they identify as 'the foreign community' that shares their village. 'Local' people have learned to incorporate change and modernity by selectively maintaining those aspects of 'traditions' that can be adapted to meet the needs of the present and their new requirements without altering the status quo. Deianencs are not being held back by 'tradition'; rather they are interpreting it in their own 'local' terms. Tradition is not static, but is constantly being made and re-made: it can be adapted to changing conditions. Resident foreigners and tourists help the Deianencs to assert their identity by not understanding or sharing the 'local traditions' on which Deianencs base their identity. However, all foreigners are not the same, and many long-term resident foreigners identify more with the Deianencs than they do with the newer residents or tourists who are now part of village life.

I think the fact that Deià has become one of the most popular and at the same time exclusive resorts on the island of Mallorca is due to the symbiosis of insiders and outsiders, who have taken advantage of this relationship to preserve the way of life, the landscape and the architecture that attracts so many outsiders to their village. In Deià, the presence of resident foreigners and tourists stimulated the local desire for 'modernity',[1] an increased demand for material goods, salaried jobs with more free time (away from the drudgery of working the land), easy access to distant places and global communications. Foreign residents and visitors offered advantages that, when combined with local social life, made village life more varied and simultaneously stimulated a revival of interest in 'traditional culture'. Shared social, religious and everyday activities marked out Deianencs in contrast to the 'others' who inhabited their village. Religious celebrations became popular celebrations of Deianenc identity in contrast to the cosmopolitan life of the 'others' in their midst.

Stokes noted that 'Groups are self-defining in terms of their ability to articulate differences between self and other, but issues of colonialism, domination and violence have to be taken into account. Recognition of difference is seldom reciprocal' (1994). Dominant groups may oppose the construction of difference when it conflicts with their interests. By observing the two-way process of identity construction and de-construction in Deià, we will see how the perceptions of 'local' and 'foreign' have altered with the changing conditions of local and national politics and world affairs. As world communications bring the most 'remote'[2] areas closer and closer together, people begin to redefine distance, time and one another. Outsiders, seeking rural beauty, tranquillity and 'a return to nature', have moved into rural areas and villages in Europe, Indonesia, Kenya, the United Kingdom, the United States or anywhere else they can buy up property, convert old houses into facsimiles of what they once were (with a few added modern conveniences), and build cheaply or modernise interiors while maintaining the external continuity of 'local' architecture. In the more developed areas, some occupants commute to nearby towns or cities to work during the week, revel in the new-found joys of nature at weekends, and soon feel that they 'know more than the natives' about what is best for the area (see the examples in Strathern 1981; A. P. Cohen 1982).

In other areas, like Deià (Hawaii, Tahiti, Corfu, etc.) some of the foreigners who purchased properties settled there to pursue the arts: painting, writing poetry or prose, composing or performing music or observing and appreciating the creativity of others. They tried to learn about the local people, their language, customs, and histories. Some developed local properties, combining their requirements with local means and ways. A few outsiders attracted more outsiders to share their particular 'paradise'. Other 'absentee owners' lived and worked in other countries and 'escaped' to their retreats for their holidays (which could range from two weeks to three or four months each year). Local people in each setting had different responses to the 'outsiders' in their lives.

Travellers in large numbers are now called 'tourists' and have invaded all these areas (Smith 1989). 'Local' people have been affected to one degree or another and have seen changes occur. Some have benefited at least materially from the influx, but many more believe they have traded their 'traditions' and sense of local identity for access to material goods (Greenwood 1976; Pi-Sunyer 1982; Boissevain 1992). They have re-structured their lifestyles and values to cater for outsiders. Men and women from rural areas have immigrated to towns, cities, and resorts to take up a variety of jobs, which required them to learn different concepts of time, language, customs, gender, etc. In many areas, the maintenance of village life has been left to old people, mothers and small children, and the fabric of social life is almost threadbare except on annual festival days, when 'native' sons and daughters try to return from near and far. Many 'new' houses in small villages have been built while their owners worked abroad, dreaming of coming home to retire.[3]

In many areas, the 'foreigner' (*estranger*), once seen as a potential patron or benefactor and treated with respect and awe, has become an intruder who needs to be controlled from imposing 'foreign' ideas and values on the 'locals'. However, foreign residents and tourists and the prosperity brought in by foreign investment and tourism are now essential parts of local, national, social and political economies. Statistics for the island of Mallorca listed 13 million tourists for 1995. 'Tourists' in this instance included every person who came on to the island via ship or plane. Obviously many of these 'tourists' are islanders returning from business or other trips, foreign residents, Spaniards, Europeans and people from many destinations coming for work, play or various other purposes than tourism. 'Tourism', 'tourists' and 'foreigners' are terms with multiple meanings. This study of Deià offers a long-term view of the changing significance of foreigners in local life and the processes of identity-construction and de-construction behind the terms 'locals', 'foreigners' and 'tourists' at various periods in the history of the village.

Foreign Visitors to Deià

Foreigners in search of unspoiled beauty and tranquillity 'discovered' Deià during the last century. The arrival of a small number of 'travellers' from mainland Spain and other European countries to the village added to the interests of local life. Two *pensions* and a few individuals had been providing services and housekeeping for foreign visitors and a dozen or so resident foreigners since the mid-nineteenth century. Peasants[4] began to gain some cash by letting small houses to foreign travellers who came to paint or write or contemplate the scenery. The reward was prestige among their fellow villagers, as well as a new sort of pride based on sharing their village with outsiders. Hospitality was a reflection of their village to the outside. However, as the numbers of foreign visitors increased, attitudes changed.

It is interesting to read what visitors to Mallorca wrote at different periods to gain some idea of their various experiences and of local reactions to them. The French novelist Georges Sand and the composer Frederick Chopin came to the island in 1838 and remained for a few months. This was the period of wars between the Bourbons and the Carlists, the dynastic disputes that lasted throughout the nineteenth century. Mallorca was in the throes of military law, and armed parties that committed robberies and other crimes made the people wary of strangers. Sand was appalled that she did not get better treatment from the local aristocrats; she wrote in her book *Winter in Mallorca* that 'one had to have a letter of introduction to the leading families on the island to gain access to coach and horses, or any information about accommodations . . .'. Sand's attitudes and behaviour seem to have challenged every value sacred to Mallorquin society at the time. A local journalist responded to her critical view of the people she dealt with in the village of Valldemossa by writing that 'Sand disillusioned in her search for the rustic ideals romanticised by Rousseau wrote scathingly of the inhabitants of Mallorca. As she was one who received favours as dues, who publicly jeered at the faith and quaint customs of the villagers, it should be no surprise that her house was avoided by most people and that she was pointed out as one accursed by God . . .' (Quadrado 1956 [1841]).

Thirty years later, the Archduke Luis Salvador of Austria (Habsburg Dynasty) travelled around the island, and later returned to buy up many estates in Deià and along the north-western coast. He wrote that 'The Mallorquins' innate good nature makes them all the more sensitive to those less fortunate and it is a question of honour for the Mallorquin to greet a stranger, and share with him the goodness and beauties of their islands. All foreigners, even those completely unknown represent welcome visitors' (1869).

Since Spain had lost the last remnants of its empire in 1898, a deeply conservative view blamed this loss on the 'corrosive effects of reforms based on foreign models imported first by the Hapsburgs, then by the Bourbons, and later borrowed from the French Enlightenment' (Balfour, 1995). It is interesting to note that the foreign societies that were blamed for bringing reforms to Spain were the ones whose members came to the islands seeking the simplicity of life, traditions and hospitality of the island inhabitants in contrast to their own countries' sophistication or development. Sand, Chopin and the Archduke Luis Salvador of Austria paved the way for other foreign visitors with their writings and music inspired in Mallorca.

Santiago Rusiñol, a Catalan artist, humorist and writer, describes a local Deià innkeeper's attitude to foreign visitors in his book, *L'Illa De La Calma* (1905):

> The times have changed a great deal from those days when the sight of a man oddly dressed or behaving queerly would cause a commotion amongst the villagers of Deià. So many of those once called strange have passed through Deià in every imaginable dress that the people have reached the point where if someone arrives and does not distinguish himself by exotic action or dress, he is considered of no importance and no one pays any attention to him (English translation 1958).

This early experience with a certain type of foreigner allowed Deianencs to develop a passive acceptance of visitors who were so completely different to anyone they knew that they were never seen as threats, but rather as entertainment and fascination. Deianencs were said to be *curats d'espants* (shockproof). Deià became a haven for individualists and eccentrics. Individualists were those who saw themselves as different from the parent societies they had left behind. They travelled seeking enlightenment from unknown places. They were perceived as eccentrics by the local population. The Mallorquin history of welcoming strangers served the interests of both foreigners and locals. The outsider gained access to the beauty, space, lifestyle, goods, information and services they required, and the local hosts were involved in the acquisitions of the foreigners. There was reciprocity between people of various levels of social and economic standing. The existing social structure included hierarchical relationships between peasants and *senyors* (landowners) as a normal part of life. These foreign, gentlemanly types were easily accommodated within the senyorial category, to whom the locals were accustomed to proffering services. A senyor had 'smooth hands',[5] dressed well and gained his income from the work of others. In fact, their continued presence reinforced an existing social order.

The relationships of foreigners to village social organisation over the past century can be seen by the forms of address that have been used for them. This is a subtle means by which the villagers transmit information about people both to one another and to future generations. Deianencs are recognised by house-names and nicknames, seldom by surnames. A man or woman is recognised in the village idiom by the name of the house or nickname associated with their family. The continuation of a house-name is what Bourdieu called 'symbolic capital', which each family is capable of maintaining or accumulating through the generations (1984). By purchasing village houses foreigners gained 'symbolic capital'. The new owner would be known in the village as 'el senyor de . . .' (the occupant of that named house). He and his family would be given a place within the village through their connection to a house that had a particular place in village history and social organisation (Waldren 1996: 58–80). We can begin to perceive the struggle for coherence in a changing world through the social evolution of the house, the family and the value system. The village was composed of families, houses and shared activities over time. Just as the members of families changed through birth, marriage and death, so the occupants of houses might change, and, although the occupants of a particular house were foreign, the house remained part of the village. Identifying someone with a local house gave that person a kind of fictive kinship with the village.

Including foreigners in the village by giving them house names or nicknames allowed the village to feel they were still in control of their lives. Each new person that stayed in the village was placed into some recognisable category. Foreigners in small numbers depended on the locals for information about available houses, food, transport and every other necessity. They were slotted into the local vernacular, and their individual differences were seen as 'colourful'. This mode of including foreign residents as part of the known village continued well into the twentieth century. Senyor and Senyora with a house name or a surname were used by locals to identify foreign residents until the early 1960s; then Christian names replaced surnames; and by the late 1970s the titles were dropped and foreigners were greeted by their Christian names or their children's names. The social class differences that once caused locals to separate themselves from 'others' with smooth hands were no longer relevant to village life. The prosperity from increased demand for goods, services, land and houses had broken down the huge gaps in social class and income; property acquisition and sales had made some who were once considered peasants into landlords.

Adapting to Economic Change

Until the end of the 1950s the Spanish economy had been in a precarious position. The state was faced with bankruptcy: unable to curb inflation, reduce trade deficits, or attract foreign investment. A policy aimed at attracting foreign investment was implemented. Foreign capital from tourism (begun on a large scale at this time), remittances from Spaniards working abroad and foreign investment made the acquisition of machinery, technology, raw materials and energy sources possible. The tourist boom that brought six million visitors to Spain in 1960 rose to thirty million in 1975 (Riquer i Permanyer 1995). Mallorca was one of the early destinations for these tourists.

Over the past thirty-five years (since 1960) an entire service sector has been created to deal with the massive influx of seasonal visitors to Mallorca. Prior to this time there had been a large peasant sector and an inflexible dominion of large landowners and religious mechanisms for social control. Migration out of the rural areas to the city or newly developed coastal 'resorts' had brought about a decline in agricultural activities, turned small villages into dormitory towns and led to an enormous increase in those employed in the service sectors. In most areas development was initiated and financed by foreign companies to comply with the necessities of foreign-organised tourism.

The development of the first tourist facilities on the island was initiated by foreign investors and took place on the southern and eastern coasts. Hotels, bars, restaurants, cafés and souvenir shops replaced the tiny kiosks that once supplied tepid drinks to local Sunday picnickers. Other areas of the island developed aspects of folklore, geology or history to attract tourists for a few hours each day and an increasing number of complementary services grew up around these attractions. For example, the difficult stay of Georges Sand and Frederich Chopin in Valldemossa, which caused her to write 'I have to affirm that I hadn't a single financial dealing, however trivial, with the Majorcans without their showing a very obvious bad faith and gross stupidity', has been cleverly forgotten by the heirs to the rooms where they stayed. These were part of the secularised cells of the Carthusian monastery,[6] which have been converted into an image of the surroundings experienced by the composer and his sophisticated partner, with period furniture, musical scores, a piano and busts of the composer strategically placed to allow the flow of thousands of tourists to walk through without disturbing the relics. Although Sand described their three rooms as 'pleasing to the eye', much of what one sees today has no relation to the contents of the cells inhabited during the cold winter Chopin and Sand spent in Valldemossa. This re-creation of the past for tourist consumption is more fiction than history.

The service sector attracted young people from outlying villages with the offer of regular wages, social security, and fixed hours of work and leisure amidst a vast array of strange and colourful tourists whose northern complexions cried out for sun and whose hearts yearned for Latin lovers. The freedom of the 1960s reached Mallorca, and allowed at least some of its local youth to taste the fruits of previously denied experience. Foreigners were attractive for their differences and for the access to outside ideas, customs and pleasures they could provide to those from the previously 'closed world of the villages'. Those left behind in the villages felt deprived and backward compared to their friends who had managed to find work in the ever-increasing resorts springing up around the island's beaches. It would take some time for most of the village people to derive some personal benefit from the increased demands for their products and services. The landscape, once the livelihood of generations, became an attraction for more and more admirers. The first hotel (there were three *pensions*) built in Deià in 1965 could only find two or three local people to work, as those who might have qualified had left and settled in the city. By the time the second large hotel was built in 1985 there was an entire generation of local young people ready to work in it. Social security, secure jobs, and dual incomes for couples provided the means for yearly holidays to ski resorts or to London, Paris or Goa for young people employed in the service sector in Deià.

More foreign visitors and residents in the village meant that more local people could experience the prosperity of the past fifteen years; but it also meant an alteration in the social relations between the two groups. By the 1980s, as increasing numbers of foreigners arrived, instead of relying on the local people, they turned to other foreigners for advice. The symbiotic relationship of locals and foreigners that had been beneficial to both groups was no longer possible. Five or ten foreign eccentrics added entertainment and distraction; but two hundred foreigners was another experience altogether. Foreigners no longer represented the wonders of the outside world once unattainable by a local person. On the contrary, they now posed a threat to the local 'inside world', buying and selling property, renting accommodation and involving themselves in local politics. The presence of another group that could threaten their very existence has strengthened cohesiveness and drawn locals together despite individual differences.

In the local terminology people are categorised as *Deianencs, Forasters* and *Estrangers*. In the strictest sense, *Deianencs* are those who were born in the village of Deià, 'the natives or insiders' who share a common heritage, language and customs. *Forasters* are Spaniards from other villages or mainland Spain. An *Estranger* is a stranger; *Estrangers* are foreigners/outsiders/persons from other countries. Tourists are referred to as *estrangers*. I will endeavour to describe the way in which these terms are used, how people label and group one another, and how they determine these labels. I will develop the argument that these terms are basically circumstantial. People categorise one another according to the situation and the desired results. Categories are important, but they don't get in the way of ongoing relations. Identities are relational terms, defined in interaction. These terms are only headings under which people are described, and they are contracted, expanded and reinterpreted to fit the constantly changing 'reality' of the society. Boundaries and definitions are shifted to meet the needs of the moment.

The category *Deianenc* ranges from generations of men and women born in Deià and wed to others from Deià, to affines from other Mallorquin villages or from mainland Spain, to Spaniards who reside and vote in Deià, and may be extended to include children born to foreign parents in Deià and foreign-born residents who act in the interests of the village. There is both respect and resentment for those who cross social boundaries. At the same time that one is identified by Deianencs as 'one of us', they point up their astonishment at the fact that a foreigner can do things (for example speak Mallorquí, catch fish, dance local folk dances, etc.) 'as well as or better than us'. It is only through involvement in local reciprocities and activities that one can enter into local life. The definition of a Deianenc is seen to be tied up directly with the conception of the village as shared knowledge, space, time, related people, activities and beliefs.

The significance of being a Deianenc, an 'insider', once meant that one had a birthright, a home that gave one a sense of belonging over all others who lived in the village. Today, this is no longer specifically a right of Deianencs. Half the houses in the village are owned by foreigners, some of whom have been residents for forty years. Their children and grandchildren also claim a birthright and a home in Deià. *Estrangers*–Foreigners, *Forasters*–other Spaniards, and *Deianencs*–locals, are now competitors for the same resources. Competition for land, houses, consumer goods and services has replaced the interdependence of the earlier years. Both groups identify with the place as 'home'.

I believe that in Deià, one group has learned to 'play off' against another: Deianencs contrast themselves to resident Catalans owing to their differing political allegiances in the past and at present; Catalans have little interest in resident mainland Spaniards on account of their own regional priorities; Deianencs see Spaniards as gentrified; Spaniards wish there were fewer foreigners; while foreigners sometimes prefer their own nationals, especially the French and the Germans. Europeans and Americans are clearly outsiders both culturally and geographically; but Catalans and other mainland Spaniards can also be outsiders in terms of their inability to understand local values and desires in other than value-laden terms. One hears people saying: 'Poor Deianencs, they are just slaves to rich Germans and they do not even realise it!' On the other hand, the same people can be heard to comment: 'The Deianencs would have lost everything if it were not for the foreigners who have bought houses, built hotels, given them work, etc.'

English is the *lingua franca* of the foreign contingents, Castilian Spanish is the everyday public language of the village, and Mallorquí, a dialectal variant of Catalan, is the local language. Each person develops different relationships with locals in terms of the location of their house, whether they have local neighbours or live outside residential areas or on the hillsides, whether they speak Spanish or Mallorquí, and multiple other factors that allow people to feel they have a special relationship with 'the village'. The question remains: Who are the village people; who are the insiders and who are the outsiders? Most important, who makes these distinctions and in what circumstances?

Locally perceived boundaries delineate separate entities under different headings in each new set of circumstances. The village to a Deianenc is not just the place, it is generations of kin, houses, land, work, rituals, religion, values. It is the vantage point from which they form their view of the world. From their perspective, they are the insiders. The foreigner describes the village from the distance: an outsider's view of beauty and tranquillity, an idealised setting that satisfies personal needs, an economically viable alternative lifestyle, an investment, a 'paradise' offering a beautiful landscape, sun, drink, and many like-minded persons with whom to share these expatriate experiences.

This picturesque village in the mountains of Mallorca, depicted by artists and writers and the home of an 'agricultural' populace now oriented toward the tourist industry, seems to be inhabited by groups of people with quite different perspectives on the village they inhabit. They manage to live side by side with really quite different perceptions of the space they all refer to as 'the village'. When decisions about the future of the village are needed, the conflict of interests becomes a political issue. In the past few years, minor internal difficulties in village politics have been absorbed in a mounting desire to 'unite' Deianencs against the opposition from outsiders. As Pitt-Rivers noted so long ago, 'the recognition of foreigners as part of the social milieu allows them to be used as scapegoats, which implies a degree of proximity and co-operation' (1954: 143). This dual role of resident foreigner as both neighbour and outsider complicates relationships both with locals and with other foreign visitors. The title of this paper is meant to reflect the dilemmas faced by foreign residents, especially when the tourists start arriving and residents, like locals, feel protective of 'their village'. This is the time when foreign residents feel most vulnerable, when they want to assert their identity as residents in contrast to other foreigners who are 'just tourists' on short holidays.

I hope it has become evident that 'the village' as a community with its own symbolic boundaries and identity is a changing entity, not despite outsiders, but because of their presence. Against a clear 'other' the local identity of *Deianencs* as a group can be asserted; but the foreign residents can only assert their identity in contrast to other foreigners, and this identity is not articulated by the Deianencs. *Estrangers* are *estrangers* . . . The events of the past decade have caused Deianencs and foreigners to reinterpret their relationships with one another and the village they share, so that some form of coexistence can be maintained. The meanings and uses of the terms Deianencs and *estrangers* have developed to their fullest and most manifest forms during the past ten years' coexistence with increasing numbers of foreigners. The terms are being elicited to articulate symbolic boundaries between those who 'form' the village and those who 'merely live' there.

De-constructing Identity

Outsiders–Insiders do not just define one another, and changing attitudes affect the use of these terms in different situations. Some people are more insiders than outsiders in various circumstances, and after more than a hundred years' coexistence between Deianencs and foreigners of all sorts it is more a question of degrees of inside-ness and outside-ness. These terms were not often used during the Franco regime. The regular use of the terms *Deianenc* and *Estranger* to distinguish 'Insiders from Outsiders' is a local manifestation of the general pattern provoked by the national constitution of 1981, which divided the country into seventeen autonomous regions and forced areas to turn inward to rediscover their local and regional identities in contrast to the rather contrived 'unity of Spain' so long espoused by the Franco government.

The political turmoil of the twentieth century emphasised being Spanish, rather than Mallorquin, and forced regional and local identities to go 'underground'. The continued surveillance of local communities by members of the Falange during the Franco regime (1939–75) and the suppression of regional identities during this period may have subdued the assertion of local identities; but they were subtly expressed at every opportunity through language, rituals, modes of address, clothing, gestures, food consumption, etc. The image of Spain promoted by Franco was of a traditional and unified country. This was the myth of Spain symbolised by religious processions, bull fights and flamenco music and dance, an ideological weapon to establish a cultural identity at a time of rapid social and economic change. However, this image of continuity and national ideology was pierced by discontinuities.

By the time democracy was acclaimed in 1976, it was clear that national identity had little meaning, and the focus of people's attention was on regional interests and the reconstruction of regional identities that had been prohibited for decades. On the island of Mallorca, the well-kept and productive land, forests, olive trees, stone terraces and citrus trees (once the source of local pride and identity) were in various stages of neglect. People were too busy (or too old) to care for them, agriculture had become unprofitable, and tourism in all its forms (accommodation, services, food, transport, fuel, etc.) offered the kinds of security that most people wanted. A large number of curious outsiders forced Mallorquins to identify themselves as a regional culture in contrast to other parts of Spain, to revitalise their traditions, their language, their customs in order to entertain and attract more visitors than other parts of the country. The result of combining their cultural specificity with the beauties of the island gave them a unique opportunity, which led to Mallorca's popularity as a summer holiday spot for Scandinavians, Germans, British, French and other Europeans.

Tourism and Development in Deià

The new democracy has made possible various public political confrontations between foreign residents and local voters in Deià concerning the future development of the municipality. Expansion of any sort, either housing development or the opening of new roads or the improvement of old ones, has been a major cause of disagreement between the two groups. From the foreign resident's point of view a new road or an improved old one opened the village to too many people; but from the local point of view, roads provided easier access to and from the village and many advantages for Deianencs and their families. At various Deià council meetings between 1977 and 1985 it became evident that Deianencs and other residents (including Catalans, mainland Spaniards, British, Germans and Americans) had quite different concepts of what 'the village' was and how it should evolve in the future.

For centuries, Deianencs had served and supplied the product Deià as identified and desired by outsiders. The landscape, stone houses, church perched on top of the hill, the wide expanse of mountains behind and the blue Mediterranean were what attracted people to Deià. The landscape and environment of Deià were products that people from other countries wanted to consume. The Deianencs felt they were responsible for maintaining this product as desired by those who came to view and appreciate it. The foreign residents in the village wanted Deià to remain unchanged so that they and other foreigners could continue to live their 'ideal lives in paradise'. What they did not consider was that their residence had begun to turn this particular paradise into a viable commercial product, and made a marked social and economic impact on the local population. No longer 'just peasants', but acquisitive individuals and families, the Deianencs were in a position to re-identify the product Deià in their own terms. It was time that their needs and those of their children came first. They were concerned with improvements that would provide employment and housing in Deià for Deianencs. After over a hundred years of coexistence and reliance on outsiders as potential clients, patrons or benefactors, constructive criticism by outsiders provoked antagonism and resentment where symbioses once existed.

Since the 1920s, outsiders had maintained the material symbols of the past while the locals were struggling to find work and have enough to eat.

During the period from 1950 to 1975, while Deianencs were putting work, time and energy into improving and modernising their lives and their homes, foreigners were buying up the 'past' as enthusiastically as the Deianencs were putting it aside. By the time there was work for all and rewards were many, Deianencs were ready to reinterpret their own past. They were able to 'capitalise' on the qualities that had attracted outsiders to their village. The very symbols of the material past once discarded by their parents and purchased and maintained by the foreigners were those adopted by the young Deianencs to express their collective identity: refurbished stone houses, agricultural implements as artefacts hung on walls, rough stone floors, rustic beams and hand-crafted materials for upholstery and curtains, ironwork and pottery. Local costumes once seen as part of an oppressive past were remade for village festivals to identify Deianencs and to distinguish them clearly from the many observers who come to the village on these occasions. Many of the details for the design of costumes, furnishings, ironwork and other implements of the past were gleaned from the collection of drawings and writings compiled by the Austrian Archduke Luis Salvador in 1868. The seven volumes of *Die Balearn* are full of historic fact and detailed engravings that represent one of the finest records available of the Mallorquin past.

While so many areas of Mallorca have been altered beyond recognition by outsiders and tourism, Deià has been able to maintain 'village' continuity visually, culturally and socially through its relationship with visiting tourists, many of whom became permanent residents. By adapting and reinterpreting 'traditional' activities, attitudes and values to meet the demands and aspirations of modern life Deià has maintained its image of 'paradise'. The selective use of traditional relations and symbols has marked the community's responses to changing political, social and economic conditions and opportunities. Reliance on 'tradition' reveals history as a legitimator of action and expresses and symbolises the social cohesion of 'the village' as an enduring combination of land, kin, houses, occupations and shared experience, in contrast to the *estrangers* (foreigners) who in ever-increasing numbers have come through Deià. Resident foreigners have aided this process of reidentification, and they too rely on similar symbols of the past, including knowledge and experience gained over their decades of residence in Deià. Both of these identities are placed in contrast to tourist developments and modern building styles in other areas of the island.

The Deianencs use 'selective traditions' as a cultural self-identification that serves as a form of collective identity; an assertion of their sense of solidarity through the symbols of everyday life. It is not just a reaction to social change, but an element in determining social action. Family, neighbour and religion are very different institutions now from what they were in the past. Yet they remain as idioms for social associations. Nuclear and extended families have become more important, while neighbour relations have altered considerably. Vatican II and post-Franco democracy have greatly altered the religious ritual of ceremonies; but the celebrations continue to reaffirm familial and community ties. These familial and community linkages are gradually rearranged to enhance current aspirations.

In Deià today, both religious and calendrical rituals mark locality and other aspects of communal identity. The structured forty-hour week has made every weekend a celebration, instead of the periodicity associated with Church festivals. Religious services have become celebrations of the community. Heightened social life once associated with the sacred has become more secular and matter of fact, as Boissevain notes for Malta (1992: 147). The sacred has become popularised, and membership in the religious community is another expression of identity.

By using the categories of Deianenc-*Estranger*, the local population are expressing symbolic boundaries. Deianencs are those who understand the meanings behind the symbols. These concepts of insiders and outsiders are based on a perceived social distance between those who 'understand one another' through a common language, traditional associations, and shared knowledge and experience and those who lack these qualities. Insiders maintain an image of 'a traditional people' in a 'traditional setting' and an ethos of continuity and timelessness. This image is an effective device behind which changing attitudes and material acquisitions can be assimilated. Insiders have drawn ideas and practices from the outside for many years. By marking at least some parts of their social life as unchanging and invariant they have been able to respond to innovation and change by bringing the changes inside their homes and families without disrupting the appearance of the social order.

Rather than collapsing under pressure or giving up their culture and community to outsiders, Deianencs have found ways to resist total change by revitalising their own cultural heritage within the changed conditions brought on by the continuous presence of outsiders. By maintaining a semblance of traditional life they retain a sense of continuity, a personal and social security based on previous generations' experiences.

The village has prospered and been able to evolve new attitudes and aspirations within the time-honoured institutions of marriage, home and family. Foreigners were often drawn into local life through being given a house name, a form of fictive kinship that allowed them to feel part of 'the village'. Together, they have developed a secure framework on which to base their future. They have learned to appreciate the past as the source and legitimation of 'their community'. They want to reclaim the material symbols of that past before they are completely lost. Landownership, once the basis for social status, the source of life and individual identity, has become a commodity sold to the highest bidder.

Long-term foreign residents 'fear' the opening up of the village to more and more foreigners who share less and less of the values to which their expatriate lives were committed. Outside the mainstream or accepted norms of their own and the local culture, each was endeavouring to create an identity based on the criteria of creativity, knowledge, and freedom of choice in all aspects of their lives. Although there was never any attempt to assimilate with their neighbours, there was a mutual respect for one another's differences. The 'new foreigners' show little interest in their local neighbours, and their actions seem to imply that money speaks across languages.

The Deià of today is only a romantic illusion of the agricultural village of the past where peasants welcomed foreigners and accepted their eccentricities without question. Deià is becoming a 'chic' area of Europe, where young upwardly mobile and retiring people are buying second homes. The demand for houses has increased to the extent that prices are doubling and tripling each year. Increased house prices have altered inheritance patterns, the community structure and the social relations between locals and foreigners. Few local people can afford to buy a house in their native village, nor can struggling artists afford to live in Deià any more. The setting is the same, but 'paradise' is harder to attain. Long-term residents as well as Deianencs are caught up in the demand. They all feel compromised. They know the village needs the revenue provided by the new residents, but they resent the 'intrusion into their village' and feel a price tag has been put on all aspects of life in Deià. No one can ignore the changes, and no one can say for sure who will be insiders and who will be the outsiders in the next generation.

Tonkin *et al.* pointed out that 'the definition and self definition of human groups and the relationship of these definitions to history reveals how history is used, experienced, remembered and created' (1989). In Deià we find that long-term foreign residents have merged their varied histories with what they have gleaned from local histories to join in claiming their rights to local identity. Their myths of Deià include stories about various events, colourful personalities and relationships and the many well-known artists and writers who have lived and worked in the village. The retelling of these stories reinforces the effect of an ongoing community with a past, a present and a future, in contrast to the many short-visit tourists who are now a regular part of daily encounters. When they go to the cove to swim and sun, the area is filled with unfamiliar tourists. Local cafés and restaurants serve more drinks and meals to tourists than they do to locals and foreign residents.

The terms 'locals', 'foreigners', 'tourists' and 'tourism' mean many different people, and require detailed description to reveal their varied meanings. In Deià, the local Deianenc identity has been formed and re-formed in contrast to the many different groups that have lived within the village over its hundreds of years of history. Foreign residents have developed their own sense of identity with the place Deià, the people, and their combined histories. These may not be the same identities; however, they have developed from similar criteria of opposition with 'others' within the same environment. As Edwin Ardener noted 'That there is a multiplicity of identities that coexist from any single perspective is not strictly speaking a problem theoretically. It is one of the proofs – and one of the costs – of the apparent paradox of the continuity between the space and individuals that constitute it. They are defined by the space and are nevertheless the defining consciousness of the space' (1989). Foreign residents in Deià feel they have much more in common with Deianencs than they do with the increasing number of tourists coming through the village, and they want to participate in the decisions made by the village. This identifying with the place, people and history they have experienced over at least three generations of coexistence with Deianencs makes them feel they can claim that 'We are not tourists; we live here'; but their self-professed identity is still not fully accepted by those who profess to be Deianencs. The ongoing reconstruction of identities is a form of control over their environment and those who pass through it, and will probably be renegotiated many times in the years to come.

Notes

1. 'Modernity', 'modernisation', 'modern' are problematic terms. They are used in this paper to include 'the process of capital-driven social, economic, political and cultural change occurring at differential rates over the past two hundred years across Europe and the United States' as discussed by Graham and Labanyi (1995). It must be clear, though, that the effects of these processes can be quite different in different areas, and I am discussing their impact on life in Deià particularly.

2. 'A place is remote to those who have not been there, but to those within it is just another place' (Ardener 1989: 213).

3. Many men emigrated from Mediterranean countries to the Middle East where work was better paid. They were able to send funds home to build houses for their future retirement. When the Gulf War occurred they were forced to return to their villages in Egypt, Greece or Turkey, where their houses remain half-built.

4. 'Peasants' in the local sense is a collective representation of a 'class' and an agricultural way of life that was once predominant in Mallorca. Although there are many distinctions made within this group according to the actual job one did, it is used to identify those who work with their hands from those who live from the work of others. It is contrasted to *senyors* (landowners). As is pointed out by Bestard (1986) for the Balearic island of Formentera, 'although these class structures have altered dramatically over the past thirty years, the "identity" is often used as a collective affirmation of a mode of social communication which ignores the differences between the forms of life of the past and those brought in by tourism. It suggests a continuity of traditional forms in the present among those who identify with this history.'

5. 'Smooth hands' is the expression used to imply that one does no menial work.

6. The monks abandoned this monastery after a law (*Ley de Cortes* 1820) deprived monastic orders and other non-tax-paying persons of dominion over any land. This was intended to break the aristocratic and church monopoly on landownership in Spain. Only tax-paying citizens were permitted to buy these lands.

References

Ardener, E. (1989). 'Remote Areas' – Some Theoretical Considerations. In M. Chapman (ed.), *The Voice Of Prophecy*. Oxford: Basil Blackwell.

Balfour, S. (1995). The Loss of Empire, Regeneration, and the Forging of a Myth of National Identity. In H. Graham and J. Labanyi (eds), *Spanish Cultural Studies*. Oxford: Oxford University Press.

Bestard, J. (1986). *Casa y Familia*. Palma de Mallorca: Institut D'Estudis Balearics.

Boissevain, J. (1992). Play and Identity. In J. Boissevain (ed.), *Revitalizing European Rituals*. London: Routledge.

Bourdieu, P. (1984). *Distinction*. London: Routledge and Kegan Paul.

Chapman, M. (1989). *Edwin Ardener: The Voice of Prophecy and Other Essays*. Oxford: Basil Blackwell.

Cohen, A. P. (ed.) (1982). *Belonging. Identity and Social Organization in British*

Rural Cultures. Manchester: Manchester University Press.

Graham H. and Labanyi J. (1995). Culture and Modernity: The Case of Spain. In H. Graham and J. Labanyi (eds), *Spanish Cultural Studies*. Oxford: Oxford University Press.

Greenwood, D. (1976). *Unrewarding Wealth.* Cambridge: Cambridge University Press.

Luis Salvador, Archduke of Austria (1869). *Die Balearen in Wort und Bild geschildert.* Leipzig.

Pi-Sunyer, O. (1982). Two Stages of Technological Change in a Catalan Fishing Community. In Estelle Smith (ed.), *Those Who Live by the Sea.* New York: West.

Pitt-Rivers, J. (1954). The People of the Sierra. Chicago: Chicago University Press.

Quadrado, J. Ma. (1956). To Georges Sand: A Refutation. In *La Palma: A Weekly Journal of History and Literature.* 15 May 1841. Reprinted in Georges Sand (1956 [1845])*Winter in Mallorca* (translated and annotated by Robert Graves). Mallorca: Ediciones Valldemossa.

Riquer i Permanyer, B. (1995). Social and Economic Change in a Climate of Immobilism. In H. Graham and J. Labanyi (eds), *Spanish Cultural Studies.* Oxford: Oxford University Press.

Rusiñol, S. (1958 [1905]). *Majorca: The Island of Calm.* Barcelona: Pulide.

Sand, G. (Dudevant, A. L.) (1956 [1845]). *Winter in Mallorca* (trans. R. Graves). Mallorca: Ediciones Valldemossa.

Smith, V. L. (ed.) (1989). *Hosts and Guests* (2nd edn). Philadelphia: University of Philadelphia Press.

Stokes, M. (ed.) (1994). *Ethnicity, Identity and Music.* Oxford: Berg.

Strathern, M. (1981). *Kinship at the Core.* Cambridge: Cambridge University Press.

Tonkin, E., M. McDonald and M. Chapman (eds) (1989). *History and Ethnicity.* London: Routledge.

Waldren, J. (1996). *Insiders and Outsiders: Paradise and Reality in Mallorca.* Oxford: Berghahn Books.

More than the Beatles: Popular Music, Tourism and Urban Regeneration

Sara Cohen

T his chapter uses a case study on The Beatles and Liverpool[1] to consider the relationship between music and the city, and the implications of that relationship for the study and development of tourism. The first part of the chapter discusses some of the ways in which the music-making of The Beatles and other musicians could be said to 'produce' Liverpool socially, culturally and materially, and it indicates the particular, and generally hidden, significance of music to tourism. The second part of the paper highlights the contested nature of this process, illustrating some of the ways in which The Beatles' connection with Liverpool is represented and debated by different resident groups in the city. One of those groups is then discussed in further detail in order to try to contextualise and explain such debates and consider the questions they raise for tourism theory, policy and practice. Such questions are to be more thoroughly addressed in a two-year ethnographic study of popular music, tourism and urban regeneration to be conducted at Liverpool University's Institute of Popular Music.[2]

Tourism, Liverpool and The Beatles

Culture, Tourism and Urban Regeneration

The potential contribution of tourism to regenerating depressed urban areas has been increasingly emphasised, and most British and American cities have turned to it as a component of their economic policy.

Tourism is viewed as one means of improving the general image of cities, enabling them to compete with other cities to attract not just tourists, but potential investors, transnational corporations, and national and international funding bodies. The past decade has witnessed increasing emphasis in America and Europe on the role of culture and the arts in this race between places to create distinct place identities (Robins 1991), leading to an emphasis upon 'cultural tourism', involving the commodification of local culture and heritage, and to interconnections between tourism, art, education, shopping, etc.[3]

Several influential economic impact studies (NEFA 1981; Cwi 1982; PANYI 1983; Myerscough 1989) have suggested that the arts are a major factor affecting people's choice of places to visit or reside, and hence spend and invest in (cf. for example Bianchini 1989; Myerscough 1989; Cameron 1991). Such studies represent an important shift from a view of art and culture as merely a subsidised adjunct to the economy. They point out the economic and social benefits of using the arts to attract more visitors and investment, creating job opportunities as well as contributing to the quality of life for residents. The studies ascertain the role, and potential role, of the arts and cultural industries in economic development by looking at expenditure on goods and services by arts and cultural organisations, and at audience expenditure on arts activities, and the 'ripple effect' of such expenditure through other local sectors (hotels, restaurants, etc.). The most significant audience spending is that by visitors, in that it brings new money into the local economy.

Whilst many British cities began to take an interest in tourism, culture and the arts following the recession of the early 1980s, Liverpool's Militant-dominated City Council was understandably concerned to concentrate instead upon an urgent local need for housing, and regarded tourism as a poor substitute for secure employment. The Council didn't allocate any funds specifically for tourism, and in 1981 handed all responsibility for tourism over to Merseyside County Council, whose development of it was due largely to one individual. At that time the linking of Merseyside with tourism was still a rather alien, and to many a rather amusing, concept in view of the region's notorious social, economic and image problems.

After the 1981 riots in Liverpool, the Government Minister for the Environment, Michael Heseltine, established the Merseyside Development Corporation (MDC), which promoted investment into the city as a cultural attraction in order to reap economic benefits. The MDC set up the Liverpool Garden Festival and an award-winning dockland and development scheme that mixed residential, retail and leisure facilities.

The latter was the subject of much controversy in the city, but its success in attracting visitors and enhancing the city's image has been widely acclaimed, and it has been seen as a spearhead for change, contributing to a shift in attitudes toward tourism within the city.

Liverpool's post-Militant City Council, following Labour councils in cities such as Sheffield, Birmingham and Glasgow, began to view tourism as a quick route to generating investment and employment and improving the city's poor economy and image (although in a sense the Council had little choice but to respond to the dictates of the MDC and central government). The seriousness of the Liverpool's current economic decline was marked in 1994 when Merseyside became 'Objective One' status, which is the European Community's highest funding category. This is the latest in a long line of Central Government and European funding schemes targeted at the region, which has contributed to a surprisingly large number of locally-based agencies involved with tourism and the arts. Today the city has a weak private sector, a mass of voluntary and community groups, and a powerful set of central government quangos that are neither locally electable nor accountable.

Alongside the latter, the City Council now emphasises Liverpool as a place that can be 'professionally' developed, packaged and sold to visitors and potential investors. The reports and conversation of such bodies contain a language of visitor services, 'key assets', 'core products', 'destination marketing', product 'quality' and 'style'. Much effort has been made to promote the city as a place of excellence, fine architecture, leading universities, etc., with a strategy based around the theme of Maritime City. Yet for some time now The Beatles have been a focal point for debates concerning the city's image and heritage and the development of its music and tourism industries, and although a vast amount of literature exists on The Beatles, little has been written on the ways in which they are used and discussed in contemporary Liverpool.

Liverpool and The Beatles

The Beatles are of course the most famous Liverpool pop band. With other local bands of the early 1960s they contributed to the so-called Merseybeat phenomenon, and they eventually signed a recording contract and moved to London. Their last live performance in Liverpool was in 1963 at the famous Cavern Club. The band split up in 1970, and hopes of a reunion were thwarted by the death of John Lennon ten years later.

The Beatles were the first British band to 'make it' in the American market, and they have also been described as the first rock/pop band to make their local origins a part of their 'global' success. An article in *Music Week* (22.1.1994) began: 'Think Liverpool and you immediately think The Beatles.' Literary and media accounts of The Beatles have linked them with a particular Liverpool sound, character or culture. Beatles literature often, for example, emphasises the band's working-class status, and represents the band in a manner that constructs an opposition between them and their middle-class (and homosexual) manager, Brian Epstein. An issue of the London-based Beatles fanzine describes Brian ordering smoked salmon and 'fine wine' from a posh London restaurant while 'the boys' preferred 'cheese sarnies' and 'cups of tea' (Barrow 1993). The article typically emphasises the quirky humour of the boys in contrast to the seriousness and moodiness of Epstein. In such literature it is 'the boys' rather than Epstein who are taken to embody Liverpool, and through them representations of Liverpool as northern, working-class, cheeky, disrespectful, and masculine 'other' are reinforced. Such representations are particularly strong in Beatles films such as 'A Hard Day's Night', where the band are also linked to kinship, Irishness and roots.

Through sounds, images, events and artefacts The Beatles have represented Liverpool in many other ways, influencing how people think about the city and imbue it with value and sentiment, and how people act in relation to the city. A city is a material setting comprising the physical and built environment; it is a setting for social practice and interaction; and it is an idea, concept or symbol used to convey meaning. To describe a city as being 'produced' is to emphasise the processes that shape the city's material, social and symbolic forms. Music is part of such processes. Music reflects aspects of the place in which it is created: hence 'different cities . . . make different noises' (Street 1995: 259); but music also produces place. The musical influences apparent in The Beatles' songs in some ways reflect Liverpool's historical development and geographical, social and economic circumstances (with, for example, American rock'n'roll and country influences reflecting the city's strong trading links with America, and melodic Irish influences reflecting the city's large population of Irish origin); but the following section illustrates some of the ways in which the Beatles have also played a role in 'producing' the city. It does so through a brief account of Beatles tourism in Liverpool, which links The Beatles with the commoditisation of Liverpool: the packaging, promotion and sale of distinct Liverpool identities and experiences.

Beatles Tourism

Despite the successes of The Beatles and other local bands, Liverpool has a dilapidated music industry from which hardly anyone in the city profits. The small businesses that it comprises undergo a continual struggle for survival,[4] and when local musicians have achieved some degree of success (such as signed contracts with London-based record companies) they have often left Liverpool. It is not just musicians who have left the city. Over the past thirty years Liverpool's population has decreased considerably (from 800,000 in 1961 to 500,000 in 1991), with many leaving the city for economic reasons (for example to seek work elsewhere).

However, The Beatles' association with Liverpool has brought music fans, journalists, and other visitors to the city. Beatles tourism began in Liverpool during the 1970s, when several local Beatles fans organised a few informal social gatherings and tours for fellow fans. A Beatles shop opened up and a small Beatles convention was organised. In 1980 John Lennon's death triggered an urgent desire on the part of many Beatles fans to travel to Liverpool; in 1981 Liverpool City Council agreed that four new streets could be named after the individual members of The Beatles; and by 1982 an employee of Liverpool County Council, working largely on his own initiative and without the support of his colleagues, had begun promoting the selling of Liverpool as the 'birthplace' of The Beatles. He organised a regular Beatles Walk, a group of tour guides, and a guidebook; he helped establish The Beatles convention as an annual event; and he introduced Beatle coach tours and package weekends.

In 1983 Cavern City Tours was established, a private company that became the main promoter of Beatles tourism when Merseyside County Council was abolished in 1986.[5] It was set up by three official Beatle Guides, and it remains the only Liverpool-based tour operator, producing Beatles-related postcards and guides, organising an annual Beatles convention and festival, and running the Beatles bus tour, walks and weekends and the new Cavern Club, which was built near the site of the original club. Besides Cavern City Tours, the other major players in the current local Beatles 'industry'[6] are The Beatles shop, selling souvenirs, memorabilia and other Beatles-related merchandise, and a museum entitled 'Beatles Story'.

During the second half of the 1980s the small Beatles 'industry' struggled to survive, and Beatles tourism has remained a small-scale affair dominated by a few private sector businesses. Most Beatles visitors are day-trippers with limited impact on the city's economy. Those connected with Beatles tourism describe it as a case of always 'missing the boat', 'a story of missed opportunities', and the city 'shooting itself in the foot', whilst overseas visitors, particularly Americans, have commented on how badly managed it is (Brocken 1993). The demolition of the original Cavern Club in 1973 on the orders of Liverpool City Council is seen as the prime example of such incompetence.

In 1993, however, Cavern City Tours successfully organised a street festival in conjunction with the annual Beatles Convention. The festival had a Merseybeat focus, but also involved other musical styles. It was seen by its organisers as a means of reaching locals as well as visitors, and as a means of attracting convention participants and their spending out of the hotel that hosts the convention and into the city. That same year the Merseyside Tourist Board was disbanded and Liverpool City Council employed its first-ever tourist officer. Part of that officer's brief was to investigate Beatles tourism and review the possibilities regarding a role for the Council. The Council recently promised funding and support for Beatles-related tourism.

Beatle City

For visitors interested in The Beatles, Beatles tourist officials point out bars, club, pubs, exhibitions and other places or events where Beatles music is played. The music often marks such spaces as tourist spaces, and it encourages visitors to enter a previous time, culture, world. Hence promotional literature on Beatles Story proclaims 'see it, hear it, feel it', advertising the exhibition as an 'experience' that will bring the past back to life. Time is constructed in other ways – through, for example, the marking of Beatles anniversaries and other calendar events. A Beatles geography in the city has also been mapped out, consisting of places and buildings in which the band lived and performed, or places referred to in their songs.

The song 'Penny Lane', for example, refers to a rather run-down, suburban-looking street in the city. The lyrics describe the street and its shops and residents, whilst the musical sounds and structures symbolically associate the street and city with particular images, characteristics and feelings. Today Penny Lane is represented on souvenirs, postcards, etc., and it is a central feature of the 'Magical Mystery' Beatles bus tour. Some city councillors have advocated renovating the street and installing plaques, signposts and a monument to commemorate The Beatles (*Liverpool Echo* 25.10.1993). They suggest that its current state is an embarrassment to the city and gives visitors a bad impression. Cavern City Tours argue that tourists appreciate the fact that Penny Lane is run down and remains 'just as it was', i.e. just as they pictured it through the song. They also stress the dangers of overdoing things in 'tacky', 'mickey mouse' style, pointing out that 'if Penny Lane was in the US it would be a theme park by now'. Hence song represents street and now street represents song.

The Musical Production of the City

The above brief account of Beatles-related tourism has indicated just a few of the many ways in which music contributes to the production of Liverpool, indicating that music's role in tourism can be extensive, varied and significant. Firstly, music regularly informs place image, influencing the ways in which people identify, categorise and represent places. This can involve music recordings, film and video soundtracks, the use of music in advertising or live music performance. For cities like Liverpool and New Orleans, music has been bound up with their image and distinctiveness for some time, and there have been various debates over particular musical styles and artists chosen to promote them. As popular culture music is a particularly powerful and accessible resource in the production of place. With regard to tourism in Ireland C. Lincoln (1993: 226) wrote:

> If any image of Dublin entered the European consciousness in 1991 it was due to music: 1991 was the year of U2's 'Achtung Baby' and, most power-fully of all, the year of The Commitments or, at least, of the film version of Roddy Doyle's novel with its depiction of a city which is characterised by its very lack of physical distinctiveness. And, appropriately enough, it was with a concert by the Galway-based band, the Saw Doctors, that Dublin's year as European City of Culture ended . . ..

Meanwhile, Craik (1991: 16) suggests that the rapid growth of Australian tourism has been due, in part, to the popularity of Australian films such as 'Crocodile Dundee', and Boniface and Fowler (1989: 27) refer to the impact on US tourism of the film 'Dances with Wolves'.

Music's peculiar ability to affect or articulate mood and atmosphere, and consequently to trigger the imagination, contributes to people's experiences of places and attitudes toward them, and this occurs in a multitude of different ways and contexts. Musical sounds and images are produced, marketed and distributed in various forms through a variety of media, and are consumed through everyday rituals and routines, or through special events or occasions. Music thus constitutes a focus or frame for social practice, and it establishes, maintains and transforms social relations.

For these and other reasons music is highly valued by people in Liverpool, as it is in many other places, and travel writers and journalists often single music out as representing the essence, soul or spirit of a place. For some people music acts as a publicly acceptable means of expressing ideas and emotions that aren't so easily expressed through other means, which can make music a particularly precious resource in the social, sensual and symbolic production of place and local subjectivity.[7]

Music's contribution to the material or economic production of place can also be significant. Music plays an important, though often hidden, role in the local economy and 'visitor industry' (through, for example, an evening economy of bars, clubs, pubs, etc., and through festivals, street music, and exhibitions). In New Orleans in 1990 the total primary spending of the visitor industry was $3.2 billion, and primary and secondary spending attracted by music was calculated at $593.6 million. During that year, music tourism created 38,000 jobs, excluding musicians (US Travel Data Service). In addition, the music industry is increasingly transnational and highly profitable. In the UK, for example, the industry is a substantial net earner of foreign exchange, with a net surplus of £571m. that is similar to the net overseas earnings of the UK steel industry (British Invisibles 1995: 5). The industry is monopolised by five multinational companies and concentrated in capital cities such as London, New York, and Tokyo, making it hard for cities like Liverpool and New Orleans to retain the income of their successful musicians. It may now be possible, however, through communications technology, to develop international networks of production and distribution that would help develop more profitable local music industries; but more research is needed to investigate the best way of achieving and capitalising upon this.[8]

The first part of this chapter has pointed to music's influence on social relations and activities in the city, on people's sensual experiences of the city, and on the city's economic and material development. It has also suggested ways in which music is used to represent or symbolise the city, distinguishing it from other places and associating it with particular images and values. The implications of this for tourism have been indicated. Music can be the focus of tourism, as it is for Beatles fans who travel to Liverpool; but music also plays a more general social, symbolic, sensual and material role in the place-selling process. The following section illustrates the contested nature of this process by highlighting some of the ways in which the relationship between The Beatles and Liverpool is discussed and debated by young Liverpool rock musicians and those involved with Beatles tourism. The debates are related to social and economic practices and circumstances peculiar to those groups, in order to try to explain some of the concepts and attitudes underlying them.

Cultural Tourism and the Contested City

Sacred Journeys

For many Liverpool fans and followers The Beatles are something to be proud of, and their connection with the city something to be commemorated and celebrated. In Liverpool tourists are often stereotyped as Japanese Beatles fans wandering around Penny Lane with cameras round their necks and lost, bemused expressions on their faces.[9] Meanwhile, those working within the Beatles industry classify Beatles visitors in terms of nationality, length of stay, the amount of money they spend, and frequency of visit. Besides those with a general interest in The Beatles, they identify 'pilgrims' who make a once-in-a-lifetime-trip to Liverpool, and 'fanatics' who make repeated visits.

The Beatles fanzines emphasise the religious, pilgrimage aspect to Beatles fandom, featuring articles with titles such as 'A born again Beatle fan' (*Across the Universe*, Autumn 1993). Brocken (1993: 7) refers to the 'completist' nature of Beatles fans (as with many other fans): their desire to read every book, buy every record, know every fact and figure. 'The Beatles have been transformed', he states, 'from musicians into a collector's hobby, like bus or train numbers.' He also suggests that there is a desire to view The Beatles in terms of a comfortable linear historical narrative with a beginning, middle and end; hence the disappointment that often greets any attempt by a former Beatle to continue his recording career, and the unease over the musical collaboration between the three remaining Beatles. The death of John Lennon heightened a sense of closure and finality experienced after the break-up of the band. Thus for Beatles fans Liverpool may be a collector's item, another link in a chain of Beatles connections to be traced, or experiences to be had, or some sort of Mecca to be visited in order to get closer to The Beatles or expand knowledge about them.

Indigenous Interpretations

Overriding the categories of Beatles visitor outlined above, those working within the Beatles industry, in conversation and in written reports, distinguish between 'the fans' and 'the people of this city', viewing them as two separate markets that can't be mixed, partly because they are seen to reflect different attitudes towards The Beatles and partly because of their different spending power. The local market is described as 'extremely difficult to reach'. There are, of course, local Beatles fans, and a Liverpool Beatles fan club was re-established in November 1993. According to its fanzine: 'For many years the one thing that has dismayed Beatles fans more than anything else has been the way that The Beatles heritage . . . has been neglected . . . There has certainly been a reluctance by the city authorities to maintain the legacy we have' (*Across the Universe*, Autumn 1993).

Thus for many local fans The Beatles are a source of pride, a credit to the city. Their fanzine, along with Beatles tourist literature and souvenirs, emphasises Liverpool as the creative origin of The Beatles, the source or author. Liverpool is described as the place 'where it all began', the place that gave 'birth' to and 'shaped' The Beatles, hence the frequent reference to The Beatles as Liverpool's 'sons'. That same desire to point out 'a beginning' is revealed by fanzine articles in which people recount the moment they first became a Beatles fan, or 'The Day I First saw The Beatles' (ibid.).

The local Beatles fanzine and Beatles industry also construct a connection or opposition between Liverpool and 'the world'. The Beatles are described as 'four lads from Liverpool who shook the world'; and the phrase 'From Liverpool to the world' is emblazoned across tourist literature. A printed Cavern City Tours Beatles guide refers to the media focus on Liverpool at the time of Lennon's death, and to press reports implying that people in Liverpool didn't care. It continues: 'But Liverpool did show the world how it cared in a very splendid way'. A Liverpool fan said of The Beatles:

> They were ours, they were Liverpool's, they belonged to us . . . they were there one minute and gone the next . . . [it was given] out that they were going to London, expecting everybody to be pleased, but . . . for the ordinary fans, we felt a bit deserted . . . Why did they have to go and leave us? . . . We lost them to the world . . . After they'd gone, after they'd made it, I didn't go to any of their concerts, I didn't buy any of their records ('Celebration' programme on the Cavern. Granada TV, Aug. 1993).

Deserting, betraying

> I also agree, as quite a number of the committee have said, that once they left Liverpool that was it. They haven't put a penny back into this city that they've taken their living out of (Liverpool City Councillor quoted on Radio 4 29.19.1982 – 'Dancing in the Rubble').

In my long life of public work I come across people who I think statues should be erected to far more than The Beatles – people who have really contributed to the city (another Liverpool City Councillor, ibid.).

The description of The Beatles as 'deserters' is quite common in Liverpool. A tourist official suggests that it is a major reason for a general lack of local interest in Beatles tourism (personal communication). Some resent the idea that the city's fortunes should depend upon four pop musicians, with its image summed up by them, emphasising that the city is 'more than' The Beatles. Others – Liverpool Development agencies, for example, promote instead an image of the city linked to 'high' culture.

Left behind

A 1994 report (unpublished) from the Beatles industry refers to: 'a question that locals and journalists always ask: "What have The Beatles ever done for Liverpool?" . . . still the Scousers say: "So what? They left Liverpool in 1964. The Beatles themselves have never done anything positive to help this area."'

In response to what it calls 'this betrayal theory' the report argues that The Beatles have never forgotten their roots; that they have paid homage to those roots in their music; that they have donated to local charities, and that Paul McCartney is establishing an Institute of Performing Arts in the city. The report refers to debates over who should be awarded the title of 'the fifth Beatle',[10] and states that 'the fifth Beatle was and always will be the city of Liverpool itself'. It concludes, 'The Beatles may have left Liverpool, but Liverpool will never leave them.' The first article in the first newsletter of the new Beatles fan club is entitled 'Did The Beatles turn their backs on Liverpool'? (*Across the Universe*, Autumn 1993). The article goes on to say: 'Genuine fans know that The Beatles were too big for any one city, or any one country. They were true megastars and belonged to the world.' This is followed by an article on the Institute of Performing Arts, suggesting that it represents 'perhaps the best indication of Paul's true feelings for Liverpool'.

In their struggle to get Beatles tourism recognised by the public sector those working in Beatles tourism adopt a pragmatic approach, trying to convince people in the city of the value of using The Beatles as a 'tool in improving the city's image' and developing the local economy, 'packaging [the city] on the backs of The Beatles', as one tourist official put it. They point out that The Beatles are perceived worldwide as 'synonymous with Liverpool', and that the city must capitalise upon its 'direct links with the most important and successful entertainment phenomenon the modern world has ever witnessed'. In 1994 the organiser of the local Beatles convention and festival told an audience of local rock musicians[11] that although for many of them the heritage of The Beatles: 'may be a big yawn . . . The Beatles will be here forever . . . The Beatles are to Liverpool what the Pope is to Rome and Shakespeare to Stratford. If you can milk it then you should. But believe me, if there is one thing that sells this city worldwide then it's The Beatles, whether you like it or not.'

All this points to The Beatles as a contested symbol, and to the contentious nature of Beatles tourism in Liverpool. Cultural tourism policies and initiatives often give rise to controversy. Some suggest that they enhance the quality of life, self-image, local pride and creativity of local residents, whilst others criticise them for, among other things: only benefiting visitors and economic élites; investing in 'flagship' events and infrastructure that are little utilised by local residents; focusing on city centres rather than outer areas; promoting misleading economic arguments; lacking adequate planning, co-ordination and consultancy with local residents; depending upon an insecure tourist industry that fluctuates according to seasonal and outside factors; creating unskilled, part-time, low-paid jobs in the service sector, rather than investing in training and job-creation for production and manufacture; and promoting fixed and restricted or false representations that obscure, misrepresent, and commodify the richness of local cultural tradition and heritage, and mask real social problems (see, for example, Hewison 1987; Bianchini 1989; Cohen 1991b; Craik 1991; Hughes and Boyle 1991; Aldskogius 1993).

Liverpool Rock Musicians and the Struggle for Success

Relations between music, musicians and the city are the subject of much critical debate among those involved with contemporary Liverpool guitar-based bands performing a so-called 'indie'[12] style of rock music. These bands, like The Beatles, usually comprise four or five musicians on drums, bass guitar, lead guitar and sometimes keyboards. The vast majority of these musicians are White, working-class, often unemployed men in their twenties or thirties. They join and form bands for social, economic, and cultural reasons.[13] A band offers, for example, a particular way of life, structuring time and space through various rituals, routes and routines (band meetings, rehearsals, etc.), and it provides its members with goals and ambitions. Many have an overwhelming desire to 'make it' with their band, which involves signing a deal with a record company that will bring their band's music to a wider public and provide them with an income.

This intensifies their commitment to, and statements of belief in, their band, and their investment of emotion, money, time, etc. in their music-making. Such music-making provides young men with a means of communicating ideas and sentiments that they cannot convey through other means, and for many of them musical performance can be a frustrating, agonising experience, but one that can also give intense pleasure and a sense of achievement.

Young Liverpool rock musicians might be influenced by The Beatles and other bands, but at the same time they strive to make music that is original and different. In order to achieve success with that music they have to try to attract the attention of record company representatives in London, where the record industry is based. However, attracting the attention of such companies is a continual problem, and many musicians visit London in order to see those record companies. There are, moreover, a large number of bands in Liverpool, only a tiny minority of which get signed. Competition between bands for resources and attention is thus intensive.

The Curse of The Beatles

British and overseas media typically relate Liverpool's contemporary music scene to The Beatles, describing it as lying 'in the shadow of The Beatles'. Not surprisingly this is a view resisted by young local rock musicians. Many of them acknowledge their debt to The Beatles and to local history and heritage, but The Beatles are also felt to be a constraining factor on their music, image, and career. Resentful comments, such as 'every other band wants to get away from the legacy of The Beatles', are commonly made. Hence a recent article on Liverpool's rock music scene in an Israeli national newspaper was entitled 'The curse of The Beatles' (*Ha'aretz Weekly Supplement*, 2.9.1994). In 1990 a large concert was held to mark the tenth anniversary of Lennon's death. Members of the local rock scene, resenting the funding and attention lavished upon this event, organised their own concurrent festival entitled 'Liverpool Now'. A local journalist wrote on that festival, 'while the city wallows in nostalgia, on the other side of town 1990 fights back.' (*Melody Maker* 26 May 1990).

A seminar on the music business held at Liverpool University in 1994 attracted many local rock musicians, and raised familiar debates over the departure of local musicians from the city, particularly the 'successful' ones, like The Beatles, who take their earnings with them. As one band manager put it: 'Liverpool is good at producing good artists and product, which we then send to London.' He criticised the belief that musicians have little choice but to leave the city, and advocated 'keep[ing] success local'. 'We've got to stop the haemorrhage' added a local musician. The rhetoric of rock in Liverpool is thus pervaded by a sense of loss. Musicians are seen to leave Liverpool because they are greedy, misguided, and 'sell out'; because to use music as a 'way out' is part of rock ideology; because there is nothing for them in Liverpool, and they are thus forced to leave; because if they do become successful their activities and lifestyle necessitate living elsewhere.[14]

A 1991 report on Merseyside's music industries, entitled 'Music City', states that 'Liverpool, unlike its neighbour Manchester, seems to have established a trend for its successful bands not investing in major projects in their city.' The report suggests that Paul McCartney's plan to set up an Institute of Performing Arts in his old school building 'set[s] a valuable precedent' (ibid.). A well-known Manchester music entrepreneur repeatedly contrasts Liverpool musicians and their commitment to their city with Manchester musicians, often in a deliberately provocative manner that plays on a long-standing rivalry between the two cities. During a lecture at Liverpool University in 1990 he suggested that 'If The Beatles had done to Manchester what they did to Liverpool' (i.e. left the city to set up base in London), the people there would have been 'furious'. 'Well-known bands from Manchester . . . it's nice because they are seen around . . . No-one has put anything back into [Liverpool, which has] . . . a history of leaving and not reinvesting.' Paul McCartney's recent initiative was, he suggested, 'too late'.

The discourses of loss at the music business seminar surrounding the departure of The Beatles and other musicians from Liverpool represent those of powerlessness, revolving around notions of dependency and opposition between Liverpool's musicians, music scene and industry, and the policy-makers or London. London was described during the seminar as 'the glittering bright lights at the end of the motorway'. Its music industry constantly beckons and dominates. Its music press defines and controls. Local musicians are described as being 'sucked out' of Liverpool to London, and Liverpool is described as a music colony whose sub-servience to London is maintained through various means. This is reflected in expressions of hostility towards London. The Beatles are thus implicated in a spatial politics involving local relations and inequalities (The Beatles are, for example, linked to suburban South Liverpool, which is commonly opposed to Liverpool's working-class and less affluent 'North End');[15] local–regional relations (hence the common references to The Beatles and other musicians in order to emphasise an opposition between Liverpool and nearby Manchester); local–national relations (hence through bands like The Beatles Liverpool is opposed to London, and the British North to its South); and local–global relations (hence through The Beatles Liverpool was opposed above to America or to the world).

Debts and Dependencies

The above debates and discussions on The Beatles and their connection with Liverpool show how musicians and their audiences are bound to a city physically, conceptually and emotionally through relations of kinship, friendship, fandom, etc. The relationship between The Beatles and Liverpool is even presented as a kinship relation, with Liverpool as mother–creator and The Beatles as her favourite sons, which carries the implication that The Beatles' obligation to the city parallels that of children to a parent. Like all social relations, the relationship thus involves notions of exchange, reciprocity, investment, and indebtedness. People are seen to 'put something in' to such relations and to 'take something out'.

The notion of debts to places (for instance, what The Beatles owe Liverpool) involves the personification of place, and is a reified notion of debts between people. Liverpool uses The Beatles, just as some might see The Beatles as having used Liverpool; but the relationship between The Beatles and Liverpool is an unequal one, involving negotiations for power and prestige and notions of accountability and responsibility. One party is usually perceived as contributing more than the other, or as more needy, deserving, or exploitative than the other. Relations between musicians and the city are thus contested, ideologically informed, and shaped by particular socio-economic circumstances. Liverpool's depressed economy, poor media image, and political 'emasculation' have strained such relations and influenced the debates that concern them.

Bleeding Cities, Breaking Bands

The city of Liverpool has inspired strong feelings and declarations of loyalty and identity, as have the city's rock bands, along with other social collectivities. Both city and bands could be perceived as being 'on show', performing identity and projecting difference to various audiences; and both are seen as being under threat, pressurised in different ways, and engaged in a continual struggle for survival. All this has emphasised images of integration and fragmentation linked to bands and city. Both are perceived as fragile, porous or fissile entities that need to be continually reproduced and have their boundaries reasserted.

Liverpool city councillors, journalists, and other spokespersons often depict the city as a large extended 'family', promoting an image of solidarity in the face of social and economic pressure and hostility. Meanwhile Liverpool rock musicians also commonly describe their band as being like a family, and use many other images of integration or bondedness to emphasise the sense of security and belongingness a band provides. However, although a band offers them a means of establishing and maintaining social relations, pressures to succeed, the tensions of collective creativity, and the competitive nature of the local music 'scene' make bands inherently unstable; hence the preoccupation with bands that split or break, like cities that bleed or haemorrhage.[16] Musicians proclaim the solidarity of their band whilst trying to prevent it from splitting up. They declare loyalty to their city, censuring other musicians for leaving it; yet the city can also seem a 'prison', as one musician described it, with popular music offering one of the only 'ways out'. If musicians achieve success, their relationship with the city becomes intensely scrutinised, and lines of debt and accountability become more tightly drawn. Those who remain may be perceived as relatively immobile and dependent, and as tied to the city.

Conclusion

In Britain the role and potential role of popular music in tourism policy, and in economic development generally, has tended to be neglected and treated with disdain by policy-makers, partly because it has been commonly perceived as overtly commercial and as entertainment rather than art or industry. Furthermore, the relationship between music and place, and the role of music in the place-selling process, has been little researched.[17] The few relevant ethnomusicological debates have been rather narrow in emphasis, focusing largely on the detrimental effects of tourism, and lamenting its commodification of traditional musics. There is a small but expanding literature on tourism within 'Cultural Studies', but it lacks ethnographic research and analyses of tourism's socio-political, economic, and cultural effects within particular localities. Hence the implications of tourism for local and cultural identity have rarely been discussed, and contribution to policy debates is limited. The emphasis is, furthermore, overwhelmingly on the visual (for example Urry 1990), and on culture as consumption, play and spectacle rather than culture as practice and production. The discussion in this chapter on the social, symbolic and material aspects of Beatles-related events, activities and debates in Liverpool has pointed to some of the ways in which a city could be said to be 'produced' through music, and has indicated the complex and contested nature of this process, exposing underlying concepts and values, preoccupations and tensions. Music is closely bound up with a politics of place, the struggle for identity and belonging, power and prestige, and this has implications for the study and development of tourism.

Local tourism is not an issue that directly concerns Liverpool's young rock musicians, yet the account of Beatles tourism indicates ways in which tourism initiatives can expose and exacerbate particular tensions experienced by such musicians. Developments and discussions surrounding Beatles-focused tourism have foregrounded tensions between success and failure, fragmentation and integration; contradictory urges to leave the city and to stay, to look outwards and to turn parochially inwards; issues of debt and dependency; and boundaries between us and them, insiders and outsiders, then and now, here and there. If tourism is to be a focus of urban regeneration strategies in Liverpool, the challenge for local decision-makers is to initiate policies that are aimed at both locals and visitors; that are sensitive to locality – to particular social, historical and economic situations and circumstances; and that adopt a broad approach, linking or integrating different local industries and sectors, such as, for example, tourism and music industries, incorporating musical production and consumption, the musical past and present.

Further investigation on music and tourism could seek to understand, critique and even contribute to such policy-making, and this chapter represents preliminary thoughts on a two-year ethnographic project that aims to explore the relationship between music and the city in much greater depth. The study will revolve around research on music tourism initiatives in Liverpool and New Orleans. The two cities were officially twinned in 1988, and they share many common social, cultural and economic characteristics (for instance population size and image problems). Both cities have identified tourism and the arts and cultural industries as a primary focus for regeneration, and both are renowned for popular music. The project will compare music's role in each city, looking at the relevance of this for the study and development of tourism.

Notes

1. The case study is drawn from ethnographic research on popular music-making in Merseyside.
2. We would like to thank the Economic and Social Research Council for funding this project.

3. Common examples of cultural tourism include: the construction and restoration of historical buildings and waterfronts; the organisation of festivals, conventions, and other special events; the development of museums, galleries and heritage centres; participation in competitions such as European 'City of Culture'; and geographical theming and sloganeering ('Robin Hood Country'; 'Glasgow's miles better', 'Manchester: the life and soul of Britain').

4. See Cohen (1991b).

5. The Merseyside Tourism Board, which took over responsibility for local tourism from Merseyside County Council, placed little emphasis on The Beatles.

6. The term 'industry' is used by many of those involved with these organisations and activities.

7. See Cohen 1995 for further discussion on this.

8. Existing relevant studies include Wallis and Malm 1984, 1990; Cohen 1991b; Malm and Wallis 1992; Frith 1993.

9. An image that probably reflects a common view of both fans and tourists as unimaginative, undiscerning, and undiscriminating.

10. For example Stuart Sutcliffe, the band's original drummer, or George Martin, who produced the band's music.

11. At a seminar on the music business held at the University of Liverpool.

12. 'Indie' rock music is neither 'light pop' nor 'heavy rock'. The term 'indie' is usually used to refer to music that is associated with independent record labels and music that is 'alternative' rather than mainstream, although much of this music is now mainstream in that it features strongly in the national charts, and most independent record labels are now linked to major labels.

13. See Cohen (1991a).

14. See Cohen (1991a).

15. Assumptions made about the working-class status of The Beatles are thus hotly contested in Liverpool.

16. Two things are typically said to split up a band: women and money (see Cohen 1991a).

17. See Loukissas 1982; Crick 1989; and O'Connor and Cronin 1993 for discussion on the limitations of anthropological and sociological literature on tourism.

References

Aldskogius, H. (1993). Festivals and Meets: The Place of Music in 'Summer Sweden'. Unpublished paper presented at 'The Place of Music' conference, University College, London.

Barrow, T. (1993). Brian Epstein's Secret Hideaway. In *The Beatles Book*. London: Beat Publications Ltd.

Bianchini, F. (1989). *Urban Rennaissance?: the arts and the urban regeneration process in 1980s Britain*. Working Paper No.7. Liverpool: University of Liverpool.

Boniface, P. and Fowler, P. J. (1989). *Heritage and Tourism in 'the global village'*. London: Routledge.

British Invisibles (1995). *Overseas Earnings of the Music Industry*. London: British Invisibles.

Brocken, M. (1993). Some Theories About Signification: Postmodernism and The Beatles' Cover Versions. Unpublished MA thesis. University of Liverpool.

Cameron, C. M. (1991). The New Arts Industry: Non-profits in an Age of Competition. *Human Organisation*. 50(3): 225–34.

Cohen, S. (1991a). *Rock Culture in Liverpool* Oxford: Oxford University Press.

Cohen, S. (1991b). Popular Music and Urban Regeneration: The Music Industries on Merseyside. *Cultural Studies* 5(3): 332–46.

Cohen, S. (1995). Sounding Out the City: Music and the Sensuous Production of Place. *Transactions* 20: 434–46.

Craik, J. (1991). *Resorting to Tourism: Cultural Policies for Tourist Development in Australia*. Sydney: Allen and Unwin.

Crick, M. (1989). Representations of International Tourism in the Social Sciences: Sun, Sex, Sights, Savings, and Servility. *Annual Review of Anthropology* 18: 307–44.

Cwi, D. (1982). The Focus and Impact of Arts Impact Studies. In C. Violette and R. Taqqu (eds), *Issues in Supporting the Arts*, pp. 22–4. Ithaca, NY: Graduate School of Business and Public Administration, Cornell University.

Frith, S. 1993. Popular Music and the Local State. In T. Bennet, S. Frith, L. Grossberg, J. Shepherd and G. Turner (eds), *Rock and Popular Music: Politics, Policies, Institutions*. London: Routledge.

Hewison, R. (1987). *The Heritage Industry*. London: Methuen.

Hughes, G. and Boyle, M. (1991). The Politics of the Representation of 'The Real': Discourses from the Left on Glasgow's Role as European City of Culture, 1990. *Area* 23(3): 217–28.

Lincoln, C. (1993). City of Culture: Dublin and the Discovery of Urban Heritage. In B. O'Connor and J. Cronin (eds), *Tourism and Cultural Identity in Ireland*. Cork: Cork University Press.

Loukissas, P. J. (1982). Tourism's Regional Development Impacts: A Comparative Analysis of the Greek Islands. *Annals of Tourism Research* 9: 523–41.

Malm, W. and Wallis, R. (1992). *Media Policy and Music Activity*. London: Routledge.

Music City (1991). Report by Ark Consultants commissioned by Liverpool City Council. March.

Myerscough, J. (1989). *The Economic Importance of the Arts in Merseyside*. London: Policy Studies Institute.

NEFA (New England Foundation for the Arts) (1981). *The Arts and New England Economy*, 2nd edn. Cambridge, MA: New England Foundation for the Arts.

O'Connor, B. and Cronin, J. (eds) (1993). *Tourism and Cultural Identity in Ireland*. Cork: Cork University Press.

PANYI (Port Authority of NY and NJ and the Cultural Assistance Centre Inc.) (1983). *The Arts as an Industry: Their Economic Importance to the New York – New Jersey Metropolitan Region*. New York: Port Authority.

Robins, K. (1991). Tradition and Translation: National Culture in its Global Context. In J. Corner and S. Harvey (eds), *Enterprise and Heritage*. London: Routledge.

Street, J. (1995). (Dis)located? Rhetoric, Politics, Meaning and the Locality. In W. Straw, S. Johnson, R. Sullivan and P. Friedlander (eds), *Popular Music: Style and Identity*. Proceedings of the seventh international conference of the International Association for the Study of Popular Music. Montreal: Centre for Research on Canadian Cultural Industries.

Urry, J. (1990). *The Tourist Gaze: Leisure and Travel in Contemporary Societies*. London: Sage.

Wallis, R. and Malm, K. (1984). *Big Sounds from Small Peoples*. London: Constable.

Wallis, R. and Malm, K. (1990). Internationalization, Localization and Integration: The Changing Structure of the Music Industry and its Particular Relevance for Smaller Nations and Cultures. Unpublished paper presented at ICA conference in Dublin.

5

Whose New Orleans? Music's Place in the Packaging of New Orleans for Tourism[1]

Connie Zeanah Atkinson

If tourism is chosen to be a major currency earner, it would appear to be impossible to avoid the detrimental effects on local culture.

(Wallis and Malm 1984: 293–4)

Despite such dire warnings, policy-makers in many localities have embraced tourism in their economic development and urban regeneration planning, and towns and cities that may have lost their traditional industries have opened their cultural activities to tourists. In this competitive tourism market, music has been identified as important in what Robins has termed 'the race between places to create distinct place identity' (Robins 1991).

For many of these places, music plays an important role in the development of a distinct culture, and provides an important context for personal and collective identity. What are the consequences of the commodification of these regional musics on traditional music practices and local identity? And to what degree are the musicians passive or engaged players in these activities?

Wallis and Malm's caution quoted above appeared in their pioneering study of the influences of the international recording industry on local recording practices; but an equally comprehensive international study on tourism's influence on local music has yet to be done. This chapter will address a few of the kinds of issues that may be raised in such a study, using as an example the New Orleans music community and its relationship

91

to the tourist industry in that city. New Orleans' particular historical identification with music, and the resulting expectations of people who visit there, as well as the determination of the city's tourist industry to exploit a particular musical image to attract tourists, make the city's musicians and their activities, social relations, and interactions an interesting focus in observing the processes through which ideas of locality are formed, negotiated, and reformed. In addition, focusing on the part music plays in the image and packaging of New Orleans as a tourist site, and the consequences of tourism initiatives for the city's musical traditions and the musicians who live there, may help to point out the role of music in the way places may be identified and packaged for economic development.

Background

With the decline of the port and the subsequent decline in the offshore oil industry, tourism became the primary income-producer of the city of New Orleans in the 1980s, with a resulting new interest from policy-makers in the hitherto neglected music community and the potential role of the city's musical reputation in attracting visitors and conventions to New Orleans.

Policy-makers are often pushed reluctantly in the direction of arts and cultural industries as a base for economic regeneration, perhaps because of their unfamiliarity with the arts as compared to more traditional industries, such as manufacturing. However, the arts are often a substantial, if overlooked, economic force. The music industry in New Orleans, for example, had an economic impact of $1.45 billion on the New Orleans economy in 1990 (Ryan 1990). Over 38,000 jobs were produced by the music industry; $94 million was spent on music education, and $433.3 million accrued in tax revenues. The 1990 New Orleans Jazz and Heritage Festival alone had an economic impact of roughly $71.6 million. The number of national and international visitors to the 25-year-old festival in 1993 exceeded 350,000. According to the US Travel Data Service, visitor spending attributable to music has a total impact of $593.6 million on the New Orleans economy, almost 20 per cent of total annual visitor spending. Said a Greater New Orleans Tourist and Convention Commission report in May 1992: 'For tourism officials, these figures are important. The history and culture of New Orleans music are key elements that attract visitor to the city.'

New Orleans's Identification with
Music — Music and Place Imaging

New Orleans holds a unique place in the American landscape. Probably the most Africanised city in the United States (Hall 1994), with its French and Spanish, rather than English, colonial background, its Mediterranean culture and Catholicism, its history of a black majority population, racial ambiguity, and native American integration, it is a part of, yet distinct from, the American South. Surrounded by water – the huge Lake Pontchartrain to the north, the Mississippi River to the west and south, and lakes and marshland to the east – New Orleans is geographically situated on an island, or more accurately in a bowl, seven feet below sea level, with a series of levees holding back the recalcitrant Mississippi River from finding its way through the Atchafalaya Basin to the Gulf of Mexico. These natural boundaries separate the city geographically from the rest of Louisiana, the South, and the nation. Cultural activities brought in by the Africans, Italians, Spanish and French flourished unchecked in this isolation, and merged with those of the indigenous population to produce rituals and cultural events largely unique to the United States, such as second-line parades, jazz funerals, Mardi Gras Indians, and Carnival.

Today, with the advent of cheap air travel, visitors to the city's old French Quarter, the chief tourist area, can imagine themselves visiting another, more dangerous, more romantic time and place. The French colonial architecture of the Quarter, its narrow streets, iron-lace balconies, and lush courtyards, reinforce this perception, as do the many Hollywood films that have portrayed New Orleans as the scene of unusual wickedness (*Blue Angel, Angel Heart, Walk on the Wild Side, Kid Creole*). The infamous privateer Jean Lafitte's blacksmith's shop lies just down the street from the strip joints and gay bars of Bourbon Street, and just a few blocks from the Ursuline Convent. Close by, Pirate's Alley runs alongside the oldest Catholic cathedral in the United States – iniquity and Catholicism sitting comfortably side by side. Visiting New Orleans, therefore, gives the white middle-class American tourist the chance to play out fantasies of sin and danger from the safety of the balcony of a Holiday Inn, or through the window of an air-conditioned tour bus.

The city is a multiracial one, with an approximately 60 per cent black population, including the mayor and most of the city council. Unlike the rest of the American South, New Orleans has a long history of racial mixing. People of the city are of all colours, and racial identity is often blurred. For US-Americans, the exotic look of the people contributes to the sense of being in another country, another place in time.

The climate and festive inclinations of the city of New Orleans conspire to open up the out-of-doors. The streets are still often the place of music and celebration, of day-to-day interaction, commerce, and community. Entertainment spills outside buildings on to the sidewalks and courtyards of the Quarter, extending the tourist space to include the streets and *banquettes*, liberating the tourist, who can now 'own' the entire space. Street bands can be heard for blocks, and music clubs leave their doors wide open. 'Private' cultural celebrations, such as neighbourhood jazz funerals and parades, have no boundaries between locals and tourists. Tourists watch and listen from doorways, out on to the sidewalk, as well as inside the clubs. Liberal drinking laws allow outdoor drinking, extending the 'tourist space' into the streets. But music is used to assist in marking spaces where revelry is permitted. Music serves as a signal that a space is open for occupation. Within the French Quarter, where the music stops, tourists hesitate to venture.

In the mid-1980s, as the city government and private interests in New Orleans began to take tourism more seriously, the riverfront was targeted as a tourist area. Riverside warehouses, once a part of the port, were brought down to create a park, and an aquarium was built by the city as part of its riverfront development. Music is used to lure visitors to the new riverfront tourist space. The riverboat *Natchez* blares out familiar tunes ('Waitin' for the Robert E. Lee' 'Way Down Yonder In New Orleans', etc.) on its steam calliope, creating a corridor of sound that tourists can travel, marking out and extending their space from the Quarter to the river. Bands play on bandstands by the riverbank, street musicians serenade visitors on the 'Moonwalk' that runs atop the levee, and concerts are held at the Spanish Plaza, on the river, using the river as a backdrop for the music. Debates over the use of a park on the opposite side of the French Quarter have included reference to there being no music to 'draw the tourists to this side of the Quarter'.

Music's Part in Packaging New Orleans — Music and City Tourism Policies

There has been extensive study on the impact of *literature* on the way cities and places are recognised and accepted and the influence of *literary* images on the portrayal and development of culture.[2] However, the relation between *musical* images and place recognition has rarely been studied. Often overlooked, music is a powerful conjurer of place, as music's role in television, film-making, and advertising will attest. Music is frequently thought of as culture-specific, and sounds are often identified in place terms: an Irish air, the Texas two-step, the Nashville sound, and so forth (John Skinner, personal communication).

New Orleans' image has been bound up with music from its founding, with one of the longest histories of musical activity in North America. Early visitors often commented on the abundance of music in the city. In 1802, a visitor remarked, 'New Orleanians manage during a single winter to execute about as much dancing, music, laughing and dissipation as would serve any reasonably disposed, staid, and sober citizen for three or four years' (Kmen 1966: 6).

New Orleans' role in the evolution of jazz gave the city an international association with that musical style, which persists. However, for decades policy-makers in New Orleans tried to dissociate the city from its 'jazz reputation', which was thought to hurt business and project an immoral, salacious lifestyle. This was parallel to the segregationist 'Jim Crow' policies that finally reached Louisiana in the 1920s.

In the 1940s, city policy-makers reversed this strategy and adopted the romanticised image of the city as the 'birthplace of jazz' to attract tourists. This interest in the city's music, however, developed along limited lines; promotion of city's music was organised into 'safe' cultural channels, such as traditional jazz museums, archives, newsletters, performance halls, and festivals, and the Franco-African performance activities, still alive in the black neighbourhoods, went unsupported and ignored. This paralleled the movement in black intellectual circles, starting with the Harlem Renaissance, of decrying African-based musical styles in favour of the styles that most closely matched the European performance aesthetic of the concert hall (see Floyd 1995).

In the 1950s, the city regained the national musical spotlight, with stars such as Fats Domino, Lloyd Price, and Little Richard heralding the new age of R&B and rock'n'roll. But despite this limited success, the local music industry remained small and fragmented, with little support or interest from the city's business leaders or politicians. Meanwhile, music continued to be an integral part of the family and community life of many New Orleanians (Berry *et al.* 1990).

In the 1970s, in the midst of the offshore oil boom, the city's tourism initiatives were confined primarily to convention trade, and the city's musical reputation was considered 'frivolous' and detrimental to attracting business and developing into a top convention destination. The city concentrated on building facilities (hotels, a convention centre, and the 80,000-seat Superdome) and attracting national political and sports events.

In the mid-1980s, with the oil industry in a downward spiral, the convention centre only partially booked, and new hotels standing half empty, the hotels passed a self-imposed $1/room tax to finance the New Orleans Tourism Marketing Corporation. Its brief was to market the city to the *discretionary tourist* – the non-convention visitor. This commitment to tourism for urban regeneration placed New Orleans in competition with other cities in attracting people for entertainment and leisure activities. The marketing group commissioned research to discover what distinctive quality of the city would be the most competitive. This research indicated that discretionary city travellers list 'excitement' most often as the goal of their travels, and the images of New Orleans as a city of spontaneous celebration, sin, and so forth, fed into this. The tourism marketing board once again decided to exploit the city's music image.

As the tourist board's director put it, 'Music is integral to our market-ing plan. Our theme is "come join the parade" and all our television and radio spots use New Orleans music. The whole spirit of the city is summed up in its music' (Esolen 1994). Instead of inviting tourists to come and be entertained, therefore, the tourist is invited actually to participate, to join in. The city thus uses music in its efforts to engulf the visitor in the 'New Orleans experience'. From the airport, where the only music played is that of New Orleans artists, through the taxi ride into the city, where the cab drivers (graduates of a city-run two-week course in tourist relations) regale the visitor with stories about musical legends, to the Riverwalk shopping mall, where again only New Orleans music is played, to the street musicians in Jackson Square, the visitor's experience is outlined and grounded in music.

What are the implications of these initiatives for local musicians, and how do they affect the musicians' images of themselves and their city? Again, Wallis and Malm:

> All along the line, tourism appears to provide short-term employment advantages but leaves cultural disadvantages. The tourist hotels attract talented musicians who have to play a repertoire suitable for the majority of tourists who come to relax, not to learn the intricacies of [local musical traditions] . . . Few government[s] seem to be concerned about the cultural dangers of tourism . . . the tourists must be given the entertainment it is assumed they want' (Wallis and Malm 1984: 284).

These comments reflect the sometimes contentious relationship between the tourism industry and local musicians, and the conflicts that can arise when tourism strategies include packaging complex local cultural activities and rituals for sale. However, these and other commentaries on the implications of tourism for regional musics are often lacking in ethnographic research that could show the degree of involvement of local musicians in the decisions that affect repertoire and musical performance. Are musicians passive pawns in the tourism game? Or are they actively involved in how their music is represented? What patterns emerge in the presentation of local music for tourism in specific places, and how does this reflect greater patterns of acculturation, power, and consumption?

There has been little research specifically on the implications of New Orleans marketing policies for musicians and locals. However, in interviews that I have collected in New Orleans over the last decade, New Orleans musicians often have talked about tourism and its implications for the future of the city's music and how they have interacted – and many have refused to interact – with the tourist marketing strategies of the city. The way that New Orleans musicians negotiate with the industry points up ways that, through music, issues of political, social, and economic identity, as well as creativity and ownership, can be addressed.

Musicmaking in New Orleans

Andrew Kaslow has documented how the New Orleans musical community is linked through family ties and membership in social aid and pleasure clubs, carnival organisations, churches, and clusterings of other organisations and institutions (Kaslow 1981). Through individuals holding multiple memberships in widely different associations, these connections proliferate, revolving around charismatic leaders, who maintain the continuity of the groups over time. The extensive kinship networks within the musical community of New Orleans are celebrated in Jason Berry's book *Up from the Cradle of Jazz* (Berry *et al.* 1990). In New Orleans, journalists and musicians commonly describe their music in terms of family relations.

Kaslow has written, 'Through conditions of economic deprivation and social injustice, sociocultural adaptations, including the traditions of benevolent societies, carnival organisations, the ecstatic religions, and music have enriched the lives of Orleanians in ways that have served to give a different focus to the meaning of "community" than in other settings.' Kaslow described the musical community of New Orleans as composed of 'overlapping thick social and kinship networks that generate a cohesiveness and integration which makes New Orleans atypical of other major American cities.'

For the predominantly African-American musical community of New Orleans, people use music to construct various social networks that shape notions of locality, reinforce family unity, and provide an important context for the issues of ownership and control of music and responsibility for the way music is used. Music has been a locally valued activity in which the African-American community's leadership has been acknowledged by non-African-Americans. As Monson (1994) has pointed out, this is of extreme symbolic importance in African-American communities such as New Orleans. Since this inversion of the usual relationship does not extend to the economic sector, however, conflicts can arise when dealing with ownership and representation. Tourism initiatives have been the site of such conflicts.

Implications of Tourist Policies for Local Musicians and Residents

The implications of the city's marketing policies for local business, the music community, and residents have been varied. Attempts to attract discretionary tourists have been successful, and some businesses have prospered. Implications for musicians and locals vary from anticipation that tourist strategy will contribute to increased employment opportunities to complaints that distinctive music-making practices are changing with the inclusion of 'outsiders'.

One of my informants, Gary, is a 41-year-old native New Orleanian who, with his friends, often patronises the small music clubs of his neighbourhood. He is bothered by changes that he has noticed since visitors have arrived to participate in local musical activities. In 1986, the Glasshouse was a tiny, run-down club in what is called the 'back 'o' town' area of the city. Every Tuesday night, the Dirty Dozen (one of the most popular of the new bebop-oriented brass bands) would play. Says Gary

> At the Glasshouse, they don't charge to go in. It's just a neighbourhood joint. But the man who owns it told them they could play there, pass the hat around, you know. They were just starting out.
>
> For the Dozen, you see, their crowd, only the guys dance. The women sit and cheer them on. The dancing gets rowdy, you know, with the guys jumping up in the air and dropping to the floor and spinning around, twisting.

As the Dirty Dozen started getting popular, some writers (including British DJ Andy Kershaw) 'discovered' the Glasshouse, and, says Gary, 'tourists started coming in cabs. They'd join in the dancing, women and men. Pretty soon, at the Glasshouse, the men and women dance together, just like everywhere else.'

On the other hand, some musicians feel that the tourist industry fits uniquely into musical practices that already exist in New Orleans. Says one musician who has achieved a great deal of success both in the city and nationally:

It's given musicians a place to play. Yeah, you can't usually make it as a full-time thing. But in New Orleans, music has always been a part-time job. Louis Armstrong played all over town, yes, but he also had a job in a mattress factory. Lee Dorsey had all those hits, but he still had his car body shop, through it all. And where do you think Aaron Neville got those big ole arms of his? That was from the docks. He worked the docks until his music hit the big time.

The head of the city's music commission agrees:

Playing for tourists can be a way to prepare yourself for the general music industry, for recording purposes. It is a strategy that will work if it's done right. I tell people all the time, music in New Orleans, working with music in New Orleans is the best part-time job in the world. It is much better than Burger King, you know, it is so much better than doing all those other things. You work four hours and even on a poor scale you get 100 dollars [£66] for the four hours. I don't know many part-time jobs that pay 25 dollars [£18] an hour. I talk to people all the time in other places, like at SXSW (a large, regional music conference in Austin, Texas), who want to be in the music business, and I ask them, why don't you have a day job? and they say well no, it just can't happen like that. I have to do my music full time.

That attitude is very common across the country, and it is an interesting thing because here, we don't see it like that. I don't see why you couldn't do them both, but their perception is that to be a musician I have to be a full time rock or jazz musician. I couldn't compromise myself on doing that, working at it part time, but to me it sounded like they were saying they just would not get up at eight o'clock in the morning. Of course maybe that's why in the industry as a whole a musician has a life expectancy of about seven years, when in New Orleans you play all your life.

These people here are professional musicians, even though they may work at different jobs. They play music every Saturday and Sunday and then some of them are playing maybe two or three times a week. So they get an opportunity to mature a music style, they get a chance to be able to become much more at ease with what they're doing. Instead of playing for seven years and talking about it for the rest of their lives, or trying to regain that seven years for the rest of their life, or having that seven years kill them, here they play thirty years, and they're always playing, and that is just being honest. Who is one of the new stars of the New Orleans musical scene now? Harry Connick Sr.

[district attorney of New Orleans, father of Harry Jr.] and he is in his sixties. He's in the park riding his bike, singing songs, I'm telling you he is out there and he is at the piano and he is singing, not necessarily half bad. The tourists love him, and he is still the D.A. He does gigs three or four nights a week now. And Frank Minyard [New Orleans coroner], he is still playing, playing all the time. They look for opportunities to play, and tourism provides those opportunities. And if they get a hit, and make it to the big time, and they're the next Michael Jackson, that time they spent working another job isn't going to hurt them at all.

Donald, a 23-year-old horn player who has received a lot of local media attention, has recorded with local rock and roll bands, played locally at clubs, and still works at a local radio station during the day:

> It depends on what you think it's all about. If music is about getting that big hit, well . . . Where in New Orleans, being a musician is, you know, say on a Sunday I am playing in churches, in the morning, and then I go over and play Commander's Palace [restaurant] for a brunch, and then I might have a gig laid on at night, and over the time period of the day, I've played music for about eight to ten hours and I have made x number of dollars and that is fine. On Saturdays, I might play Saturday night at House of Blues with a rock band, or R&B band, or behind some big name who came to town and needs a horn player, or sometimes I might play Saturday nights with this guy Mickey Easterling and his orchestra and you know that is cool and we play for hours and I get the standard union scale and that's not bad at all. And then there may be a wedding in the afternoon. On Friday nights I am there playing a function, say a convention gig or a gig at Tipitina's; they both pay, the tourist gigs pay more. I played the other Saturday afternoon at the airport. These people wanted a band to meet a plane. It all adds up. It's all music.

George, a musician who achieved quite a bit of fame in the 1960s, speaks from his experience:

> If you don't watch out, trying to run around trying to be a great success in the recording aspect of the music industry then god, it'll run you insane, and drive your wife and family insane, to a point you can't have one, and you find what you wind up doing is you lead this very disconcerting existence that really hurts you and your playing, because you don't have someone to worry about you, someone you can belong to over and beyond your playing buddies, your fellow musicians, and then you don't have to come home and you don't have to get up and take the kids to school, you don't have to get to work at a certain time, you don't have to do all those things that ground you and keep you sane. You can kind of wallow in your self pity, and that's when your

playing really gets bad. You need to have this grounding, this balance, to be a musician.

Can you make money in the tourism industry? Yes, but you have got to really work at being a part of what they're doing and in reality you may be able to get to that point of say $50 [£33] an hour, which is not bad in New Orleans for any job, for a four-hour set on a Sunday playing from eight till twelve. You still got time if you want to go to church in the morning, to catch the Saints [football team] with your kids in the afternoon. Well if you do this on Saturday and Sundays every week that's four hundred dollars [£264] a weekend that you are making extra. So this is like an addition of 1600 dollars [£1056] a month, and this four hours that you have just gotten into the groove of doing, and then of course the extra weddings that you might play and the thing you might play in the evenings, and you see also this kind of playing, the tourism stuff, is over by midnight or 11 o'clock, they don't really go on late at night. So you could go on to play a club, since music starts so late in the clubs, or you could go home, and be home for 11 o'clock. That's the kind of thing a lot of people never realise, that tourism gigs end early. Believe me, 999 times out of 1000, in the long run it pays better than if somebody gets signed and goes off to Los Angeles, for sure. And every year or two you can get time off to go to Europe in the summer for a festival. Like Joe Simons, he plays on the riverboats. He has 25 standard gigs a week, and he is home at ten o'clock every night if he so desires. His band plays Mr B's (restaurant) for brunch every weekend, he also has the riverboats seven nights a week, and he does other gigs around town. Now he is making very, very good money, let me tell you.

The majority of musicians interviewed confirmed the notion that the tourism industry required that the musicians play a certain kind of music. One young musician who leads his own band put it this way:

They don't require that you do anything, they are just not going to hire you if you don't play what they want to hear. They only hire the group that play that kind of music, so they don't tell you to change and they'll hire you – they don't care that much about you. We have lots of band, they can choose somebody else. So no, they are not going to tell you that they don't want you to play whatever, blues, rock, Irish ditties. They'll say they just want to hire your band. But if you don't play what they expect you to, you won't get hired again.

Another group leader:

It goes this way: They'll say, 'I need a blues band, you are a jazz musician, I'm not telling you that you got to be a blues musician, I want to tell you I only hire blues bands. So I'm not telling you to change your life ambitions, I was just saying this is why you are hired', so yes, musicians do feel held back by the way they have to play. But that's also why most everybody plays most every way here, so you don't have those categories attached to you that can keep you from getting hired. You just let it out that you're a drummer, or a trumpet player, and you're ready to play. So the situation with tourism causes the musicians to have to be broad based.

There is general agreement that tourism provides opportunities for young people to play, but there are conflicting opinions about how this affects their future prospects. A music educator at the University of New Orleans:

Music requires discipline and especially commitment. It is very hard to be a young musician training to be a professional musician. There is that initial burst of talent, where people say a child is going to be great – well he may be very good at eight years old, but by 12, they have to move beyond the very good eight-year-old status, to having to make a commitment. That's when the training comes in. Those who practice, they are better musicians. It becomes a thing of time, a thing of hours. It is a solo activity, it is an activity about developing the individual and it is an individual effort and that is what kids don't have anymore in this country, in lots of places; they run in packs. So music is a great social engineering tool for the city of New Orleans and it has always been a great social engineering tool. Here music has been used as a gang that kids got involved with, to develop a sense of who they are.

You also have to be able to improvise; New Orleans music is a music of improvisation, so at one point or other you have to step out from the crowd. You have to make your statement, inside, of what is the overall group statement. So the tourism industry provides a place for all this to happen, and for young people, they can play on the streets, in the Quarter, and get that practice in, and also make a pretty good piece of change. You can get hired for these afternoon events, and on the weekend, while you're still in school, and make some pocket money. Look at Harry Connick Jr. He was playing on Bourbon Street when he was 13, 14. But you have to be able to compete. You have to keep your level of musicianship up or the tourist will just walk down to the next group. But playing, the more you play the better you are as a musician, and the tourist industry gives lots of opportunity to play.

At the same time, there are doubts about the staying power of these opportunities afforded to young people. Teachers in local university music departments, including Ellis Marsalis, father of jazz giant Wynton Marsalis, have expressed worry that young musicians, given the opportunity to make a little money playing for tourists, will not continue their education, and their talents may be stifled at a young age by their dropping out of jazz studies available in local institutions. 'Yes, they're cute playing out there at 12, 15 years old. But how cute is that same musician at 35, when he hasn't progressed, and doesn't have a diploma because he dropped out of school to work for the tourists?' On the other hand, others, including a member of the local public school board, disagree with this notion:

> It's easy for some people to say all children should go to college and all young musicians should take college jazz studies, but the reality is that college is not an option for many young New Orleanians, and playing music, at any level, is an honourable and fulfilling occupation especially with the limited options available to many young poor people in an urban area. And as a musician, I believe playing for years only improves musicians . . . So just because a young person begins to play early, outside the institutions of learning, because of the opportunities given by tourism, that doesn't necessarily mean that that young person won't have a long and successful career. It happens all the time. That's a case of 'let them eat cake.' Well, 'let them go to college to study jazz' may sound like an idea for everyone, but frankly, it's not.

The Twinning of New Orleans and Liverpool

As New Orleans opens up its private cultural activities to the outside, the city is wrestling with questions such as what effect new tourism initiatives will have on a city such as New Orleans, and whether these changes will, in fact, translate into economic regeneration and sustainable growth for the local music industry. Looking for balanced strategies that will facilitate control and ownership of representations and cultural products, and at the same time provide economic support for the community, New Orleans has looked to other localities for innovative ideas and information.

In the late 1980s, for example, the city of New Orleans and the city of Liverpool became what is called in the United States 'Sister Cities' and what officials in Liverpool City Council call 'friendship-linked' (which, they explain, is less expensive than twinned, since links don't involve international trips by city officials and exchanges of scrolls). Previous attempts to adapt programmes from such 'music cities' as Nashville, Tennessee and Austin, Texas had proved impractical for New Orleans owing to what local policy-makers described as 'economic, social and historic differences' in the cities' experiences. The predominantly African-

American musical community of New Orleans felt little in common with
the experiences of the predominantly white musical communities of Austin
and Nashville. For instance, despite the efforts of the New Orleans city
government and a good relationship between the city's music business
community and the annual South by Southwest Music Conference in
Austin, few New Orleans musical groups attend the conferences, thereby
missing opportunities to make links with the recording industry. Samples
of remarks made by New Orleans musicians when asked why they didn't
participate were: 'They aren't interested in our music'; 'We don't play
for free'; and most often 'We can't afford to drive 500 miles to play for
some record industry cat who came to hear some hillbilly punk band.'

In contrast, the musical community of New Orleans shared a common
belief that in Europe lay possibilities of business success. The popularity
of New Orleans music in Europe creates opportunities for playing
international festivals, and many New Orleans musicians have travelled
to Europe who have never travelled within the United States. Musicians
often mention 'Europe' as a place of musical discernment where New
Orleans music is appreciated, reaffirming feelings of local difference and
worth. An invitation to play overseas can be seen as a reapprobation and
endorsement of a group's talent and creativity.

At the time, some informal links between the cities carried the news of
current initiatives in both places to boost their local music industries, and
articles appeared in both cities about the other's attempts. Liverpool, it
was felt, shared many common traits with New Orleans: historical trade
links, a similar population size, heavy unemployment. Both cities have
international musical traditions and reputations, yet neither has benefited
in any substantial way from these. Both cities have been linked with crime
and violence by their national media, and were looking for a way to
overcome that image.

Feelings of powerlessness and frustration with the music industry and
belief that their contribution to popular music (jazz and R&B for New
Orleans, the Beatles and the many successful bands in the 1960s and
1970s for Liverpool) never resulted in adequate remuneration, together
with a perception of lack of support from their own local and national
governments, fed into common notions of being both geographically and
economically isolated from the centres of power, creating a bond between
the two cities based on perceptions of common experience. The groups
involved in the twinning felt that mutual exchanges of ideas and projects
would benefit both localities, and that, given the similarities of
circumstances, any initiatives for music business development that had
succeeded in one city had a good possibility of success in the other. The

twinning of New Orleans and Liverpool points out how music can generate notions of community that may transcend national borders.

Conclusion

This look at New Orleans points out the often overlooked role of music in the way cities and places are recognised and accepted and the influence of musical images on the portrayal and development of culture. As towns and cities embrace tourism for economic development, decisions on how local cultural activities are commodified for tourist consumption could become important factors in the shaping of local identity. In addition, the way that New Orleans musicians relate to the tourism industry points up ways that economic pressures may affect local cultural products and styles.

Notes

1. Interviews with sources are drawn from research done in New Orleans, Louisiana, over the last decade, both as a doctoral candidate and as a journalist in the city.
2. See, for example, Jan Nordby Gretlund, *Eudora Welty's Aesthetics Of Place*, Odense, Denmark: Odense University Press, 1994; Leonard Lutwack, *The Role Of Place In Literature*, Syracuse, NY, Syracuse University Press, 1984; David Kranes, 'Space and Literature: Notes toward a Theory of Mapping', in *Where? Place In Recent North American Fictions*, ed. Karl-Heinz Westarp, Aarhus University Press, 1991; and Violet Harrington Bryan, *The Myth Of New Orleans In Literature: Dialogues of Race and Gender*, Knoxville: University of Tennessee Press, 1993.

References

Berry, Jason, Tad Jones, and Jon Foose (1990). *Up From the Cradle Of Jazz*. Athens: University of Georgia Press.

Esolen, Gary (1994). Interview with the author, March 1994.

Floyd, Samuel (1995). *The Power Of Black Music: Interpreting Its History From Africa to the United States*. New York: Oxford University Press.

Hall, Gwendolyn Midlo (1994). *Africans in Colonial Louisiana, The Development of Afro-Creole Culture In the Eighteenth Century*. Baton Rouge: LSU Press.

Kaslow, Andrew (1981). Oppression and Adaptation: The Social Organization and Expressive Culture of An Afro-American Community in New Orleans, Louisiana. Unpublished Ph.D. thesis, Columbia University.

Kmen, Henry (1966). *Music In New Orleans, The Formative Years 1791– 1841*. Baton Rouge: LSU Press.

Monson, Ingrid (1994). Improvisation and the Art of Signifyin(g). *Critical Inquiry* 20(2) (Winter 1994).

Robins, Kevin (1991). Tradition and Translation: National Culture in its Global Context. In J. Corner and S. Harvey (eds), *Enterprise and Heritage*. London: Routledge.

Ryan, Tim (1990). *Economic Impact of Music on the New Orleans Economy. Report to the City of New Orleans*. University of New Orleans.

Wallis, R. and Malm, K. (1984). *Big Sounds From Small Peoples. The Music Industry In Small Countries*. London: Constable.

6

The Ideal Village: Interactions through Tourism in Central Anatolia

Hazel Tucker

A
nalyses of tourism and tourist culture have tended to work through a purely visual framework, responding to the perpetual visualisation in tourism-related discourses. Indeed, Urry (1990) argues that tourism is all about gazing upon particular scenes that are different from those encountered in everyday life. Furthermore, this view of tourism has led Urry to the conclusion that, since postmodernity is marked by 'the proliferation of images and symbols' (Lash and Urry 1994: 256), tourism is coming home, since it is now possible to '*see* many of the typical objects of the tourist gaze . . . in one's own living room, at the flick of a switch' (Urry 1990: 100).

Whilst it cannot be denied that visual images and experiences do play a major role in postmodern tourism, I would argue that there has become something of an *over*-visualisation in tourism industry and tourism discourse.[1] Tourism theories that only emphasise the gaze can themselves set the tourist experience in frames, and thereby gloss over what actually takes place in touristic processes and tourists' interactions with the visited environments. Beyond gazing, 'traveller-type' tourists in particular, whose discourse revolts against the '*tour*-ists' who bus around glimpsing at *sights*, seek prolonged and close encounters with the landscapes and cultures they visit. The 'tourist site' then becomes participatory in touristic interactions, rather than being merely an object of the tourist gaze. This chapter focuses on the nature of tourist expectations and encounters in Göreme, a Cappadokyan village in Central Turkey, and considers the extent to which the physical and social environment meets the imagined ideals of tourists who go there.[2] In analysing tourist motivation and discourse through the representation and construction of Göreme as a 'tourist site',

I look at how the local environment responds and adapts to the expectations of tourists who go there for a combination of both 'fun' and 'authenticity'.

The Site and the Tourists

The area of Göreme consists of soft volcanic rock that has gradually eroded to form natural cones and columns, which are locally termed 'fairy chimneys'. For centuries the chimneys have been carved and hollowed to form the dwellings, stables and places of worship that pattern the troglodyte village of today. Through most of the village, the streets are steep and often narrow, and have a haphazard appearance, with most houses built half into rock faces and 'fairy chimneys'. There are many empty and crumbling 'chimneys' and cave houses giving certain areas a ghost-town appearance. Today many of the older houses have been restored as *pansiyons*, or small hotels, which are dotted throughout the village. Except for these, all the tourism businesses are down in the centre. These newer buildings, which house restaurants, bars and travel agencies, line the central roads, acting rather like walls that seem to separate this central tourist area from the older residential areas behind. For this reason, it is possible to refer to the 'front' and 'back' regions of touristic Göreme, presenting an architectural and social duality in Göreme, which, as I will show, suits the duality in tourists' quests.

In the Cappadokya area, tourism has developed fairly rapidly since the mid-1980s, and the villagers of Göreme are continuously trying to find a suitable niche for themselves in the touristic processes. Since the area became a national park in the late 1960s, the Ministries of Culture and Tourism have imposed strict regulations concerning the preservation of the rock cones and caves, especially those containing Byzantine period churches. As a consequence, the building of large hotels is not permitted in the Göreme valley, so that unlike what has happened in other Cappadokyan towns, Göreme's tourism has remained relatively low-key and low on capital investment. The majority of tourists staying in the village are thus young, lower-income tourists, travelling independently of package tours.

The type of tourism most prominent in Göreme thus pertains to the *new petit bourgeois* tourists, whose 'exploratory extended self-testing adventurous style' is described well by Graburn:

> Prototypical tourists in search of new experience – in the extreme form in their wandering youth – who to varying degrees wish to 'consume' (like television) the rest of the world, its sights, its history, its peoples and their

cultures – their clothes, artefacts, bathing styles, cuisines, etc. – and who compete back at home in prestige rankings based on distance, exoticism, crises overcome, variety of tourist experiences etc. (1983: 20).

This description can be linked with the ideas of MacCannell (1976), who emphasises the postmodern tourist's quest for *authenticity* in other times and other places. Tourists, for MacCannell, are alienated by the conditions of contemporary life, and engage in a 'modern ritual' in order to 'overcome the discontinuity of modernity' by 'incorporating its fragments into unified experience' (ibid.: 13). For tourists in Göreme, I would argue, this process is sought through their particular interactions with the local environment. Following an ideology that insistently values the 'unique', 'natural' and 'traditional', these tourists seek *authentic* experiences within the village. At the same time though, it is important for these tourists to experience 'adventure' and 'fun', and to confirm, through the presence of other tourists and tourism services, the *consecration* of Göreme as a 'tourist site'.

Adventure in the Landscape

Tourists are enticed to Göreme by images of the moon-like landscape and troglodyte dwellings. Tourists seek to 'go into a cave to experience it for [themselves]. It's like being a child, exploring, finding something which no one else has found' (Dutch tourist). Alluding to a discourse of uniqueness, romanticism, and adventure, the landscape around Göreme is perfect for discovery and the feeling that you might find a cave, church or even a valley that has been forgotten for hundreds of years. The landscape is ideal to suit both the serendipity of these tourists, and the quest for 'a personal semi-spiritual relationship' (Urry 1990: 45), which is what these 'romantic' tourists seek to have with the tourist site.

Describing the area as 'beautiful', 'bizarre', and 'out of this world', tourists are attracted to the landscape because of its otherness and the idea that it is 'like a huge adventure playground for adults'. An imaginary moon-world of fairy-chimneys and troglodytes, Göreme is an ideal of the tourist imagination. Indeed, Bruner has argued that, 'In tourism, the Third World becomes a playground of the Western imaginary, in which the affluent are given the discursive space to enact their fantasies' (1989: 440). However, although Bruner follows Baudrillard (1983) in the idea that the 'preference for the simulacrum is the essence of postmodern tourism' (Bruner 1989: 438), it is important that Göreme is only 'like' a playground because it is actually 'real'. The fairy-chimneys are naturally eroded, and the doors, windows and churches are carved out in the real lives of other people. Referring again to MacCannell's idea that tourists seek authenticity and an experience of the real, Göreme is a perfect destination for these young tourists because the landscape is 'like a playground' and yet at the same time is 'natural', and is importantly perceived to be so by the tourists. The tourists here do not have a preference for simulacrum, quite the contrary, they consider Göreme to be 'heaven on earth' because it is both a playground and real at the same time.

Moreover, the idea of an 'adventure playground' implies some sort of bodily involvement rather than mere *gazing*. With grazed hands and bruised knees, tourists coming back after a day of hiking and clambering through caves and fairy chimneys, look vibrant in comparison to those climbing out of a mini-bus after a day's tour of the *sights*. Whilst the Göreme landscape is on the one hand a *spectacle* that is framed for and by tourists in their touristic activities, it is also a place to get involved with, where tourists can indulge in an almost carnivalesque celebration of the physical senses. In addition to gazing upon the landscape, eating, smelling, listening, and especially crawling and clambering amongst the caves are all ways in which Göreme's environment is experienced. What is more, as one Australian tourist said, 'The mosque calling to prayer and children asking you for bonbons are all part of the landscape', so that adventure is sought by 'getting into the culture' as well as through interaction with the physical landscape.

The Tourist Village

Just as the moon-like valley is a 'natural adventure park', tourists seek from the village both 'authenticity' and some element of 'fun' and relaxation. From these quests arise certain representations of the village and the village community. These, in turn, involve the representations that the local people have of both the tourists and themselves. Even though the tourists are in a Central Anatolian village, they expect to be serviced in a way generally prescribed by Western tourism. At the same time, though, services must be consistent with tourist representations of Turkish villages and Turkish people, so that whilst providing tourists with what they need, the tourist 'front' must somehow be appropriately 'other'. Their expectations include a rather tumultuous but friendly production of services that play well to the liminal nature of their experiences.[3] The expectancy that things will not go smoothly is all part of the 'adventure' in Turkey, and the amicable terms on which services are conducted provide the close encounters that these tourists are seeking.

Time spent in the village is in many ways characterised by the experience of disorder and the awareness that anything untoward, either good or bad, could happen at any moment. As Turks are constantly saying to tourists, 'everything is possible in Turkey'. Many tourists comment on how their experiences in the village are enriched by such happenings as the mosque calling to prayer and the loudspeaker announcing village news and events from the municipality office. Every few days a municipal truck goes around the streets billowing out insecticide spray, inciting comments, coughs and clicks of the camera from the tourists. Every weekend the streets are alive with wedding parties or circumcision processions. There's always someone to talk to: if it is not some other tourists you have met, then it is a waiter inviting you into a restaurant or a carpet salesman engaging you into friendship in order to seduce you into eventually buying a carpet.

Catering to a low level of tourism with small guest houses and other services, local entrepreneurs are to some extent able to condition the tourism in Göreme in their own way. Besides the economic gains to be had from their businesses, the local community wishes to offer hospitality and friendship to tourists in relationships of mutual respect. Some confusion occurs in these interactions, however. Tourists are often sceptical about the behaviour and motives of the men they meet in this environment. They are suspicious of the perceived over-friendliness of the salesmen and waiters, so that some tourists reach the point of complete mistrust, and ignore virtually anyone who speaks to them. This puts the local men on something of a knife-edge, caught between being 'too friendly' and not 'charming' enough. Their images of themselves are constantly contested through their experiences with tourists.

Many of the men working in these services complain that backpackers expect the local people to adapt to them and always to help them when they have no money: 'they just bargain, bargain, bargain, and then they complain about the service'. As tourism is becoming more important in the economy, the local entrepreneurs are becoming less patient with 'hard-up travellers', as well as disillusioned by their attitudes. As an example, I heard a woman from the USA telling some other tourists how she likes Turkey because it is cheap. She went on to explain that whenever she arrives in a new place, she begins to flirt with some guy so that she will get free meals and accommodation for the rest of her stay. Although this woman is by no means typical, there is something in her quest for 'free' services that rings true for many of the tourists who come to Göreme. The mistrust guiding interactions in this arena therefore becomes mutual.

However sceptical the local people are, they are still reliant on the tourists, and must continue to try to attract their custom. Aware that they are untrustworthy in the eyes of the tourists, many of the businesses are now employing the casual help of tourists. Indeed, it was evident from my observations that tourists more readily buy carpets or take tours that are sold or promoted by fellow-Westerners. The cultural self-confidence attributed by Graburn (1983) to seemingly forthright tourists such as those in Göreme is perhaps not as evident as expected. Lacking in the cultural self-confidence necessary to deal comfortably with the Other, they are perhaps not quite so serendipitous after all, preferring to deal with and glean information from their fellow tourists rather than Turkish people.

Whilst Graburn only seems to consider the cultural self-confidence of the tourists, it is also necessary to assess that of the local people, especially those who are dealing with tourists in the tourist realm. I would argue that in Göreme there is a narrative of pride if not actual confidence, and the quest for mutual respect in relations with tourists is paramount. The Göreme people carry a fierce pride in their culture and social virtues, and are continually negotiating a worthy image within and through tourism. This pride was displayed clearly one evening in the disco when a group of about ten Australian men were overheard criticising and cursing Turks. Word quickly got around, and within a few minutes a crowd of local men arrived and sat near to the Australians. Nothing was said, but their intimidation was enough that the Australians soon left the disco. Unprepared to put up with such criticism, the local men had displayed a strong sense of cultural pride, without doing damage to the tourism industry.

Whilst tourism relations bring an inevitable renegotiation of identity with reference to the Other, at present, since much of the tourism business in Göreme is locally owned and managed, identity is negotiated through relationships of reasonable equality. As the tourists are *their* guests, the local people are largely able to condition the level of their hospitality and of the interaction they have with tourists. However, entrepreneurs from outside Göreme are slowly moving in, and this may bring a gradual loss of control over relations and identity in the service arena. When locals change from being entrepreneurs to employees, their tasks become more menial, and their position in relation to tourists more subservient (a point observed in Greek tourism by Williams and Papamichael 1995).

Without intending to conduct an 'impact' analysis of tourism in Göreme, it is right to point out that where processes of social change bring loss of local control, the renegotiation of culture and identity is increasingly in the hands of 'others'. There are now significant grumblings within the community that the 'local culture', especially that of the young men, is being 'ruined' by tourism'. What is meant by this is that the men are losing their grip on the moral codes of life, by turning their backs on the village and only looking to the 'tourist front'. Whilst it is generally accepted as positive that tourism brings economic gains, the increasing frequency of sexual encounters between female tourists and local entrepreneurs and service employees has stirred up some disillusionment and discontent.

According to one local man training to be a tour guide, for many of Göreme's men working in tourism-related businesses, tourists mean 'dollar, dollar, dollar, sex, sex, sex'! Whilst equal numbers of men and women may arrive in the village, more women tend to stay around for longer periods of time. Almost all the foreigners working in Göreme are women, and many are having relationships with Turkish men in the village. Indeed, it has been recently pointed out that we should be paying more attention to the issue of gender in tourism studies, since 'women and men are involved differently in the construction and consumption of tourism' (Swain 1995: 249). A further assertion suggests that 'Gendered "realities" shape tourism marketing, guests' motivations, and hosts' actions' (ibid.). Women's motivation and self-transformation through 'independent' travel, for example, could be viewed differently from that of men undertaking long arduous trips. Women might be asserting stronger statements about the self, concerning their freedom, independence and capability.

Certainly the production of tourist experiences is dictated by gender relations in the 'host' environment. There is in Göreme a strict segregation of the sexes, and it is so obviously men who work with tourism there that many tourists comment on the fact that they never have contact with Turkish women. Indeed, they are not likely to in Göreme, since, for the people indigenous to Göreme at least, the tourist front is strictly the domain of men.

The large number of sexual encounters between female tourists and their Göreme 'hosts' are premised on a set of both understandings and misunderstandings about Turkish male and foreign female sexuality. For Göreme's men, female tourists represent 'sex'. Whilst local women are under lock and key, female tourists are perceived 'not to care about virginity, and so represent limitless opportunities for local men to prove their own sexual prowess. Many of the men are convinced that women actually come to Göreme for sex, so that through tourism, local male sexual identity is constantly strengthened.

For the foreign woman, not only do the liminal experiences of tourism allow for certain moral constraints present in normal life to be put aside, but she has found a place where she is charmed by numerous attractive young men. As one North American woman explained, 'I don't get looked at at home, then I come here and I've got ten guys all looking up admiringly at me.' Sex tourism clearly influences power in sexual identity and presents opportunities that may be perceived as lacking in the tourist's home environment. However, whilst some women enjoy the admiration, many of the female tourists perceive the attention they receive as annoying 'hassle'. In particular, many women find themselves 'attached to' for the duration of their stay in Göreme. After they are claimed by a certain man, wanted or unwanted, their interaction with other people in the village becomes limited. The local men become fiercely possessive, and tourists find themselves embroiled with one particular man and one particular web of relations and unable to break free. For the local men, the tourist season is experienced as a series of 'friendships', whilst for the tourists, this practice is restricting on the 'play' and 'freedom' that their liminal state requires.

The fact that female tourists *do* have sexual relationships with local men confirms representations about their own and the men's sexuality. A good time is undoubtedly had by many; but various disputes arise between these partners, as well as within the local community. Numerous married men pretend to be single whilst dealing with tourists, and there are competitions and games regarding 'conquests' in this realm.[4] In other respects, these relationships are taken very seriously, often with a view to a kind of 'personal salvation'. Despite their 'backpacker' image and constant bargaining in Göreme, tourists are perceived to be 'rich', and even some local women, who are evidently marginalised by these practices, appear to be tolerant for the sake of potential economic gain.[5]

The young men in Göreme are developing what Picard (1993) has called 'touristic culture', or are becoming 'touristified' through the process of tourism production (Picard 1995). That is, tourism has become an integral part of their culture with the development of new styles of living and working as well as of relating to women. They are negotiating a new identity for themselves that includes relating with foreign tourists. Although villagers (including these men themselves) fear that the young men are 'losing their culture', they are generally open to change; this change being an ongoing process of cultural invention. Of course, this process is not always smooth-running, being conditioned by a set of often conflicting interests; but as long as it remains largely in the community's control, then Göreme village and the people who live there will become 'touristified' in their own way.

A problem lies, however, in the tourists' perceptions of a touristified

Göreme. Whilst they expect to be serviced comfortably and enjoy the 'fun' to be had in the tourist realm, the tourists here are generally seeking to 'be transported to somewhere completely different – a sixth-century village – to experience a different time and place' (Canadian tourist). They therefore consider the tourist arena to be something of a necessary evil as it provides the services that they need and enjoy, yet clashes with their ideal imagined village.

There is a belief amongst Göreme's tourists that 'tourism destroys the culture' since, through tourism, 'the people have contact with the Western way of life'. In other words, the Other culture has then become too much like us, and, since tourism is all about going to extraordinary and Other places, there is a danger that the social and physical environment will no longer constitute a suitable tourist site. Some tourists feel in Göreme that they are 'not in a real Turkish village', perceiving Göreme to be a 'tourist village' instead. The judgement of authenticity is based largely on perceptions of the level of touristic involvement in the social and physical environment, and the tourists in Göreme are constantly wary and sceptical of anything that might be staged for them. If something has been altered or packaged for tourism, or sometimes if it has been 'polluted' merely by the *presence* of other tourists, then it is perceived not to be real.

It is doubtful, however, that all the tourists in Göreme are equally in quest of authentic experiences. For the tourists in Göreme, there is a very fine line between that which is considered worthy of tourist attention, and that which is perceived to be too touristy for 'real' experience. Since they spend much of their time in Göreme in conversation with, and competing with, other tourists reliving their 'authentic' interactions in the village, authentication of experience becomes a way of obtaining 'symbolic capital' in Bourdieu's (1984) sense, being more a marker of taste than of alienation in modern society. In this case, it is the signs of experience collected by tourists while they are in Göreme that must find the balance between being tourist objects worthy of collection, yet not blatantly packaged for tourists.

In any case, the concept of authenticity is relative and socially constructed (Cohen 1988), and must be viewed as such when considering tourist experience and touristic relations. All tourists bring with them an image and certain expectations about what they will find in Göreme. First impressions range from the perception that Göreme is too quiet and lacking in tourist fun, to its being ruined by tourism and no longer a 'real Turkish village'. Tourists differ both in the extent of their quest for authenticity and in the extent to which they are prepared to put up with perceived inauthenticity. In general, the Göreme environment does seem to strike the right balance and stays worthy of tourist attention. Of interest here, though, is the production and maintenance of this balance, which makes Göreme the ideal place that it is for these tourists.

The Preservation of Göreme as a 'Tourist Site'

Sites become 'tourist sites' through a system of symbolic and structural processes that are guided by the power of tourist discourse. Urry (1992) argues that tourist discourse conditions the way that environments are 'read', appropriated, and exploited. For landscapes to be suitable for aesthetic appropriation, tourist discourse narrates that they must be unique, unpolluted and authentic (authenticity here implying a consistency between the natural and built environment, ibid.: 21). The dominant narrative asserts authority over landscapes, which become tourist objects, even though certain participants in the environment may bring conflicting representations to the tourist setting.

In the Göreme valley, various laws operate to protect the 'authentic' buildings and rock formations, as well as to keep a check on the aesthetic quality of new building developments. These laws are not always observed, and there is much building work that is incongruous with tourists' representations of how the village should be. New buildings and tourism businesses appear inconsistent with the 'original' cave-dwellings, and consequently many tourists find that Göreme is not the 'real' sixth-century village that they had hoped it to be. They constantly look at the physical environment and wonder if it has been altered or constructed for tourists. Here again, is MacCannell's idea that people become tourists in order to find authenticity in 'the real lives of others'; others who appear to be more attuned to the authenticity of human life (Sack 1992).

This sort of touristic attitude is said to be essentially conservative, orientalist and reflective of imperialist ideals (see Errington and Gewertz 1989; MacCannell 1992; Munt 1994b). The consumption of certain touristic experiences, described by such adjectives as *alternative, adventurous, unique* and *authentic*, serves an ideology that separates so-called 'travellers' from the perceived crassness of package holidaying. However, as Munt points out, 'While mass tourism has attracted trenchant criticism as a shallow and degrading experience for the Third World host nations and peoples, new tourism practices have been viewed benevolently and few critiques have emerged' (1994b: 50). Munt, himself, is critical of the *new petit bourgeois* tourism, arguing that behind their disguise as socially and environmentally sensitive travellers, the middle classes are in fact strong proponents of ethnocentric imperialist values.

Indeed, the 'travellers' in Göreme do show a marked desire for the village to somehow remain static in a primitive and untouched state. An Australian woman told me that she 'would hate the Göreme people to all be driving cars in twenty years. Donkeys and horses and carts are much nicer. It's nice for time to stand still in some places.' Another tourist pointed out that the telegraph poles in the village provided a rather quaint link with our time, since they marked 'modernity', and yet were sufficiently rusty and decrepit to be consistent with [his ideas of] the village. Such tourists look in Göreme for 'part of the past still being used today, because it is comforting to see a place which is living in an era earlier than ours'. These tourists are then troubled to find a place 'polluted' and rendered 'inauthentic' by modernity, and even worse, tourism.

This presents interesting issues concerning the preservation and restoration of the cave dwellings. There is no doubt that parts of the village are crumbling, and, since the 1960s, the Disaster Relief Director (AFET) has declared parts of the village dangerous. If erosion continues, more residents will be moved out to new housing, and Göreme village will become a 'ghost town' like the nearby villages of Uchisar and Cavusun. The preservation issue would clearly have arisen with or without tourism; but it has become particularly important now that tourist discourse is at work. As Urry (1992) and Munt (1994b) point out, the emergence of the new middle-class 'real' and 'romantic' tourism has led to a rise in environmental consciousness whereby conservation of the natural and unique is considered of major importance. Of interest in Göreme is the contestation of what is natural or authentic and worthy of conserving.

Tourism brings the preservation issue in Göreme village to the forefront on two counts. First, tourist discourse asserts certain representations of the village according to aesthetic value. Second, tourism itself is perceived to spoil the environment, since it renders that environment no longer authentic. Both of these assertions are currently embedded in the actions of a 'Save Göreme Committee', started by a non-Turk who has managed a *pansiyon* in the village for a number of years. According to him, profits from current tourism should be used to restore the old village, rather than the AFET and tourism organisations continuing to construct new buildings 'which are spoiling the natural beauty of the environment'.

Instead of being moved out into safer new houses, it is considered, for the sake of tourism, that the people should be kept in their chimney houses, so that the houses and the culture contained therein will be retained. If the houses are neglected, the houses will ruin, and 'then, this natural and architecturally historical unique monument – a natural open-air museum

– will no longer be around for future generations to see' (Leyssen and Idiz 1993: 13). Besides having political and economic motivations, in advocating a 'Save Göreme Committee' the writer shows clear ideological representation of the village and its cave dwellings as 'monuments' worthy of preservation.

For the villagers on the other hand, the meaning of the troglodyte houses concerns the practicalities of life rather than anything else. Many people view their cave dwellings as dark, impractical, and often downright dangerous, expressing a wish to move out into safer and more 'prestigious' accommodation. Aesthetics and authenticity are not high on the priorities of local building practices, and many people cannot afford to restore their houses in the prescribed way.

The difference in tourist and local representations of Göreme were shown to me when looking at photographs taken to represent Göreme in a book to be published by the Göreme Tourism Co-operative. The tourist photographer largely chose images of village scenes showing decrepit cave houses, old doorways, carts and people in 'traditional' dress. These depicted the 'traditional' and 'authentic'. The official from the Co-operative whose task it was to select photographs from this photographer chose only the more holistic pictures of the *physical* landscape. He chose to represent Göreme through the rock formations in the valleys, rather than through the everyday lives of the community. Tourists, on the other hand, view the living people as a necessary part of the landscape, their 'real' lives being crucial to the authenticity of the environment.

Tourism presents Göreme as a living museum, and renders the local people museum objects along with the fairy chimneys, churches and houses, to be gazed upon, photographed and encountered. However, the villagers now realise the value of their old houses as tourism assets (to be turned into 'cave' hotels), and their own valuing of the chimney houses is slowly changing to be more consistent with tourist representations. One day in the village, when a woman was complaining to me about the impracticality of her family's cave house, her six-year-old son contested, 'but the tourists like it – that's why they come here'. Without this idea, the erosion would eventually drive the villagers away, and the village would be left to collapse in on itself. There would be no more living museum.

Interactions in the Living Museum

Tourists staying in Göreme enjoy 'hanging around to get into the culture'. Their time in Göreme is therefore fairly unorganised, and their interactions with the local people unmanaged by guides. As I said earlier, they seek from the village both authenticity and some element of fun and relaxation, and from these quests arise certain representations of the village and the village community. These, in turn, involve the representations the local people have of both the tourists and themselves. Although tourism in Göreme is not blatantly 'culture tourism', as is the case in Bali or Papua New Guinea for example, an accidental by-product of promoting the surrounding *physical* landscape is the emergence of images of 'primitive' troglodyte dwellings. Without fully realising it, Göreme village is asserting an identity of the past to tourists, thereby creating an image of itself that most tourists will come here and find. Tourists regularly explore the back regions of the village, seeking authentic encounters with the 'real lives of other people', in order to 'experience the simpler, pure life that we've lost'. For tourists then, Göreme *is* a living museum.

Again, it is clear that such postmodern social movements as environmentalism and cultural preservation (Munt 1994b), guide tourists' encounters within the 'tourist site' of Göreme. In interactions the tourist narrative, based on the 'traditional' troglodyte culture of the tourists' imagination, is dominant. Göreme's people are imagined to be 'living in the past', living a life other than our own, a purer life free from the burdens of modern civilisation. Making contact with this pure other life is experienced by these tourists as enhancing their own humanity, their own selves. For 'travellers', Errington and Gewertz write, 'the encounter with what was seen as the "primitive" – the exotic, the whole, the fundamentally human – contributed to their own individuality, integration and authenticity' (1989: 42). Moreover, these tourists are endeavouring to affirm their distinction, thus engaging in a competition for symbolic capital, this capital gleaned from experiencing the most 'authentic' encounters with these 'real' people of the village. In this, taking photographs as proof of their encounters is important.

In Göreme, tourists seek to photograph the 'authentic', and preferably no signs of modernity should be present. That is unless the photographer can compose an interesting juxtaposition between the traditional and the modern. They prefer their human subjects not to pose, since it would show that the villagers were temporarily pulled out from their 'real' life, rendering the picture immediately inauthentic. Photography has become such an important part of tourism that it actually 'gives shape to travel' (Urry 1990: 139) and influences much of the interaction taking place between tourists and local people. Many tourists in Göreme wander around the village with the specific purpose of accumulating photographs. This activity causes some distress in the village, mainly because of the negative meaning attached to images in Islam; and numerous disputes arise when tourists take pictures of people without asking.

The power in the photographic gaze is evident both through the symbolic representations 'captured' within the pictures and in the actual process of taking photographs. Here we return to the idea of Göreme's being a 'living museum', through which the people of the village are gazed upon, appropriated and collected. When photographed, the villagers of Göreme are rendered 'objects' both in the Foucauldian sense and in an existential sense, in which there is a constant battle to be subject or object in relation to the other. This battle occurs in tourists' photographs and in touristic encounters in general. However, whilst much has been written about the powerful gaze of tourists upon 'others', the return gaze is not so often considered. It is generally assumed that tourists have the upper hand, being the lookers, and that 'host' communities are the looked at. However, during my stay in Göreme, I observed a number of occasions that showed that the gaze, and indeed the *power*, in interactions between tourists and local people is not all one-sided.

The 'back' part of the village is generally women's domain. In the afternoons groups of women sit chatting and sewing in shaded parts of the narrow streets. Sometimes, tourists walk by and gazes are exchanged. I observed that the women, who are on home territory and in larger groups, have an equally (if not more) powerful gaze on to the tourists as tourists have on to them. One afternoon I was inside a house drinking tea with a group of young village women. Some were gazing out on to the street below, and whenever tourists walked by they called 'tourist, tourist', and mocked their clothing or their apparently ridiculous behaviour. We were behind a window, and the tourists had no idea they were being gazed upon, let alone mocked. Another time, some women sitting in a courtyard eating fruit joked that we should throw our apple cores over the wall with the aim of hitting passing tourists. Just as the Turkish men in the touristic area return the tourist gaze, these women in the 'back' regions are by no means passive.

The battle of the gaze is also a battle of cultural self-confidence. As long as tourists behave in a 'respectful' manner, they can enjoy some interaction with the local people. All the villagers are extremely sensitive to the issue of respect, and if they perceive that tourists are in any way disrespectful, then they will not interact with them. Local people are critical of the backpackers who seek only fun with their fellow travellers and do not consider the fact that they are in a Muslim village, where, for example, it is ill-mannered to walk around scantily clad. Male tourists in particular are marginalised, and not permitted much interaction with local women.

Generally, then, it is only the 'respectful' tourists who interact with the people in the back of the village. Consequently, when asked what they think about the presence of tourists, local people typically answer 'We're all people. Tourists come and they go. They are our guests and we like them. If they respect us, we respect them.' With a tradition of hosting traders passing along the silk road, this points to a local self-representation as a people most 'hospitable' to guests. Villagers generally see their role in tourism as providing hospitality, considering this to be a 'traditional' Turkish virtue.

'Traditional Hospitality'

Turkish people take pride in their 'hospitable culture' and have come to promote and perhaps *sell* it for tourism. It is interesting to consider the authentication processes surrounding this 'traditional' custom. Authentication and commodification are often discussed in reference to aspects of culture such as festivals and dances. 'Hospitality', however, takes us more to the core of Turkish culture – for it is an aspect of *daily* life that is considered by the local people to be 'traditional'. Tourists usually receive that hospitality graciously, and often discuss the great friendliness, helpfulness, and hospitality in their experiences with Turkish people. However, as I have already said, services in the tourist realm of Göreme are considered by tourists to be inauthentic, although necessary. This is because they are created *for* tourists. This point is clarified by considering the different cultural meanings attached to the idea of hospitality by Göreme's 'hosts' and 'guests'.

For the tourists, friendliness and economic relations are two opposing phenomena, whereas for Turkish people, the two can comfortably co-exist, since economic transactions are negotiated very much on a personal level. Carpet salesmen may tell a whopping lie in order to sell an expensive piece, but at the same time they may sincerely *like* their customer and genuinely wish to befriend them for the duration of their stay in the village. One local entrepreneur told me 'Turkish people really take pleasure from giving hospitality. Whether it's for money or not, it's in our culture.' There is, however, much confusion concerning tourists' interactions with local entrepreneurs. Since tourists construe a dichotomy between friendship and money, they constantly ask themselves whether an offer of assistance, for example, is 'genuine hospitality'. While this dilemma is made easier for package tourists who pay everything up front and do not witness the exchange of money, for Göreme's 'independent' tourists the direct economic relations are more blatant, and so hospitality is a confusing issue.

I observed situations in the back of the village in which 'authentic hospitality' was clearly 'staged' for tourists. Both MacCannell (1976) and Cohen (1988) discuss at length the staging of certain desired aspects of culture for tourists, describing the way in which tourists are cheated by the deliberate dressing up of back-region events to look authentic. One clear example of this occurring in Göreme involves a family who live in a cave house set into the cliff of a valley just below the top ledge, which has now become one of Göreme's main panoramic viewpoints. Bus groups of tourists often stop on this ledge to gaze over the valley, and there are now numerous souvenir stands at the site. Whilst gazing at the view, some lucky tourists may catch the eye of a 'traditionally-dressed' woman on the ledge below. She might wave to invite them down the steps dug into the rock and into her cave house to drink some tea. The group's guide will translate any information the tourists desire to know about the troglodyte family, and on their way out they may browse over and hopefully buy a souvenir hand-crafted by the mother and daughter of the family.

These tourists experience 'real hospitality' in a 'real' Cappadokyan cave house. It is unknown to them that the family has a connection with their guide, and that the whole thing is a set-up. The guide secretly phones a little earlier to warn the mother to be waiting out in her garden, so that the hospitality can be made to look like an unexpected and authentic encounter. The family obviously benefit economically from the selling of the handicrafts, although I was unable to determine whether the guides give them any fee for the visit.

It is interesting to consider here whether or not the staging for tourism of this aspect of Turkish culture in any way changes the meaning of hospitality for the family concerned. Greenwood (1989) has argued that the packaging and commoditising of culture for tourism renders that culture meaningless. Other tourism anthropologists, for example Picard (1993), take the view that local people can adequately distinguish the real, in which they are still able to find meaning, from the performances put on for tourists. Through regular observations, I concluded that this family is able to distinguish between the staged and the real hospitality given to guests. They certainly behaved rather despondently with the arrival of yet another group of tourists, compared with the arrival of friends from the village. The only people duped in the interactions described above, it seems, are the tourists.

Other quite similar occurrences take place within the village for the backpackers who go wandering through the back streets seeking authenticity. Some village women invite tourists in to look at their cave house and to give them tea. The tourists experience an encounter with 'real' village life – until the host presents a pile of head scarves for her visitor to buy at rather inflated prices. Suddenly the situation is no longer perceived to be real. The hospitality has turned into an economic event, and the two are irreconcilable. One tourist disillusioned by such an encounter said 'This place slides between being authentically real and what's done for tourists.' Indeed, we are told of the duality between friendship and economic exchange by *The Good Tourist Guide to Turkey*, which warns us that 'invitations to view the insides of houses should be seen as what they are: low-key commerce rather than simple friendliness' (House and Wood 1993: 253).

Tourists experience staged hospitality as a double let-down. It is bad enough that the encounter turns out not to be authentic, but even worse that what they thought was real friendliness turned out to be a con (at least that is how it is perceived). Women and families in the village on the other hand, seem to be making good use of tourist representations of them as being 'traditional' and 'authentic' by letting them have their desired experiences for just a small fee; the price of a scarf must be nothing, after all, compared to that of the camera draped around the tourist's neck.

The Meaning of Meetings

There are of course some encounters in the village which do not result in economic exchange. Tourists are often invited to events such as weddings, where no payment is expected. However, even then, tourists may still become suspicious that the event is somehow contrived or packaged for them, especially if there are other tourists there. Conversely, if someone finds that he or she is the only tourist present at an event, there may be doubt that the event is worthy of tourist interest. Here again is the matter of finding a balance between that which is a sanctified tourist experience, and that which is perceived to be too touristy for real experience.

During my time in Göreme, I took a young Japanese woman named Kiko to a women's wedding party that I had been invited to in the village. When I first told Kiko about the possibility of her joining me, she was very eager to go and join in a real village experience. However, at the wedding Kiko spent an hour or so taking photographs of the dancing, and then told me that she wanted to leave. It seemed that the experience had not met with Kiko's anticipation of the event. She hadn't actually enjoyed her 'authentic experience'. Instead she had used the event in order to 'stoke up on cultural capital' (Munt 1994a: 109) by taking photographs and simply being there, in order that she could say she had been there once she returned to the tourist sphere of Göreme, where she felt more comfortable.

This incident takes us closer to the idea put forward by Lash and Urry (1994) that postmodern tourism is about consuming signs and images rather than the real. In this view, Kiko's experiences, and especially her photographs, were collected as signs for use in later exchange. She was seeking some sort of real experience for its sign value, but she seemed to be avoiding interaction with the women in the village by hiding behind her camera.

However, whilst these tourists *are* clearly engaging in some sort of competition in cultural capital, and so authentic experiences are collected for their sign value, many tourists do seem to find some intrinsic value in their interactions with the local people of the village. Whilst wandering around the village, tourists might be invited to sit for a while with some local people, or to help them in their activities, such as picking fruit off the trees. Although language is viewed as an annoying barrier in such interactions, the tourists still manage to enjoy simply *being* with the local people and 'exchanging cultures' through more practical and sensual modes of communication. As Kohn states, even though our experiences of other cultures are always mediated through our*selves*, and are thus 'second-hand experiences', there is the ability to meet with other cultures through media 'beyond the scenario set with words' (1994: 25). The meeting of cultures in Göreme takes place through many such interactions, beyond the boundaries set by words as well as beyond the framework of the tourist gaze.

In such interactions, however, it is still true that the culture of the Other is *imagined* more than it is actually shared. The tourist's imagined ideal of finding 'the pure life that we've lost' is what provokes many writers to be critical of tourist discourse that projects an ideal identity on to the Other. The people in Göreme are undoubtedly aware of – and further idealise – discrepancies in wealth between tourists and themselves. Bruner argues that with this realisation 'comes the shameful realisation for the first time that they are now classified as "native" and "backward" peoples' (1991: 245). One villager's idea about what tourists think of the Göreme people was, 'they think we're interesting because we don't have anything'. I was also told by an elderly local couple that 'tourism is good for Göreme because tourists bring civilisation'. Similarly, the self-representations of young women in the village must be affected by the perceived relative freedom of female tourists of a similar age.

It would be erroneous and arrogant, however, to assume that tourism plays more than a minor part in the identities of people who are not directly involved with tourists in Göreme. A few tourists walk past their houses every day of the summer, but there is of course more to these people's lives than just this. Moreover, there is a television in almost all the troglodyte dwellings, and images of a richer Istanbul-centred Other seen in advertisements and soap operas may have a stronger influence on their self-representations than tourism. So whilst representation in tourist discourse does play a part in identity and social change, it must not be over-estimated.

What *are* becoming influential, though, are the laws concerning the physical environment in Göreme. If a 'Save Göreme Committee' gets off the ground, creating further decrees pertaining to the conservation of troglodyte dwellings and troglodyte life, then we will see the shaping of a culture in Göreme *for* the satisfaction of tourists' desires. Although touristic encounters in the village are not usually managed by guides, they are low-key, sporadic, and set in a relation of equality and respect. However, with the possibility of increasing outside control and interest in the area, Göreme might become an official 'living museum', living the aesthetic ideals of the tourist imagination.

There is an obvious paradox in tourism concerning the perceived modernisation that tourism brings about together with the tourists' quest for tradition and authenticity. Furthermore, 'travellers' believe that it is insensitive 'tourists' who spoil Other cultures, and thus claim no responsibility themselves for any misgivings. There is no doubt that the tourists who stay in Göreme fit with Munt's idea of postmodern 'real' tourists who engage in this particular style of tourism in order to distinguish as well as spatially separate themselves from the perceived masses (1994a, b). Their taste in travel necessitates 'getting into' the culture and physical environment of their destination, rather than merely glimpsing it through a frame.

The particular expectations and ideology of these tourists clearly bear heavily on the way that they interact with the Göreme environment, and the ways in which Göreme village is constructed and maintained as a 'tourist site'. Tourism anywhere leads to an aesthetic reflexivity whereby people on both sides of the equation come to reflect on and evaluate their social conditions and their society's place within the world (Lash and Urry 1994). Indeed, in Göreme the aesthetic valuing of the troglodyte dwellings and way of life shows how tourism has the power to shape landscapes and cultures to its own needs. The tourists' need here is for Göreme to be romantic and suitably Other, whilst at the same time providing the tourism services in which to 'play' and be comfortable, and the presence of other tourists who confirm that Göreme is consecrated as a tourist site. Similarly, their bodily enjoyment of the 'real adventure playground' of the Göreme valley combines the postmodern carnivalesque experience sought in fun-fairs and theme parks (Featherstone 1991) with the experience of authenticity. Importantly, though, whether the Göreme environment is real or not, the tourists there encounter an idealised environment, experiencing what they *want* to experience.

It might be concluded at this point that if the Göreme people do not mould themselves and their environment to meet the tourists' image, then tourism will decline. Perhaps a simulated Göreme constructed somewhere in the West, complete with rock cones and troglodyte dwellings, would do better than the spoilt real one. Again, this might be the view of theorists such as Urry, who argue that, since postmodern tourism is the visual consumption of signs and images, today people are tourists most of the time whether they are mobile or not (1995). In other words, there is no need actually to go there, and the simulacrum is just as good as, or perhaps even better than, the real thing.

However, I have shown how tourists in Göreme do require to experience the 'real', even though it is an idealised real. Besides the symbolic capital to be collected through encountering the exotic and authentic Other, these tourists *are* serendipitous. They seek adventure in unexpected encounters with both the physical and social environments in Göreme. Yes, the tourists' ideal influences local self-representations and shapes Göreme to its own image; but at the same time, the people of Göreme are not passive in the tourism process. As long as they can, to some extent, shape the environment in their own way to provide adventures in a way *perceived* to be authentic by the tourists, Göreme will be maintained as a tourist site.

Notes

1. This point is made by certain other authors, for example: Adler 1989; Little 1991; Veijola and Jokinen 1994.
2. This work is based on fieldwork research carried out in 1995.
3. Drawing an analogy between tourism and ritual, *liminality* refers to the experience of being removed from everyday life so that the usual order and rules may be reversed. This idea is based on Turner's (1969) description of the ritual process, which in turn is based on Van Gennep's earlier work of 1909 (Van Gennep 1960 [1909]).
4. Similar processes are described by Bowman (1989) in his discussion of sex tourism in Jerusalem.

5. Much of this information was obtained through personal communication with C. Bezmen.

References

Adler, J. (1989). Origins of Sightseeing. In *Annals of Tourism Research* 16: 7–
29.

Baudrillard, J. (1983). *Simulations*. New York: Semiotext.

Bourdieu, P. (1984). *Distinction*. London: Routledge.

Bowman, G. (1989). FuckingTourists: Sexual Relations andTourists in Jerusalem's
Old City. In *Critical Anthropology*, 1X(2): 77–93.

Bruner, E. (1989). Of Cannibals, Tourists and Ethnographers. *Cultural Anthropology* 4: 438–45.

Bruner, E. (1991). Transformation of Self in Tourism. *Annals of Tourism Research*
18: 238–50.

Cohen, E. (1988). Authenticity and Commoditization in Tourism. *Annals of
Tourism Research* 15 (3).

Errington, F. and D. Gewertz (1989). Tourism and Anthropology in a Postmodern
World. *Oceania* 60: 37–54.

Featherstone, M. (1991). *Consumer Culture and Postmodernism*. London: Sage.

Graburn, N. (1983). The Anthropology of Tourism. *Annals of Tourism Research*
10: 9–31.

Greenwood, D. J. (1989). Culture by the Pound: An Anthropological Perspective
on Tourism as Cultural Commoditization. In V. Smith (ed.), *Hosts and Guests*.
Philadelphia: University of Pennsylvania Press.

House, S. and K. Wood (1993). *Good Tourist in Turkey*. London: Mandarin.

Kohn, T. (1994). Incomers and Fieldworkers: A Comparative Study of Social
Experience. In K. Hastrup and P. Hervik (eds), *Social Experience and Anthropological Knowledge*. London: Routledge.

Lash, S. and J. Urry (1994). *Economies of Signs and Space*. London: Sage.

Leyssen, N. and M. Idiz (1993). Göreme – Saving a Unique Historical Combination. *Turkish Daily News*, 16 May: 12–15.

Little, K. (1991). On Safari: The Visual Politics of a Tourist Representation. In D.
Howes (ed.), *The Varieties of Sensory Experience*. Toronto: University of
Toronto Press.

MacCannell, D. (1976). *The Tourist*. London: Macmillan.

MacCannell, D. (1992). *Empty Meeting Grounds – The Tourist Papers*. London:
Routledge.

Munt, I. (1994a). The 'Other' Postmodern Tourism: Culture, Travel and the New
Middle Classes. *Theory, Culture and Society* 11: 101–23.

Munt, I. (1994b). Eco-tourism or Ego-tourism? *Race and Class* 36: 49–60.

Picard, C. (1993). Cultural tourism in Bali. In M. Hitchcock *et al.* (eds), *Tourism
in South East Asia*. London: Routledge.

Picard, M. (1995). Cultural Heritage and Tourist Capital: Cultural Tourism in

Bali. In M. Lanfant, J. Allcock and E. Bruner (eds), *International Tourism – Identity and Change.* London: Sage.

Sack, R. D. (1992). *Place, Modernity and the Consumer's World: A Relational Framework for Geographic Analysis.* Baltimore: Johns Hopkins University Press.

Swain, M. (1995). Gender in Tourism. *Annals of Tourism Research* 22: 247–66.

Turner, V. (1969). *The Ritual Process.* Chicago: Aldine.

Urry, J. (1990). *The Tourist Gaze.* London: Sage.

Urry, J. (1992). The Tourist Gaze and the Environment. *Theory, Culture and Society* 9: 1–26.

Urry, J. (1995). *Consuming Places.* London: Routledge.

Van Gennep, A. (1960[1909]). *The Rites of Passage.* London: Routledge and Kegan Paul.

Veijola, S. and E. Jokinen (1994). The Body in Tourism. *Theory, Culture and Society* 11: 125–51.

Williams, W. and E. M. Papamichael (1995). Tourism and Tradition: Local Control versus Outside Interests in Greece. In M. Lanfant, J Allcock and E. Bruner (eds), *International Tourism – Identity and Change.* London: Sage.

7

'Alternative' Tourists on a Canary Island

Donald V. L. Macleod

This chapter will take a look at tourists and tourism on the Canary island of Gomera, which is just south-west of Tenerife. Gomera remained relatively untouched by tourism until the late 1970s, with most employment being in the primary industries of agriculture, plantation work, animal husbandry and fishing. The decline in demand for agricultural and fishing products has led to a greater reliance on tourism as an income-generator, a situation that has been promoted by government organisations.[1]

Vueltas, the focus of this paper, is a small fishing settlement on the outskirts of a magnificent valley (Valle Gran Rey, hereafter VGR) that has been visited by tourists for some years following the ferry link with Tenerife in 1975. The island's poor road network and rugged terrain has filtered out the less adventurous visitors. As a consequence, the valley itself, on the west side of the island and a two-hour journey by bus from the port (San Sebastian), has been popular with a particular type of backpacking tourist that may be classified as 'alternative'.[2]

My work in the valley led me to question certain models and proposals put forward by anthropologists studying the impact of tourism, and I began to see the importance of the type of tourists visiting an area in relation to the influences they have upon it.[3] This chapter will touch on some of the findings of my research, whilst concentrating on the tourists themselves and their identity as a classifiable type.

To give a comprehensive form to this chapter I have divided it into two main parts:

I. Whose identity is it anyway?; and
II. What difference does it make?

This division is analogous to the two general thematic approaches towards the anthropology of tourism as represented by Graburn and Nash in the edited collection *Hosts and Guests* (Smith 1989). These approaches are headed: (i) 'Tourism as a Sacred Journey', in which Graburn focuses on the individual's experience; and (ii) 'Tourism as a Form of Imperialism', in which Nash looks at the impact of tourism.

Whose Identity Is It Anyway?

In order to clarify the meaning and intention of this question I will metaphrase a line from a famous play that deals with the complexity of identity: 'Some are born with identity, some achieve identity and some have identity thrust upon them.'[4] In this manner I am drawing attention to the issue of the origins of identity, as well as to the agent categorising the object, leading us to focus on the creation of identity. In this chapter the identifying label of 'alternative' tourist is used as a means of classifying and examining a group of people, whilst concurrently being the object of analysis itself. In other words, how did these people come to acquire the identity of 'alternative' tourists?

Social anthropologists have examined historical evidence in the search for information about identity (Tonkin *et al.* 1989; Macdonald 1993a). For some investigators, history provides a useful treasure chest of clues and symbols, a means of confirming suspicions, firming-up ideas and supporting hypotheses. A look at the history of a people, a group, a self-consciously defined collection of individuals, can help the observer to interpret contemporary behaviour and beliefs. Old patterns are sometimes maintained, new patterns can reflect old, a certain continuity may be discernible. An examination of the recent history of Gomera will help us to understand the current pattern of tourism.

It is said by the islanders and long-term foreign settlers that the first visitors included a few deserters from the Vietnam war. These Americans were amongst a number of people, including hippies and explorative travellers, who sought the gentle climate and anonymity of these Spanish islands in the 1960s. Unlike Tenerife, which experienced a dramatic surge in tourism during the 1960s and 1970s, Gomera was relatively untouched, largely owing to its lack of an airport and its mountainous terrain. Most of the island remained without an electricity supply until the late 1960s, when a road-building and electrification programme was carried out. This lack of commercial development and modernisation was very attractive to the hardy travellers who ventured by boat to the island. Some of them became well-known faces to the local villagers, and most were labelled 'hippies', after the fashion of the day, because of their appearance and lifestyle.

With the installation of a ferry linking South Tenerife to Gomera in 1975 the visitors increased in numbers, but remained largely of two types: the adventurous backpacking 'alternatives', and the day-trippers from Tenerife. By 1990 the annual volume of arrivals had reached more than 75,000 (according to the Spanish environmental organisation ICONA). In the port of San Sebastian, the capital of Gomera, there is a state-owned hotel, and overlooking the fishing village of Santiago there is a hotel owned by the Olsen company. Apart from these two there are no other large hotels on the island, only apartment complexes, and in Valle Gran Rey most of these were built in the late 1980s. Up until then accommodation was in the form of apartments and rooms adjoining family homes, which satisfied the needs of the backpacking arrivals.

It is only recently that the variety of tourists visiting VGR has diversified. Owing to the relatively easy access by road from the main port and the frequent ferry services, the island is being visited by more charter tourists, one of the types categorised by Smith (1989b) – i.e. those that book rooms in advance through tourist agencies, seek modern amenities, and favour organised tours and hotel facilities. Graburn (1989) has described them as 'timid' because of their disinclination to meet local people and indulge in their ways. Together with these charter tourists there has also been a growth in the arrival of the Spanish-speaking 'veranistas' (summer visitors) from other Canary islands, especially Tenerife, mainland Spain, and occasionally Latin America. The common denominator tends to be that they have relatives on Gomera, and often they own property in the form of an old house or an apartment in a hotel complex.

This spectrum of tourists sorts itself out into a seasonal pattern. There is a clear cycle of tourist types holidaying in VGR over the year. The autumn run-up to Christmas tends to be almost exclusively the back-packing German 'alternative' tourists; Christmas through to New Year is a frenzied free-for-all dominated by the German 'alternatives' bolstered by British, Dutch and Spanish 'alternatives' and agency tourists. The winter months up to Spring and 'Semana Santa' (Easter week), see the backpackers predominating, until the Easter holidays produce another rush to the valley of seasoned regulars, many being single mothers with young children. After this short period of intense activity the place returns to a relaxed and peaceful pace ('*tranquilo*' as the locals say) until June, when the predominantly German charter tourists come for their summer holiday break, having been enticed by the literature advertising the recently built apartment complexes. They are followed in August by greater numbers of the Spanish 'veranistas', who arrive with cars loaded with food and relatives (cf. Kohn 1988), out to enjoy a month of vacation. There are fewer backpacking 'alternative' tourists around at this time, as they prefer to stay in mainland Europe.

The cycle of tourist activity, with its peak in winter (especially December and January) coincides with the fishing cycle, which experiences its most intensive work period during this time of year. However, as most of the fishermen are not directly involved with catering to the tourists they do not have double the burden of workload, although their wives and other family members will suffer the pressure, and many people complain of the hectic pace of life during these months. In the summer months the fishing activity is less intense, and some fishermen find temporary work in painting apartments and other forms of manual labour.

'Alternative' Tourists: A Description

As a general impression, 'alternative' tourists appear in a variety of guises, and often wear very colourful attire in contrast to the mainstream charter tourists. There seem to be no restrictive rules on dress or hairstyle. They may be seen wearing jeans, trousers of cotton and sometimes leather, shorts, skirts of all lengths, T-shirts, blouses, waistcoats, felt hats, cowboy boots, sandals (especially clogs), beads, facial make-up, tattoos, rings and bracelets: all these are acceptable and are commonly worn. The overall appearance is one of casualness: sometimes a statement of individuality, often a statement of freedom – a sort of structured anti-conventionality. This physical liberation is celebrated on the beach, where nudism is the norm: the 'alternative' tourists usually sunbathe with no bodily covering besides beads, rings, and oil.

Most of the visitors to the island were German – probably over three-quarters of the total during the winter period – and theirs was the dominant nationality in the group of 'alternative' tourists, which also included some British, Irish, Dutch, Austrian, American, and Spanish tourists. The 'alternative' tourists that I met followed a variety of careers at home: there were social workers, teachers, nurses, psychologists, journalists, therapists, ecologists, artists, architects, media professionals, and many students. Most were educated to a high level, and aged between 20 and 45; they might be classified as those working within the liberal professions, members of the 'chattering classes'. The Germans themselves often joked that only teachers, social workers and psychologists visited Gomera. Many were interested in the environment, and avidly walked around the island, which is blessed with an ancient forest in its centre and ample hiking routes. There was an awareness of a collective similarity, a recognition of the type of tourist visiting VGR and of the sort of experiences available. In fact, some have told me of Gomera's reputation as a meeting place for single people, and it was facetiously referred to as 'Love Island' or 'Sodom and Gomera'.

In Vueltas, the majority of 'alternative' tourists backpacked and stayed in apartments or rooms adjoining the homes of local residents, often fishermen. They would cook in these self-catering premises, occasionally going out for meals to local restaurants or the apartments of friends, and usually visiting the bars late at night. Some tried to camp out at night, which was officially prohibited; a few lived in caves by the seashore, and others lived in small shacks in the upper valley, often abandoned sheds or huts. These tourists valued their contact with local people, and many spoke a few words of Spanish, proudly testing their vocabulary on their hosts, and ostentatiously sporting Spanish dictionaries in public places. They wanted to meet the local people, to experience a different culture, to learn new ways and make new friends. There was an element of education for its own sake in this activity reminiscent of the 'Grand Tour' of earlier centuries (see Turner and Ash 1975), a search for the 'other', and a hunt for the 'authentic' (see MacCannell 1976).

This notion of authenticity can be seen as a feature of the literature that self-consciously sells a type of reality to tourists. The identity of holiday destinations as promoted by those interested in attracting tourists is constructed to reflect the interests and desires of the potential customer. Accordingly, we see in a brochure produced for the island tourist board by a resident German photographer and a German artist the presentation of the island as a rural idyll, with photographs of rustic peasants smiling and holding animals, or in a festive mood playing traditional instruments. A map of the island itself is personalised by hand drawings of traditional houses accompanied by childlike annotations. The whole effect is one of innocence and natural beauty, an image that is intended to appeal to the desires of the 'alternative' tourists who seek an escape from the formal, urbanised world of their home environment.

Activities

A typical day for many tourists that I knew consisted of a large and leisurely breakfast: coffee, cereal, bread, eggs and fruit, eaten on the terrace, followed by a midday stroll to the beach. Once on the beach the tourists made their own entertainment and were happy to do so. Most read books, listened to music or juggled on the beach and occasionally went for a swim, or, more daringly, body-surfed. Home-made snacks (banana and chocolate pancakes, vegetable omelettes, etc.) were purchased from beach vendors who were themselves tourists or short-term settlers. Some of the hippies and travellers, known as 'freaks' by the German tourists, played music on home-made drums together with accompanying guitars. The afternoon on the beach was followed by a rest at the apartment, preparation for the evening activities, a cooked meal and a visit to the bars.

The beach-based activities might be broken by a walk on the hills or through the forest, or a car journey around the island. There were not many organised activities in the valley: no boats for hire, or entertainment arcades. However, two German entrepreneurs independently of each other started a fishing-trip service and a mountain-bike excursion programme in 1991 (by the summer of 1995 a tour boat, owned by a Canary Island company, was selling a 'Dolphin Safari', employing three ex-fishermen from Vueltas). There was also a 'Sannyasin' centre (for followers of Bhagwan Shri Rajneesh) situated in an adjoining valley, which attracted a small number of serious followers, mostly German, and other interested travellers. This centre offered various services, including vegetarian meals, accommodation and meditation classes.

Certain bars were more popular than others. One, known as 'El Mago', the nickname of the proprietor, had a phenomenal sea view, and with its late bar and charismatic barman, was a clear favourite.[5] The German tourists would sit drinking, talking and surveying the clientele until intoxicated with alcohol, marijuana and the music; some would dance around the tables with the bar staff encouraging them. Groups would slowly mix together: old friends would meet up and new friends discover mutual interests and connections, whilst local boys would drink, sell drugs, pick up tourists or talk amongst themselves. Anglo-American rock music, reggae, and the Gypsy Kings were the staple musical diet, and the crashing waves added a background chorus to the changing melodies.

Other popular bars included one run by a German settler. This had a slightly heavier atmosphere of subversiveness, created by the open consumption of drugs and a more obscure brand of music.[6] Another bar, run by a group of women from Northern Spain, was popular with the tourists and especially the foreign settlers,[7] many of whom gained work through connections made at the bar. All these bars were regular meeting points for tourists, the majority of whom visited at least one daily.[8]

Over the Christmas period there was a preponderance of single mothers and their children staying in the valley. They were noticeable because they would settle on the small beach at the fishing port, which was sheltered by the sea wall from big waves. Some told me of the attractions of Vueltas: it was a safe resort where there was little hassle from men, and because of its clientele, a place for single people to mix and meet one another, a place where they could entertain at home and also leave the children with friends. This highlights the casual sociability of the tourists and foreign settlers, where the catering infrastructure accommodated the needs and desires of tourists who wished to cook, meet other tourists, meet local people and experience freedom of movement.

'Alternative' Tourists?

One thing that became apparent in my study of 'alternative' tourists was the blurring of boundaries between the tourists and the foreign residents or travellers on a long stay. Many tourists stayed for more than two weeks, and they would mix with friends who were resident and occasionally with local islanders. They shared interests and socialised widely, their social networks expanded, and many returned again within the year. One English girl visited the valley three times in six months: firstly with three friends, secondly with her brother, and finally alone. She sometimes stayed at the home of an English settler, where she could relax, pursue her interest in painting, and mix with other foreign settlers and villagers.

There are no universal markers for these tourists, no shared symbols of identity, no single common language or physical boundary; however, they do appear to share a desire for freedom of thought and movement, a need to escape constraints. This was especially apparent with the German tourists, who often told me of their desire to escape the restrictive lifestyle of Germany. They resented the regimentation of life there and the coldness of social relations, many feeling unable to express their true selves at home. They were often individualists who didn't want to be told what to do in their own time. They liked to feel that they could move around the island at will, and casually changed their rooms, moving to another part of the valley or island. Most were shocked and saddened by the continual building going on in the valley, with new roads and apartments replacing the bamboo-covered valley and the banana plantations. Some spoke of departing for the unspoilt island of Hierro nearby; others would go much further in search of paradise.

Perhaps their code of identification was in their casual dress, their openness, their easy mobility, their serious conversation and uncontrolled socialising; there was certainly a sense of anti-structure and experiment among them (cf. Lett 1983). In this manner their identity begins to form, and it becomes an opposition to the more uniform and controlled nature of the agency tourists, those that arrive with neat suitcases, in a group or with a tour guide, stay in a hotel or apartment complex for the whole period, eat in the hotel restaurant or one selected for them, and tour the island on organised outings. I met one woman, a student lawyer, who was on a package holiday with her friend, a practising lawyer, and she told me that they had never been to a village bar and had preferred to eat at the recommended restaurant. Her friend liked to stay inside and read, and neither of them had met any of the local people – well, only those serving them in the apartment complex.

A number of the German tourists actually described themselves and other tourists as 'alternative'. This adjective had gained popularity during the late 1960s as a description of a lifestyle outside the mainstream, synonymous with hippies and drop-outs; and more recently it has signified the anti-establishment stance within such diverse groups as academics and comedians. There is a general consensus that it represents a reaction against the norm, an opposition to conformity. This could be seen in the personal attitudes of many of the tourists, who wanted to be different and escape from institutionalised behaviour.

In many cases that I encountered the German 'alternative' tourists were seeking self-knowledge: some had been in, or were considering having, psychotherapy, most were deeply frustrated with their lives at home. The vacation had been an opportunity for self-discovery and learning; not so much a 'sacred journey' as a journey of enlightenment. This would seem to situate them within the class of those tourists seeking 'experiential and experimental' holiday experiences according to Erik Cohen's typology (E. Cohen 1984), although I would suggest that people often have a multitude of motivations and cannot be readily pigeon-holed. Experiment, experience, excitement, change: all of these become part of many holiday experiences, and a single primary motivating factor is not always present.

Some of the tourists that I have considered to be 'alternative' may not consider themselves as such, whilst others may have thought themselves to be 'alternative', but do not fit my description. This is a problem area, and highlights the difficulties faced when notions of identity are discussed.[9] I have in effect 'thrust' an identity upon some people, and they may not be remotely aware of it. This process of classifying others is universal, and the people of VGR themselves have a number of categories for tourists, depending on such qualities as nationality, gender, dress and age.

Local people often referred to some tourists as 'hippies' according to their hairstyle and clothing (Crick 1994 reports the same labelling in Sri Lanka). They nicknamed the Germans *cabeza cuadrados* ('squareheads'), a reference to their inflexibility and strong-minded attitudes. English youths were called *hooligans* (borrowed from the English language) after the infamous exploits at football matches and their occasional rowdy behaviour on holiday in Spain. One fisherman told me of the mess that his apartment was left in after a group of English tourists had used it; and plenty of people had anecdotes about English tourists in Tenerife. Many German women were regarded as *putas* (whores) because of their skimpy clothing and supposed sexual promiscuity. Whereas a general classification amasses all tourists under the derogatory term of *giris* (after *gira*, meaning 'outing' or 'tour'); and some of the younger men had organised violent confrontations with male tourists of any description. All this is stereo-typification, and it has a direct effect on the way that individuals and especially groups interact. It has clear parallels with ethnic categoris-ations, where large groups have their own inner differentiations that become overridden by broader common denominators dividing 'Us' from 'Them'.

Identity: Private and Public

It would seem that the creation of identity is linked to the basic human desire to organise, classify, comprehend and control. By drawing lines determining who we are, or which group someone else belongs to, we can classify ourselves and others. Delineation and description lead to a sort of understanding and a sort of control. Boundaries become sketched lines around a relatively amorphous area; movements and behaviour may be predicted, and we can decide whether we feel comfortable with and consequently belong to a group. There is an interesting paradox concerning the 'alternative' tourists who seek freedom and rebel against conformist behaviour, but who inevitably conform to certain broad patterns such as fashion in clothing and leisure pursuits. They consciously create boundaries of behaviour within which their individuality finds expression. Their anti-structural behaviour has a shape, even if it simply represents a rejection of traits belonging to the 'mass-tourists'.

I would make an analogy between the constant changeability and plasticity of identity with the workings of the human brain as described by Edelman (1992). It has been said that mental processes, particularly memory, are constantly being revised and updated, with pathways being created, strengthened and broken. The whole process is one of rearrange-ment and change: the memory is not static, like a computer disk reference file. In this manner individuals are constantly revising their own past physiologically as well as conceptually.

I liken this process to the creation and maintenance of identity, where there are few permanent facets and nothing is absolutely static, yet there are recognisable traits. The 'alternative' tourists may once have been or may well become conformists; they may differ widely amongst themselves and interpret events variously. And what was once alternative may become the norm as time passes. I would venture to say that the cultural context of ethnicity is subject to similar processes: definitions change, individuals vary with their peers, and they revise their personal opinions privately. The boundaries are not permanent and the contents are in a state of flux (cf. Macdonald 1993a; O'Brien 1993).

One of the interesting aspects of this study is the conscious decision of certain individuals to be regarded as 'alternative' tourists. This demonstrates a merging of the personal identity with the social identity. A person's intimate sense of self, of private identity or reality, can become reflected by or absorbed into a group which shares similar interests. This phenomenon indicates how personal and social identities can become combined in a tangible manner, where a person's privately felt emotions and opinions can be articulated by a group. Is this then a more truthful form of identity than those known as 'ethnic' or 'national' that have been created by others for a group of people?

At the beginning of this paper, using a metaphrase I suggested that identity may be acquired through birthright, achieved through personal determination, or thrust upon an individual, all of which processes we may apply to certain 'alternative' tourists. Similarly, we see in Europe today the ethnic and geopolitical identities of peoples acquired by birth, achieved through political struggle, or thrust upon them, for instance by the bureaucrats of the European Union as they create a pan-national European identity (see Shore 1993). The main analytical focus used in this part of the chapter, enquiring as to the source of the identity tag, attempts to offer an approach towards the question of the construction of identity and helps us to discuss this subtle issue. By asking 'Whose identity is it anyway?', I have addressed the problem of classifying groups of people and highlighted the process of creating identity, drawing attention to myself the anthropologist as active agent in the identification process. I have also addressed the issue of the relationship between private and public identity. The chapter will now examine some of the specific influences that an identifiable category of tourist can have on the host community.

What Difference Does Identity Make?

What difference does it make whether the visitors are 'alternative' tourists or mainstream charter tourists? Well, different types of tourists have a different socio-economic, cultural and environmental impact on the local people and their environs. Nash (1989) has concentrated on the impact of tourism, and in his work he describes tourism in powerful terms as a kind of imperialism (which he considers to include the invitation of others and their influences by the host community). Furthermore, it has been pointed out by De Kadt (1979) that tourism is unique in that the consumers travel to the destination of production to satisfy their needs: tourism is an export consumed on the producer's home ground. Therefore it is of great importance for the host community to know their customers, to be able to identify the type of tourists visiting, as behaviour, tastes and desires vary greatly.

It has been recognised by many writers that different types of tourists have different degrees of impact on the host community. Smith (1989b) has developed a model that suggests that the 'explorative tourists' at one end have the least impact, whereas the 'charter' tourists at the other end have the most impact on the community, and in between in ascending order are the tourists classified as élite, off-beat, unusual, incipient mass, and mass. Graburn (1989) has also written that the charter tourists have the greatest economic and cultural impact because of their numbers and spending power. Whilst undeniably useful in helping us to comprehend and analyse the influence of tourism, I disagree with both of these views, and argue that they have focused on the macro-economic impact whilst not analysing face-to-face local exchange adequately. And more importantly, they have ignored many aspects of socio-cultural impact such as the direct interaction of tourists with local people, friendships, serious relationships, and the exchange of ideas, knowledge and interests. All these forms of contact can be found in greater proportion between the hosts and the 'alternative' tourists than between the hosts and the charter tourists (those tourists that Graburn (1989: 35) described as 'timid', who travel within their own protective cultural 'bubble').[10]

Economic Consequences

One of the salient economic consequences of different types of tourism occurs with the differing accommodation preferences of the groups. In VGR the 'alternative' tourists stayed in rented rooms or apartments that belonged to local inhabitants: these apartments may be adjoining or on top of the original home – often the case in Vueltas – or constructed on nearby plots of land. They would therefore be very close to the family home itself, or if blocks of apartments they would be part-occupied by family members. One fisherman in Vueltas owned two separate blocks in which two of his daughters and their families were housed. Some consequences of this favoured type of accommodation are that the rent goes directly to the local people, and, importantly, visitors have a direct contact with the local people: a relationship that is one of equals, or one in which respect is given on both sides.

This contrasts markedly with the situation of the charter tourists, who rent apartments in large complexes owned by businessmen. In these instances the money from rent does not always go into local hands, but often into foreign bank accounts. Contact with local people is limited to the receptionists and manual workers, such as waiters, cleaners or maintenance men. Social interaction, friendship and the exchange of ideas between tourists and locals are relatively rare in this environment. For example, one 'alternative' tourist, a German teacher, told me how she had booked a room in an agency hotel after a hard journey in Tenerife, but had disliked it because the German tourists there were, in her words: 'So *petit bourgeois*: they don't mix with the Spanish and complain that their children make too much noise at the pool.' She moved into a room in Vueltas where she felt more comfortable, and enjoyed the communication that she had with her landlord's family.

As well as favouring accommodation belonging to local people, 'alternative' tourists have a greater tendency to shop locally, and would be encouraged to purchase goods sold by their landlords or friends of landlords. They also ate in local restaurants and drank in local bars; whereas the charter tourists would not cook for themselves so often, and generally favoured the restaurants within the vicinity of the apartment complex. Consequently the charter tourists buy fewer goods from local shops and do not patronise the smaller restaurants so much. Again, proportionately less money is ploughed back into the local economy and less contact made with local people.[11]

Socio-cultural Consequences

Many serious relationships develop through tourists meeting local people. In Vueltas (population about 350) there were more than nine such couples living together or married in 1991: a result of foreign women on holiday meeting local men. They often met initially through the rental of apartments. It was rare for a local girl to date a foreign man, as they were kept under close watch by family and friends, and such relationships were actively discouraged.[12] I have been told by many residents that local men are expected to chase women and to be promiscuous, whereas local women are encouraged to be virginal and shy. Such gender roles have been commented upon by anthropologists of the Mediterranean area,[13] and this ideology of clearly delineated behaviour prevailed on the island, having a strong influence on the way people perceived the foreign visitors. Female tourists who did enter into serious relationships with local men often found that they eventually became subjected to severe restrictions on their movements that were irksome and unacceptable.[14] Many settlers realised that their original perceptions of the village as an easy-going and open community were wildly inaccurate.

The tourist accommodation infrastructure therefore allows for easy socialising between the tourists, as I have pointed out, with cooking facilities, mobility between rented apartments, constant access to local people and a generally relaxed relationship between the hosts and their guests. Ideas and fashions are exchanged and, in Vueltas alone, two restaurants, one bar, a meditation centre, a small boutique and a postcard shop have been established by foreigners. One German, a man in his fifties, has started up a fishing-trip business for tourists, using a standard local 11 m. boat, as well as opening a small fishing-tackle shop. This is new to the valley, and is an example of how different ideas and attitudes have begun to arrive and change the face of the port area. Another German, originally a tourist, has started a mountain-bike touring business, and opened up a small sports equipment shop by the beach. Neither of these men expressed a desire to make money for its own sake; rather, they enjoy the lifestyle in the valley, appreciate the beauty of the place, and can manage a way of surviving whilst enjoying their lives. They reflect a more entrepreneurial feature of the individualistic, environmentally aware visitor.

An appreciation of the natural environment and an awareness of ecological issues was certainly a common denominator amongst many of the 'alternative' tourists that I met. They were attracted to the island because of its apparent unspoilt qualities – a facet exploited by tourist brochures and articles about the island. It possesses an ancient temperate rainforest and has beautiful valleys with stone terraces and abundant flora. The volcanic sand beaches have not been meddled with as they have on other islands, and there is relatively little construction along the seafronts. All this is admired by the tourists: for example, there was a notice posted in a restaurant run by an ex-fisherman and his French wife that proclaimed in German that it was a tourist petition against construction in the valley.

This notice encouraged people to sign up in protest against the roads and building projects that are ruining the valley's appearance and eco-system. Such concern for things natural has been noted by villagers, and reflects the feelings of many local inhabitants.

There was one particular incident that epitomises such feelings. It involved a protest by local people against the proposed 'development of the beach area' instigated by the local council. The plan proposed that the natural bay should be altered and fitted with groynes such that sand would not be washed away in winter, thereby giving an all-year-round beach; and that a promenade should be built, as well as vending kiosks at strategic points. The whole character of the bay would change and offer attractions to a different type of tourist. The local council won support for this idea from the government, and various bodies would have received millions of pounds for the construction from the available development funds that the island is receiving from the EU and the Spanish government. However, many local residents were most upset by the proposal, which they felt would add to the gradual ruination of the valley and beach by removing its natural beauty. Fishermen drew attention to the potential ecological changes wrought by the proposal, including the endangering of inshore marine habitats, and the potential cessation of the natural cleansing effect of longshore drift and tidal changes.

In a number of articles in the press, one man (who later ran for the post of mayor with the Socialist Party) voiced the opinion of many when he indicated the importance of retaining the natural beauty and unspoilt character of the area, which serves as an attraction for a certain type of tourist: 'Unless it is intended to scare off the so-called "alternative" or "green" tourists, the only truly profitable type for the valley and its inhabitants, nothing that is done at the municipal level makes sense' (J. Casanova, November 1990 in the periodical *El Dia*).

This man later ran as the Socialist Party (PSOE) candidate for mayor in the local elections in VGR, and made mention of the tourism in the valley, its character, and the need to approach development seriously, bearing in mind the valley's ecosystem and the type of tourism desired. Tourism is a very big issue now on the island, and within the Canary Islands archipelago it represents the major form of income. The sum of £60 million has been earmarked in a programme (POI 1990) for the structural development of Gomera, most of which is going to the construction of an airport and the improvement and building of roads. This sort of activity makes tourism an extremely important and contentious industry on the island, and indeed around the world. Many local people feel that more important things, such as the disposal of waste and the support of local primary industries including fishing and farming, have been overlooked in the rush to attract foreign visitors.

Conclusion

The tourists examined in this paper whom I have categorised as 'alternative' would probably recognise themselves; they may even regard themselves as such, and were occasionally classed as 'alternative' by other academics, local residents and one another. Yet they remain an extremely varied collection of individuals – a fact which is certainly not peculiar to this particular categorised group; in fact it is probably true of the majority of members of specifically identified groups of people. The simple classification and consequent lumping together of people masks a tremendous variety of constituent components.

Personal identity is usually a much more refined and subtle creature than group identity, and each individual is a collection of numerous 'identities': i.e. one person may be perceived (by herself and others) as a German, an 'alternative' tourist, a mother, a Berliner, or an artist, simultaneously or separately depending on the situation. In thrusting identity upon others the describing agent chooses to highlight one feature of his subject, such as 'alternative' or *cabeza cuadrado*, and risks muting a host of other characteristics, creating a monochrome reproduction of a colourful original. Conversely, the individual subject may overemphasise an identifiable facet of herself, losing a sense of proportion and balance. Thus complexity often becomes simplified for ease of understanding and communication. Such is the nature of this almost ephemeral and often metamorphic quality termed 'identity'. But this occasionally intangible quality can have very tangible consequences and act as a 'motive force in history', as Macdonald (1993b: 7) states.

I have ended on a note in which the construction of identity becomes literal in a concrete sense. Some islanders are struggling to retain a certain quality of life and identity based on their rural skills, their culture, including the image of the *mago* and the *silbo*,[5] and the livelihoods of farming and fishing. Others are defending the island's natural beauty, which they love and which attracts the 'alternative' tourists. Whereas, in opposition, there are different parties seeking to transform the island's identity into that of a modernised 'developed' resort, catering to a different type of tourist. The initial stages of this metamorphosis are manifest in material changes: more tarmac, concrete, metal and plastic appears as the roads, hotels and airport are being built.

In this chapter we can see how individuals relate to their social and natural environments, mediating through practice and driven by concept-ualisations related to personal and social identity. So the apparent subject–object dichotomy is in actuality a continuum, the private and public identities of people being inextricably linked to their social and natural environment; in the words of Descola: 'Every action, every labour process begins with a representation of the condition and procedures necessary for its execution' (Descola 1994: 3). Identity informs, interprets, and shapes our image of the present, past and future, and this highly developed self-consciousness is a fundamental aspect of our common humanity.

The construction of identity is a process shared by tourists, local inhabitants, politicians and anthropologists alike; in this case using the island of Gomera itself both as a symbol and a material object. Bureaucrats in the EU, fishermen in Vueltas, and tourists from Germany are all involved to varying degrees in a game focusing on identity, perception and representations. This game of high stakes is being played by increasing numbers of people involved with tourism around the globe, and this chapter draws attention to the importance of 'identity' in the creation of our personal, social and physical worlds.

Notes

1. The Canary Islands are politically part of Spain, but geographically part of Africa, being islands of volcanic origin situated around one hundred miles off the coast of North-West Africa. In 1990 the GDP for the Canary Islands was composed of the following: agriculture 4.1%, industry 11.3%, construction 11.6%, services 73%. Source: *OECD Economic Survey 1992–3*.

2. I have decided to use the term 'alternative', as this was used by the tourists themselves and by some local observers. The chapter goes on to explain in detail my own reasons for grouping the tourists under this term. It may briefly be explained as an oppositional category in relation to what are referred to as charter tourists (mass tourists who take package holidays booked through agencies), the 'alternative' tourists being backpacking individualists. It should not be confused with the phrase 'alternative tourism', which refers to specifically planned recreational activities (see Hitchcock *et al.* 1993: 25–7).

3. This paper is based primarily on fieldwork undertaken in 1990–1 for my D.Phil. thesis (Macleod 1993), together with more recent visits to the field in 1994 and 1995. There have of course been changes since 1991, and these are noted where relevant.

4. 'Some are born great, some achieve greatness, and some have greatness thrust upon them': Malvolio, in 'Twelfth Night, or What You Will' II:5:135 by William Shakespeare.
5. *Mago* is a nickname given to rural islanders by other islanders that is full of cultural associations. These include a pastoralist and agricultural subsistence lifestyle, the *silbo* whistling language, the *Tajaraste* (Gomeran music, dancing and singing), hand-turned clay pottery, and many other rural crafts (see Macleod 1993).
6. In 1995 this bar displayed a homemade sign forbidding the smoking of marijuana on the premises.
7. In 1986 the resident population of the municipality of Valle Gran Rey was 2,988, of whom 202 were foreign nationals (*source*: statistics office, Santa Cruz, Tenerife). In 1991 I estimated the resident population of Vueltas to be approximately 350, with around 10% being foreign nationals.
8. There were 13 bars in Vueltas (including restaurants) in 1991. By 1994 there were 3 new ones, whilst 'El Mago' had been demolished to make way for a road.
9. A. Cohen (1994: 178) draws attention to the issue of personal identity and the labels imposed upon people: '. . . we have neglected the often fraught and agonising clash between a person's sense of self and the identity imposed on her or him, a conflict which is essentially about who has the right to define an individual's identity'.
10. This argument is developed fully in my D.Phil. thesis (Macleod 1993).
11. Crick (1994) goes into detail on the different economic consequences of alternative tourism as opposed to a capital-intensive industry as experienced in Sri Lanka, illustrating the importance of backpackers to the private landlords, small businesses and informal economy.
12. Local girls told me that if local boys see them with *extranjeros* (foreigners) they criticise them and call them *loca* (mad).
13. In particular relating to the 'honour and shame' debate. See, for example, Peristiany (1965) and Gilmore (1987).
14. An interesting and comparable study has been made by Zinovieff (1990) in Greece, where she looks at foreign women (usually ex-tourists) marrying Greek men. She notes how these women often become withdrawn and isolated, partly as a result of different expectations of behaviour and their lack of a kinship support network.

References

Cohen, A. (1994). *Self-consciousness: An Alternative Anthropology of Identity*. London: Routledge.

Cohen, E. (1984). *A Phenomenology of Tourist Experience*. Les Cahiers de Recherche de Tourisme No. 52. Aix-en-Provence: Les Cahiers.

Crick, M. (1994). *Resplendent Sites, Discordant Voices: Sri Lankans and International Tourism*. Chur, Switzerland: Harwood Academic Publishers.

De Kadt, E. (1979). *Tourism: Passport to Development? Perspectives on the Social Effects of Tourism in Developing Countries*. Oxford: Oxford University Press.

Descola, P. (1994). *In the Society of Nature*. Cambridge: Cambridge University Press.

Edelman, G. (1992). *Bright Air, Brilliant Fire. On the Matter of the Mind*. London: Penguin.

Gilmore, D. (ed.) (1987). *Honour and Shame and the Unity of the Mediterranean*. Washington, DC: American Academic Association.

Graburn, N. (1989). *Tourism: The Sacred Journey*. In Smith 1989: 21–36.

Hitchcock, M., M. Parnwell and V. T. King. (eds) (1993). *Tourism in South-East Asia*. London: Routledge.

Kohn, T. (1988). Seasonality and Identity in a Changing Hebridean Community. Unpublished D.Phil. thesis, University of Oxford.

Lett, J. (1983). Ludic and Liminoid Aspects of Charter Yacht Tourism in the Caribbean. *Annals of Tourism Research* 10(1) pp. 35–57.

MacCannell, D. (1976). *The Tourist: A New Theory of the Leisure Class*. London: Macmillan Press.

Macdonald, S. (ed.) (1993a). *Inside European Identities*. Oxford: Berg Publishers.

Macdonald, S. (1993b). Identity Complexes in Western Europe: Social Anthropological Perspectives. In S. Macdonald (ed.) 1993a.

Macleod, D. (1993). Change in a Canary Island Fishing Settlement, with Reference to the Influence of Tourism. Unpublished D.Phil. thesis, University of Oxford.

Nash, D. (1989). Tourism: The Sacred Journey. In Smith 1989.

O'Brien, O. (1993). *Good to be French? Conflict of Identity in North Catalonia*. In Macdonald 1993a.

Peristiany, J. G. (1965). *Honour and Shame: The Values of Mediterranean Society*. London: Weidenfeld and Nicolson.

POI (*Programma Operativa Integrado de la isla de La Gomera (Canarias)*) (1990). Madrid. April 1990. Government document.

Shakespeare, W. (1994). *Twelfth Night, or What You Will*. Oxford: Clarendon Press.

Shore, C. (1993). 'Inventing the "People's Europe": Critical Approaches to European Community Cultural Policy. *MAN* 28(4): 779–800.

Smith, V. (ed.) (1989a). *Hosts and Guests: The Anthropology of Tourism*, 2nd edn. Philadelphia: University of Pennsylvania Press.

Smith, V. (1989b). 'Introduction'. In Smith 1989: 1–20.

Tonkin, E., M. McDonald and M. Chapman (eds) (1989). *History and Ethnicity.* London: Routledge.

Turner, L. and J. Ash. (1975). *The Golden Hordes: International Tourism and the Pleasure Periphery.* London: Constable.

Zinovieff, S. (1990). *Dealing in Identities: Insiders and Outsiders in a Greek Town.* Unpublished Ph.D. thesis, Cambridge University.

8

Mas' Identity: Tourism and Global and Local Aspects of Trinidad Carnival

Niels Sampath

Trinidad and Tobago without carnival would be like Washington without intrigue or Salzburg without music. With its two offshoots, calypso and steel orchestras, it is an ear-splitting, insomniac orgy of movement and colour, a communal catharsis. It is what Trinidad and Tobago best likes to be known for, and what best defines the country's free spirit: to say it is the greatest show on earth will endear you for ever. And although it is far from being the only big or famous carnival in the world, it is perhaps the most down-to-earth, the most participatory carnival, the one that has stayed closest to the people and furthest from commercialism and empty show.

From a tourist guide book to Trinidad (Taylor 1991: 39)

Introduction

This chapter is not so much about tourists as it is about a tourist *attraction*. For it can often be the tourist attraction that is the most salient point about a given locale, to *both* host and guest. The tourism phenomenon nurtures itself on distinct sensory images that have become attached to distinct geographic areas. The more surreal these destination images are in comparison with those produced by the reality that is regularly experienced at home, the more powerful is the effect in contrasting the tourists' own identity with foreign identity. In order to accomplish this contrast *and* gain satisfaction, the tourist must experience these foreign images in such a way that they are placed within a localised paradigm that is contextually separate from 'home'. But does this necessarily differ from the satisfaction gained by the local population?

149

Carnival in Trinidad has become a complex multi-faceted event attracting a fair degree of academic attention.[1] While this chapter cannot do more than offer brief descriptions and introduce a few interpretations, the highly related subject of tourism, both present and potential, has not really been addressed in previous writing. Rather than concentrating on the symbolic local nuances of Trinidad Carnival, this chapter will elaborate those aspects of carnival culture that reflect perceived identities of locals, viz the phenomenon of tourism.

To begin with, a brief overview of carnival, local history, and social relations is presented, emphasising Trinidadians' need to construct/re-construct a new identity. Secondly, carnival itself is described both in historical terms and via contemporary background information. Then, several aspects of carnival are examined in relation to tourism and foreign influence: present-day scandal in Trinidad's carnival; the exporting of carnival and its music; as well as gender, carnival, and the contrasting influence of the 'sister island' of Tobago. Finally, some conclusions are presented.

Playing Mas': The Tourists' Carnival?

Trinidad's carnival events, which take place off the usual beaten track of stereotypical Caribbean resorts (cf. Pattullo 1996), seem tailor-made to produce unusual sensory images. The setting is urban yet tropical. The calypso and *soca* music associated with carnival are rhythmic, yet more energetic and less familiar than reggae, and are often produced by the comparative novelty of large 'steel pan' orchestras. Self-expression, sexual and otherwise, is encouraged and alcohol flows freely as the participants go through the 'Playing of the *mas*'. 'Playing the *mas*', a Creole colloquialism derived from the French *masque*, is the local phrase applied to both formal and informal participation in the street theatre bands that make up the carnival processions. The term *mas'/masque* connotes the identity transformations and catharsis as indicated in the quotation above.

The events carry on vigorously throughout the 48 hours before Ash Wednesday. But they are preceded by many hectic weeks of 'warm-up' fêtes, starting on Boxing Day, which serve to heighten the tension and acquaint band members with each other and their upcoming performance. Children's carnivals are held, primarily as costume competitions. The music industry in Trinidad launches various calypso tents (though usually held in union halls and similar venues), which vie with each other in providing the most original and timely lyrical compositions amongst both their professional headline acts and semi-professional newcomers. Steel bands, meanwhile, are busy rehearsing every evening in 'pan yards'. Here they attract their own neighbourhood followings that will end up supporting them in their competitions.

On the Friday prior to Ash Wednesday various competitions for steel bands and calypsonians begin. Sunday evening, known as *Dimanche Gras*, is the time for intensive private partying at homes, at private fêtes, and at *mas'* camps (the headquarters of the various Road March bands – see below), where last minute arrangements and gossip can be exchanged.

Then, at around 4 o'clock on Monday morning, carnival officially begins. It is *Joovay* (from the French *jour ouvert* or 'daybreak'), which has, in effect, become a carnival within carnival, known as *'Ole mas'*. There is no competition, and no costume is required. Some merely smear themselves with mud or grease. Many carry signs that are usually a play on words derived from television commercials or some other popular reference that pokes fun (known as *picong*) at politicians or celebrities or the general social climate. Music is less organised and less electronic. Steel bands are let loose from the competitions and follow and lead groups of impromptu processions as well as organised groups.

Joovay has become increasingly popular recently, since it requires no major financial investment or planning, and starts in the cool and dark early hours (which adds to the surreal atmosphere). Thus, even the most inhibited feel free enough to participate. People throw themselves into *joovay* with all the energy they can muster, and the processions proceed until exhaustion sets in, usually when the mid-Monday sun is at its hottest. At that point some rest is inevitable, and people tend to sleep for a few hours before going back out on the streets, sometimes until late on Monday night. This is known as *Night Mas'*.

On Tuesday morning the more intensive band competition begins. Now elaborately dressed in full costumes, the themed bands that some have paid the equivalent of hundreds of pounds to participate in take to the streets. By and large and with notable exceptions, each band tries to present a 'pleasant' theme of some sort, whether it is based on Trinidadian folklore or merely on something aesthetic like flowers or birds. In contrast to *Joovay*, there are no steel bands. They would not be loud enough! Instead, there are large flat-bed 'DJ' (disk jockey) trucks loaded up to 20 feet high with amplifiers and stacks of speakers, each of which blares out the latest calypsos as chosen by the players of the band. The most popular calypso tune played on the day becomes the *Road March* winner for that year.

Starting from their respective *mas'* camps, the players march (using a shuffling dance called *chippin*) through the streets of the city. Each band waits in turn to take the outdoor stage[2] in front of judges, local television, and a paying audience. The streets and locales surrounding the competition area are filled with spectators, who occasionally join in the processions as well, even if they do not enjoy quite the same welcome as on *Joovay*. It is on the stage that any set pieces or choreographies are performed, although these are by no means mandatory. The most common dance on stage is a pelvic gyration done with the man behind the woman, called *wining*.[3] There is much congestion at the approach to this stage, and some bands wait a long time to enter it. In fact, some band organisers deliberately delay trying to come on stage until after sunset, when they feel their impact will be at its greatest. Although there are claims that Trinidad carnival is not commercialised, the balance between the artistic, the commercial, and the popular is a fine one, and it is the carnival bands that reflect this.

Once the competition is out of the way, the sun has more or less set, the air is once more cool and some energy returns to the players. Knowing there are now only a few hours until Ash Wednesday, the *Last Lap* (a final tour or tours of the city streets) begins. Because of the large size of the bands nowadays, and the fact that they are not so active when they are at a standstill waiting patiently to take the carnival stage, *Last Lap* has become popular again, as it was traditionally. In fact, it is now common to fête[4] into Ash Wednesday. This is a practice that, somewhat ironically, evokes some consternation amongst the more traditional and moralistic citizens. It is frequently blamed on degenerate foreign influences.

Having summarily described what would be a highly escapist effect on any *guest* participants in this way, a corollary can also be produced. Shrouded within the term 'Westernisation' and, even more recently, via the complementary terms: 'globalisation' and 'localisation', a narrow analysis of the *host* population at the tourist destination suggests that it adopts the base culture (i.e. usually Euro-American) of the tourist. While this can occur under the direct influence of the foreign tourists' actual presence, their agency need not necessarily demand a large physical presence. To expand the analysis: because of tourism's growing economic influence, the original imagery that attracted the tourist is often locally nurtured and commercially embellished.

In this way, the fascination of the now rather surreal tourist-attraction images can become equally powerful to the *host* population. The difference is that, for the hosts, the images have become *parallel* globalising variables of local identity,[5] rather than the variables of *contrasting* foreign exotica that they are for the guests. While the occurring images that attracted the tourist remain *ostensibly* part and parcel of the destination's apparent identity, for the host population matters have become slightly different.

The images are now essentially detached from their previous intrinsic relation to everyday life. This effectively creates a local tourism, and what might be considered a more globalised and, in many ways, a more equitable identity. It is equally accessible to both tourist and local. In fact, it is difficult to identify many stereotypical white, untanned or sunburned tourists 'playing the *mas* ". This is because many, if not the majority, of the foreigners in Trinidad for carnival are, in fact, Trinidadians living abroad and/or they have had occupational or family connections with Trinidad. Such 'tourists' approach carnival with sentimental notions as well as with foreign tastes and habits. Although much may be made locally of how many 'tourists' are visiting Trinidad, when Trinidadians discuss making Trinidad 'more appealing to tourists' they are, in effect, merely trying to globalise Trinidadian culture and identity for themselves. As evinced by the local television coverage of [white, untanned, and sunburned] tourists every time a new cruise ship decides to dock in the capital's harbour, there is a definite prestige to hosting these sorts of guests.

Tourism in Trinidad is more of an allegorical involvement in *hosting* someone from abroad to reflect a perceived local identity rather than a direct physical or economic force exercised by *guests* (although attempts are being made at encouraging the latter). After all, as a result of a local oil boom in the 1970s, many Trinidadians became avid globe-trotting tourists themselves. They visited 'nice places' and purport to 'know what tourists want'. Despite having never known much 'real' or stereotypical tourism (cf. Macleod, this volume, Chapter 7) on their island such as might be found in Barbados, Tenerife, or Cancun, Trinidadians use carnival to claim a share for themselves in the prestige that the tourist industry appears to offer the global marketplace. In other words, by affecting carnival, tourism has its role in creating a shift in local identity in Trinidad and globalising it.

What consistently relates Trinidad carnival to local identity is that it has influenced that identity in the past. As illustrated below, there have been changes since the colonial period. At that time the social dynamics that surrounded the carnival exerted a primarily localising influence. Images were utilised that were 'locally foreign' in the context of the highly segregated social structure of the time: one segment of the population could masque itself as another. In contrast, since national independence (and ostensible egalitarianism) there has been a marked shift to place identity within a global context; but, in a seemingly paradoxical fashion, this has been as a result of a greater use of much more local imagery. Brief overviews of Trinidadian and carnival history and identity will provide a useful background.

Trinidad History, Identity, and the
Localisation of Culture

Trinidad and Tobago is a twin-island republic and former British colony off the coast of Venezuela's Orinoco basin. The indigenous Amerindian population and culture were eradicated by sequential Spanish and British colonisation. A large and influential French Creole population arriving in the 1700s also made its presence felt, with English only taking over as the dominant language at the turn of this century. Today, Trinidad has a multiethnic population and, importantly, more than a third of it is under the age of 15. According to 1990 Trinidad and Tobago census figures, the East Indian diaspora made up 40.3 per cent of the population (virtually all of whom are on the main island of Trinidad), followed by those of African descent, with 39.6 per cent. The other groups include, with 18.4 per cent, a growing 'mixed' category (largely African/European Creoles or those once known as coloureds); whites, with 0.6 per cent; and a Chinese/Syrian/Lebanese category of 0.5 per cent. An 'unstated/other' category makes up 0.6 per cent.[6] Given this kind of demography one can understand that, embedded within notions of often heavily reconstructed ethnicity, it is impossible to discuss present Trinidadian identity without some brief mention of local history (Yelvington 1993: 3).

A variety of historical influences have gone into importing, and then transmuting, the constituents of the post-colonial cosmopolitan society that exists today. The chief effects came from the cocoa and sugar industries and their demand for cheap labour. The abolition of slavery in 1834, and a relative lack of success at recruiting and retaining the freed African slaves, resulted in a search for a replacement plantation workforce. For this reason, indentured Indian migration to Trinidad began. It continued until 1917.

Any view of Indian culture 'persisting' must be seen as a relative one, given the history of the African diaspora, described below. Nevertheless, each year sees new schemes, both formal and informal, to 'revitalise' Indian culture.[7] If a 'heritage industry' ever becomes fashionable in Trinidad, it will almost certainly be from the Indian community that claims of 'authenticity' will be made. The important point to note about Indians in Trinidad is that their influence in carnival is gradually increasing, not necessarily at the 'expense' of Indian culture, but in *addition* to it.

Thus, the situation of apparently ethnically-prescribed culture is palpably changing as the first generation of post-colonial Trinidadians become the working majority. To them, Trinidadian culture is now seen in a global, rather than just a local, context. Carnival is now something of a holiday from their daily cultural practice. In the global context, image is everything. It is the visible *social* features of a particular situation that are important to Trinidadians as much as, if not more than, their ethnic *origins*. In fact, some activity that may be seen as separate from ethnicity (as carnival is to much of Indian culture) merely becomes part of a wider global arena, rather than an area of self-exclusion. Indians have adopted the now-obsolete anthropological term 'creolisation'; but, particularly amongst the young, they have ascribed some positive as well as negative aspects to it (Sampath 1993).

Thus, in the south of Trinidad where Indians predominate, the carnival in the town of San Fernando has grown tremendously through Indian participation at *precisely* the same time as the recent revitalisation of Indian culture.[8] This is reflected in the way a great many calypsos in recent years have taken up themes dealing with issues important to Indians, even if there is often a mocking tone involved. In Trinidad, such *picong* is an acknowledgement of power.

The African-derived population of Trinidad today (i.e. those considered black or mixtures once known as 'coloured') is mainly urban and suburban in its residence, and is involved largely in low- and middle-income white-collar government and business occupations. In common with other post-slavery/plantation societies in the New World, the Afro-Trinidadian population has always struggled to construct and/or re-construct an identity that could distinguish notions of 'the self' from those that were imposed upon it by the former white élite and their dominant/submissive and superior/inferior racist paradigms.

A huge variety of emancipation efforts and strategies, too many to detail here, were employed with some slight successes by the Afro-Trinidadian population, not only in the 128 years between slavery's abolition and national independence in 1962, but also prior to those years. However, particularly since the First World War there have been more effective efforts. These included labour organisations (and unrest) in an increasingly industrialised economy. At the same time, there was a widespread acceptance of education as a means to social advancement. As a result of this combination of organisation and education, a gradually increasing political representation within the Colonial Government led to social policies that, upon independence, were democratic enough to justify self-rule.

These largely socio-political tendencies have continued evolving in the post-colonial period. But, in a related sense of evolution, the modern nation-state is still seen, often with good reason,[9] as an offshoot of white colonialism. This reflects and reinforces any local notions of an as yet *incomplete* emancipation. Therefore, in more purely cultural terms and as illustrated below, the predominant and reflexive agent of any emancipation of local Afro-Trinidadian identity remains the locally-produced phenomenon of carnival. It continues to provide a relief from social tensions and dislocates these tensions away from the local, officially disciplined and self-reliant (but in fact quite chaotic and constraining) national identity.

This effect of carnival's cathartic relief, mentioned in the introductory quote to this chapter (from the tourist guidebook), works via an emancipation of identity through a form of independence that has little to do with mainstream nationalist politics. Nationalism has tended to create a revised political version of colonial authority. It segregates Trinidadians from the outside world; which, for a small and young country, is a rather isolating effect. Carnival participation, on the other hand, transiently *encompasses* 'national independence' and can, for example via tourism, fuse Trinidad with the global arena. Given this perception and that of the modern nation-state described in the preceding paragraph, it is somewhat ironic that the tourist industry, with carnival as its 'centre-piece', has recently become a *government* priority in the post-oil-boom society.

Making *Mas*': History and Organisation of Carnival

That tourist industry promotion should be led by carnival makes good political sense in Trinidad, as a brief review of its history will illustrate. Carnival has been and continues to be a celebration by both the island's élite and the masses. But importantly, this celebration by the two groups, despite an apparent unity of hedonistic purpose, is not always a perfectly harmonious one. Local moralistic forces, led previously by the Roman Catholic Church, and more recently by evangelical Christians, have always been present throughout society.

Although Trinidadians claim that 'carnival began in Trinidad' and claim authenticity for its style and form (officially, it is stated to have begun with the ending of slavery in 1834), carnival *came* to Trinidad in the 1700s with French settlers and their attendant slaves. Some, though not all, were escaping the effects of the Revolution in the French Antilles (Wood 1968: 32; Joseph 1970 [1838]: 167) and arrived just prior to the Spanish ceding Trinidad to Britain in 1797. The pre-Lenten festival quickly became established amongst both the plantation and urban élites, primarily via masked balls, dinners, and late-night carriage processions, where an ostensible spirit of anonymity could literally *masque* indiscrete behaviour.

Running concurrently with the élites' activities and as an extended adjunct to Christmas, slave festivities with a heavy emphasis of drumming and dancing began to make use of the social opportunity afforded by carnival. They homogenised local traditions from the pot-pourri of African culture that the diaspora had brought with them from both Africa and other slave colonies in the New World.

The abolition of slavery in 1838 created a new class of free, albeit colonial, people. Their technical freedom allowed much of the carnival festivities to be conducted with a much freer rein on creativity of expression. To quote Trinidad historian Bridget Brereton (1993: 50): 'after emancipation the whole cultural complex associated with the pre-Lenten carnival – stickfighting or *Kalinda*, calypso, *tamboo-bamboo* percussion music, drumming, Afro-French dances like the *Bele* and *Belair* – came to be central to Afro-Trinidadians' sense of identity.'

This infectious spirit of freedom of expression resulted in two things. Firstly, one can speculate that because of the greater free population in general, carnival became a much bigger event outside the plantation. It became urban and largely centred on the capital, Port of Spain. But this must also have created a propensity for each of the social strata of Trinidadian society (ex-slaves, free coloureds, mulattos, French creoles, and British colonials) to maintain some degree of segregation and adopt particular events as their 'own', though each would in time come to be included in the totality of carnival.

Nevertheless, it can be suggested that this segregation ensured that carnival in general could survive attacks on some of its constituent parts. In this situation it could, for argument's sake, be said that an institution had divided any opponent's attention, and conquered any problem of longevity.

The second result of the abolition of slavery was an increase in the use of carnival as a form of protest. Noisy torch-lit street marches known as *Canboulay* (derived from the French 'burning cane') with an attendant ritual stickfighting became the norm. These street events became so popular and rowdy that in 1881, following a particularly riotous event, a crisis ensued when the heavy-handed police were confined to barracks as a restraining measure by the popularist governor, Sir Sanford Freeling.

These circumstances appear to have had further long-term precedent-setting consequences. They established a perceived need on the part of officials to allow the arbiters of local morals to be more actively employed to judge what was, and what was not, 'suitable' carnival behaviour, all in the name of 'public order'. It was not long before different *masque* bands gradually began to test the boundaries of local acceptability.

For example, *Dame Lorine* was a name given to a rather complex pseudo-self-parody, played in private quarters before the actual street events, by and for the élite. They first portrayed themselves arriving in very stately fashion. They then repeated this with a parodied re-enactment of the same event supposedly done by slaves, when in fact it would be the same white/coloured players made up in Negro caricature costume with much bawdy exaggeration and racially-motivated 'comedy' (Crowley 1988 [1956]: 45–6). It is interesting to note that the *Dame Lorine* masque did not suffer as harsh a treatment as the other bands, because it was purposefully discreet, and survived in one fashion or another up to the 1950s.

It was during the 1940s and early 1950s that carnival in Trinidad began to blossom into something that really made it the premier attraction or event in Trinidad. At that time, the American military bases that were built during the Second World War were at their peak of activity. While it could be argued that prostitution and other forms of vice that the American bases indirectly fostered would result in local hostility towards such foreign influence, in fact the Americans lent a great deal of legitimacy to carnival by their participation. This interpretation was particularly true for the growing coloured middle classes of the time. They had 'seen America' and admired it in Trinidad's many cinemas in the 1930s and 1940s; and now America had come to them.

In what is now a somewhat dated (but still relevant) article, Barbara Powrie (1988 [1956]) has outlined the changes over time in the coloured middle-class attitude towards carnival. Basically, having adopted an idealised mind-set with regard to a perceived white superiority, the coloured community struggled to attain the unattainable, namely: supposed white respectability, while constantly fending off what would now be considered as 'African roots'. In this exhausting struggle, carnival has been seen by many, if not most, as a relief period. And so, the carnival paradoxes continued.

Thus, while racial-mixing aspects of carnival in the 1800s were 'good' so long as white jocularity prevailed, ethnic representation and rebellious representation by blacks was 'bad', since it threatened the otherwise homogeneous élite (Trotman 1989: 268–9). But, as respectability amongst the coloured and black middle classes has in *this* century come of age, as it were, the parameters of 'good' and 'bad' were bound to change as well. Today the racial boundaries within carnival have given way to economic ones, where race is often more a matter of family history than an economic barrier. Sufficient money can buy a ticket into any carnival band or fête.

Clearly, Trinidad carnival has been a historical compromise between two opposing tendencies in the Caribbean conundrum. It is a sensory relief for those who are most blinded by the spectrum of supposed 'civilised' white colonialism and its 'respectability'. Yet it is simultaneously the heart and soul of cultural emancipation and a reaffirmation and celebration of positive identity for those who are the most negatively affected by colonialism. This latter fact continues to be valid even as carnival tries to align itself with the commercial and global tourist marketplace.

Today, 'making *mas*' and carnival in all its forms, is big business in every sense. To begin with, organising carnival events takes a lot of energy, time, and money. A band can have 2,000 players, each with a variety of sections and costumes. Finances need to be arranged and costs set. Such disciplined activities are often taken for granted as 'theirs' by the Trinidadian élite, but in fact many bands draw their support and resources from throughout the lower classes as well. What in fact has happened in recent years is that different organisers have specialised in different markets.

Participants are organised into sections within bands. Each costumed band is a separate entity, drawing on a theme to make an artistic statement and a visual and auditory impact. It has become increasingly expensive for an individual to enter a band. Although this is said to be related to the work put into the organisation of a band, there is a constant debate within Trinidad as to whether cost actually reflects artistic merit. It seems to be the general consensus that cost reflects reliability in terms of knowing that one will get good costumes that will survive dancing rigours and can be worn all day long. Another concern is the quality of pre-carnival 'warm-up' fêtes. Needless to say, some bands, which rely and recruit foreign participants i.e. 'tourists', can charge more money with favourable exchange rates, yet would need to provide less 'pre-carnival value' for their money.

Overseeing carnival in terms of its competitions, scheduling, and the way it is run, is a government-appointed 'NCC' or National Carnival Commission. As was previously suggested in terms of the post-independence government still being perceived as an oppressor as much as a benefactor, the NCC is an annual source of irritation for many carnival enthusiasts, who, in the spirit of carnival bands of the last century, enjoy testing the boundaries of local tolerance. It is frequently suggested that 'improvements' made to carnival to attract tourists or make carnival more convenient and accessible to them are, in fact, moralistic regulatory applications masked (or *masqued*?) by economic benefits. However, the ambiguity of carnival's purpose (as reflected by the NCC's mandate to balance carnival as a local and tourist release from tension versus a source of 'ill-disciplined' culture) is part and parcel of Trinidadian society. A 'real' carnival cannot be socially neat and tidy.

The result is a nation where the cultural centre-piece is an event that both reflects and contributes to a constant construction or, in some contexts, reconstruction of self-identity in relation to both the global and the local 'other'. Most of the ensuing notions of identity will find acceptance somewhere within a broad portion of what is, superficially, quite a culturally bipolar population (i.e. African/Indian). This is borne out by government policy. Because of the culturally-bipolar concept's superficiality, the key to any specific policy's success seems to have been to accommodate the rather homogeneously-transformed cultures of each of the diasporas, in addition to the global culture being imported *en masse*. This importation is via the global media, via communication with a third diaspora, i.e. Trinidadians abroad, and from the new role as hosts to tourist guests.

Carnival: An Import—Export Business

In the past two decades an interesting phenomenon has occurred with respect to the export of Trinidadian-styled carnival to various metropoles around the world. The development of these events has occurred to the greatest extent in those areas with the heaviest concentrations of the Trinidadian *emigré* or 'third diaspora' population: London (Notting Hill carnival), Toronto (Caribana), and New York (Brooklyn carnival).[10] Crowds at these events abroad often exceed the entire population of Trinidad and Tobago (1.5 million). Thus, in a contradiction to the generalisation made by De Kadt (1979), Trinidad is one of the few developing countries to have actually transported its tourist attraction for consumption, and test-marketing, abroad. But it is more than money that returns home; and, as is described below, this makes it more marketable and acceptable as a tourist attraction.

Two major aspects of these foreign carnivals affect the one in Trinidad. First of all, whether by accident or design, none of these 'expatriate' carnivals is coincident with either Trinidad carnival or with any of the other major carnivals. Foreign carnivals began to lure the formerly semi-professional carnival organisers and performers from Trinidad into a global professional 'carnival circuit'. Secondly, and not surprisingly given their similar histories, the foreign areas of concentration of Trinidadians and their culture are also areas where other West Indians, most noticeably

Jamaicans, have also settled. In these settings, it is not surprising that what may have been considered 'Trinidadian' culture became somewhat blurred in the West Indian spectrum of music, costume, food, drink, dance, social concern, and ethnic and cultural consciousness.[11]

This rapid globalisation conduit widened the creative scope of the organisers and the performers. It was not long before the costumes, lyrics, and general themes of carnival bands reflected a greater global consciousness, dealing with current events such as South Africa and Haiti. These issues are paramount to the minority West Indian and black community identity abroad, certainly to a greater extent than in post-Independence Trinidad. Music, and lyrics in particular, are now very quick to adopt more foreign themes, especially when involving Trinidad overseas in such matters as cricket, football, or some global crises. Although this may have been true to a certain extent fairly far back in this century, there can be no comparison to today's 'CNN[12] Society' (the title of a 1994 calypso).

The electrification of carnival music means that much of Trinidad's carnival music can be used 'as is' abroad. However, it also means that it can be modified, sampled, and mixed by foreign producers for foreign markets (though the producers are often the same Trinidadian producers that recorded the music originally). It also places other West Indian styles and rhythms of music on an equal marketable footing in that regard, which is important for the West Indian diaspora in Britain and North America. Having little or no interest in Trinidad's local politics or understanding of over-complex *double-entendre* when presented in very local Trinidad patois, it is usually the 'Jump and wave!' lyrical tunes and electronic music that the tourist (or potential tourist in, for example, Notting Hill) picks up and returns to his home with, expanding that market further.

With the predominance of electronic music and 'DJ' trucks, steel bands have had quickly to carve a new niche for themselves in terms of being slightly novel 'live' acts. This is ironic considering the relative speed with which steel bands grew in the 1930s, when the use of the oil drum as a percussion instrument was perfected, replacing more primitive bamboo instruments. Although still much-loved by locals and tourists alike, steel pan, as it is called, has moved from a 'mainstream' to a 'folk' form of music. In the end, it may be the foreign or tourist market that preserves the art of steel pan production and tuning (the instruments require regular tuning *in Trinidad*), and which injects the cash for steel pan competitions in Trinidad. Local authenticity could be preserved by global taste.

If Jesus was a Tourist: Modern Carnival and a Point of Contention

During the build-up to the 1995 carnival season, a quintessential carnival incident took place: a theme was set up by one of the carnival band organisers which allowed an opposition to carnival to focus on an issue and give vent to the ambivalent attitude prevailing in Trinidad towards carnival. There is in fact an 'intensity of opposition to attempts to present Trinidadian national culture as a homogeneous entity in which there exists unanimous enthusiasm for and participation in the carnival' (Green 1995).

The carnival organiser in question was Peter Minshall, a white Trinidadian who had studied art in England and had gone on to achieve fame there at the Notting Hill festival. He had been apprenticed by established organisers in Trinidad and then set out on a remarkable career of his own to the point where, today, he artistically dominates Trinidad carnival and is much admired for it.

Other artists and organisers have concentrated on forms of expression that stress the emphasis on the individual player. Here each costume is elaborate and colourful in its own right. These are really the most popular bands, since individuals, and especially women, can 'look good'. They retain some sort of identity for themselves. However, this individual attention has, by necessity, usually been at the expense of the larger theme of the section and/or band.

Minshall, on the other hand, has attempted to create more grandiose commentary themes, where the greater emphasis has been on each section of the band. The individual players are often no more than methods of transport and animation for symbolic messages in the shape of huge masks, banners, or large animal shapes, etc. that externally mirror a thematic concept. The human form is often, sometimes purposefully, lost. Perhaps the most widely recognisable illustration for this was his commissioned design of the opening ceremonies for the 1992 Barcelona Olympics.

In 1995 Minshall's theme and title for his band was 'Hallelujah!'. The plan was to incorporate a wide variety of spiritual symbols of 'human rejoicing' in different sections. The band immediately ran into a problem with the Christian evangelical churches in Trinidad. They objected to the use of the word 'Hallelujah!' on the grounds of blasphemy. There was also objection from the Hindu religious hierarchy over the use of a symbolic representation of the god Siva. Although the Hindu problem resolved itself via a slight change of design, Minshall refused to change the title of the band, claiming artistic freedom.

The interesting thing about the entire controversy is the vigorous way Trinidadians reacted to it. The evangelical churches, long the 'poorer cousins' of the more established Christian churches and the Hindu and Muslim representatives, maximised their exposure. This was done not so much with any proclamations of self-righteousness (never politically correct in Trinidad), but by merely demanding equality with other religious organisations. There is a carnival by-law which prevents bands from deliberately mocking a religion.

A University of the West Indies poll announced that 48 per cent of the population was 'for' the Minshall band, while 45 per cent were against. One of the more telling arguments put forward by the 'pro-Minshall' spokespersons was that 'if Jesus was a tourist visiting Trinidad he would want to play *mas'* in Peter Minshall's band'. Many people thought that Minshall had known that a controversy would ensue from the title 'Hallelujah' and that he had deliberately chosen it in order to maximise both exposure and numbers of people signing on to his band. In other words, a clever commercial motivation was suspected of the man most admired for *artistic* achievement in carnival. In the end 'art prevailed', and the band went ahead.

The implications for tourism come part and parcel with the question of art versus money. Minshall had always claimed to reserve certain places in his band for less well-off (i.e. black, working-class) players, by subsidising them with more expensive places reserved for well-off patrons. But if his artistic bands have had to use controversy to attract local patrons, would the bands that cater more towards foreigners and locals with money who have little artistic interest other than to 'look good' and 'Jump and wave!' become ever more commercialised in order to compete?

The key point seems to be that bands that allow some degree of a changed *individual* identity via the *mas'*, rather than subsuming it within a theme, are able to carry on without controversy. Individuals in Trinidad carnival have always been harmless to the establishment. It is the bands with a strong group identity that can incite what is really a tradition for carnival: controversy. They can have a theme that offends. They attract the local revisionist attitudes against globalisation and the influence of the outside world. If carnival continues and successfully incorporates a greater tourist development it will probably be only via the non-controversial route. Tourists cannot blatantly come to Trinidad *en masse* and offend the establishment with their 'own' artistic licence. They are free to be individuals within Trinidadian-inspired locally-acceptable collectives. But the tourists' existence can affect the thematic determination via the economics of scale.

In other words, it is possible that if tourism becomes a major force in carnival it may well do this at some expense to artistic freedom and at the expense of the unique features of Trinidad carnival that make it a tourist attraction in the first place. And this may also be at the expense of those, such as Minshall, who have made some efforts at being seen to create an equitable carnival for Trinidadians. On the other hand, if these expenses are not paid, new controversies may erupt, and the establishment may be overturned. Negative or positive effect depends on what Trinidadians evolve for themselves within their own local paradigms and what being 'global' means to them. That is how carnival has always developed.

Gender and Carnival

A great deal of the cultural discourse surrounding carnival deals with notions of gender and aspects of male and female sexuality. Much of this discourse has been, and continues to be, heavily embellished with West Indian machismo and male sexual prowess. This is not surprising considering the past and, to some extent, present situation, where economic disparity was/is highly correlated to racial phenotype. According to Wilson (1969; 1973), having few economic resources, Caribbean men were essentially reduced to building sexual reputations rather than careers for themselves. In Trinidad of course, methods of proclaiming such a reputation, or destroying someone else's, became part of carnival discourse. Wilson balances his notion of male 'reputation' with that of female 'respectability', where women uphold colonial values in their own domestic sphere of influence. In this sense, male 'reputation' can be seen as a working-class behavioural reaction to the domestic *petit bourgeoisie* (Littlewood 1993: 38–40).

However, academic criticism of Wilson's (1973) benchmark dualism does exist. Here, the claim is that the supposed relegation of women from the public sphere, so that they can uphold a 'colonial respectability', is both Eurocentric in its framework and ignorant of several areas of women's public interaction (Douglass 1992: 251–2; Besson 1993). In fact, one can see an argument parallel to this over-arching academic argument take place during modern carnival. Tourism has had its effect here.

There has been a perception in Trinidad that 'women are [gradually] taking over carnival'. The initial signs of this perception were noted in the 1950s by Powrie (1988 [1956]), but since then it has accelerated. Some carnival bands have a ratio of ten women for every male participant. The reasons for this are as follows.

To begin with, women in Trinidad, while hardly emancipated to their own satisfaction, have nevertheless made strides in that direction, as have women in other primarily Western (or Westernised) countries. But their near-predominance in Trinidad carnival is due to more than a simple trend. Carnival is seen as a time when notions of traditional 'respectability' as outlined by Wilson (1973) do not apply. The *difference* between everyday life and carnival is greater for women than for men. Indeed, some women say that 'men in Trinidad, they think every day is carnival. But women must think of work.' And so, women are more distinctly enthusiastic about carnival, and, indeed, seem to be quicker to recognise the attractions for foreigners that carnival may have in terms of escapism. Ironically, many women can maintain 'traditional' concerns about clothes and make-up and domestic gossip through carnival. But at carnival time, these concerns are dealt with in the public sphere, and with a greater cultural purpose that legitimises these activities to the women themselves, and to paternalistic society in general.

There are also economic reasons for women 'taking over' carnival. Men have traditionally been employed in plantations and heavy industry. These activities are in decline. The service sector, including tourism, is the growth industry, and here women predominate. Thus they are the steady income-earners, and are quite often in charge of domestic finances. As a result, women can have money specifically set aside for carnival bands and fêting, whereas many men, who feel obliged to try to party (or *lime*, as their get-togethers are known) on a constant basis, are invariably short of the required cash.[13]

This predominance of women in the presentation of carnival also has direct implications for attitudes towards tourism. In January 1995, on an Internet discussion group,[14] a foreign anthropologist asked Trinidadians a question that would seem obvious to any outside observer (see illustration: Yelvington 1996: 319): 'Are women taking over carnival because the festival has changed from being primarily black, male, and working-class to primarily middle-class?' Furthermore, the anthropologist suggested, was it not true that 'carnival has become more about representing Trinidad to the world at large than anything else, and that in these terms – *wining* – women [see Note 3] are more of an acceptable vehicle of Trinidadianess [*sic*] for the tourists than rebellious working-class males. Aren't Trini women happy to go along with this . . . to express some of the freedoms they may have achieved since independence?'

The women in the discussion group were clearly computer-literate, 'on-line', no doubt of middle-class background and not resident in Trinidad,[15] but still representative of the conservative élite that participates in carnival. They very much disagreed with the anthropologist's opinions and effectively 'flamed' him off the discussion. The women's particular hostility can be summarised and interpreted as follows: (i) They were being denied any active role in 'rebellion' (cf. Besson 1993) and (ii) the suggestion was being made that women were not in fact 'free' during carnival, that they were still being 'used', and thus their carnival identity was not a relief from oppression. Overall, the on-line Trinidadian women did not enjoy the idea that women in carnival are 'there for the tourists'.

This indicates three things. First, of all, the idea of carnival being 'for tourists' is not nearly as endemic as the government or media in Trinidad would like to think, nor is it really reflected beneath a superficial local discourse. Secondly, Trinidadian women's notions of 'freedom' are somewhat independent of any 'respectable' notions as put forward by Wilson (1973) and of the phenomenon of visiting tourists. Their own notions of individual self-respect are maintained as they gain from emancipation efforts. Finally, it would seem notable that *participation* in carnival is perceived first and foremost as an equitable affair, and that 'consumption' of the event by spectators is not what motivates or, in locally-moralistic terms, *should* motivate the performers. Both the tourist and the host are equally active in creating and/or servicing the event.

Reading the on-line exchange reminded this author of a particular letter to the editor of a Trinidad newspaper in 1989. In the letter an adamant reader said that Trinidadians should not succumb to the 'neo-slavery' [*sic*] imparted by tourism, and that if tourists wanted to come to Trinidad they should be treated 'no better' [*sic*] than other Trinidadians. What makes this local suggestion relevant to a gender, tourism, and carnival paradigm, is its application to the tourism that has existed less than 20 miles to the north-east of Trinidad on the smaller, but nationally incorporated, island of Tobago. The contrast with carnival- obsessed Trinidad is interesting.

Tobago is, literally, the last small and stereotypically Caribbean island in the Lesser Antilles chain as one travels from North America. It has a homogeneous African-derived population. Because of its network of coral reefs, clear water, and sandy beaches, as well as its lack of local industry and resources (in contrast with oil- and gas-rich Trinidad), Tobago has been the focus of Trinidad's private-sector financial investment in tourism, if not, until recently, its government's tourism policy.[16]

To sum up the dualism of sexual identity between Trinidad and Tobago: the smaller island's previously much more separate identity with regards to tourism has led to a different expectation there. Trinidadians (and Tobagonians one might add) perceive Tobago as a 'pure' place, an escape from carnival where women tourists should not bare their breasts on the beach nor should they lure 'unsuspecting' local boys. That would 'spoil the place'. Trinidad, through the catharsis of carnival, is perceived to be able to handle the apparently illogical moral inconsistencies (illogical given the racist and masculinist[17] ethos that can still prevail). And tourists moving from one island to the other are also allowed, if not expected (depending on the direction of travel), to change their morals appropriately. One island is passive and laid back, while the other is active and resistant. To paraphrase British Afro-Caribbean parlance: Tobago is sweet. Trinidad is wicked.

The examples of women 'taking over' carnival, and the dualistic tendencies in sex and tourism between Trinidad and Tobago, illustrate the way in which concepts of emancipation tendencies develop from within Trinidadian culture, and retain certain gender constructs. As such, the tourist industry in Trinidad is bound to reflect this endemic evolution if it continues to develop with respect to carnival.

Conclusions

Until now the palpable effect of tourism, when taken in the narrow sense of economic development, may have been slight in Trinidad. But by analysing carnival, the real and potential effect of tourism is much more interesting and substantive, especially if one concentrates on what was suggested in the introduction to this chapter: that tourism is a broad phenomenon which thrives on the foreign contrasted with the local. This contrast has increased as Trinidadians have simultaneously localised and globalised different aspects of their identity. Carnival is, both officially and unofficially, a marker for Trinidad's 'national' identity, and so, by encouraging the development of surreal tourist images it will further affect its self-identity through further local contrasts. The facility with which the local society can incorporate the resulting ambiguity into its own notions of the global and the local can affect the degree to which either the event or the society becomes a 'victim' of tourism. Clearly, certain events are better able to absorb this sort of imperial influence than others.

In conclusion to this chapter it can be suggested that, under certain circumstances such as those presented by Trinidad's carnival, it is possible that 'authenticity' can be safely sacrificed to tourism, if that authenticity is never strongly claimed to have existed in the first place. By having allowed a constant stream of 'foreign' influences to affect it during its segmented cultural construction, carnival has ameliorated negative effects on the society from which it sprang. In fact, carnival provides a celebratory forum for a society to express its fears of global influence *by displaying them.*

Finally, it is suggested that *both* locals and tourists appreciate distinct events and their sensations. But, in carnival these images are on display and *available through participation* to both locals and tourists on a near-equitable basis. Thus, once the effect of tourism becomes more palpable, global and local references become more tangible to the individual Trinidadian, who is, like an individual in any society, constantly sorting out both his own and his group identity. Already, Trinidadians are more than aware of academic interest in their culture. They see their carnival on television (while not necessarily aware that there is little or no coverage outside Trinidad[18]) and hear and see (via videos) their music brought back from abroad. They believe that they are 'world players' in the new 'sound bite' montage of world culture and tourism. In the words of one informant 'If the world is a big carnival, Trinidad is like one big band. It has plenty different kinds of people in it, but in a way they all alike. They all know how to dance and play the *mas'* real good.' The continuous question for Trinidadians is whether a 'tourist carnival' evolves as an escape from, or immersion into, a localized culture.

Notes

1. During the February 1995 carnival season, for example, the Trinidad academic grapevine indicated that 4 anthropologists (of whom this author was not one) were attempting research on one aspect of carnival or another. Balliger and Green were identified (the latter is cited in this chapter). The other two are yet to be identified. Previous work on carnival is cited throughout this chapter. My own research, involving 2 years of Trinidad fieldwork, dealt primarily with rural Indian masculine identity.
2. In Port of Spain this is the grandstand of a former horse-racing venue in the Queen's Park Savannah in the centre of the city.
3. As described, *wining* is a dance form that involves very explicit pelvic gyrating and thrusting usually, though not necessarily, with the man behind the woman. It has come to predominate during carnival, though Indians in Trinidad have adapted it into their own folk music and called it 'chutney dancing'.
4. 'Fête' is a common verb in Trinidad, akin to 'party' in North America.
5. The issue of a developing nationalism, viz Trinidadian nationalism (see D. Segal 1987 and Eriksen 1992), is a topic which, although

acknowledged as relevant, is perhaps too tangential to be detailed in this chapter.

6. Since independence, vital statistics on a racial basis (in terms of household, employment, etc.) have not been kept. Such an analysis has been seen locally as a 'political no-man's land' (A. Segal and Earnhardt 1969: 61), which has only recently been broached (e.g. Ryan 1988; 1989).

7. Roughly 85% of East Indian immigrants to Trinidad were Hindu and the rest were Muslim (Weller 1968; Wood 1968). Presbyterian and, more recently, evangelical missionaries have made inroads, but the majority of Trinidad's East Indians are still Hindu.

8. To illustrate how recently East Indian participation in San Fernando carnival has boomed, Clarke (1986: 106) notes in his wife's diary entry for 1964 at the San Fernando King and Queen [of carnival] competition: 'There were hardly any East Indians there . . .'. See also Powrie (1988 [1956]: 98).

9. Following the 1986 general elections, the Trinidad and Tobago government went to the International Monetary Fund to seek post-oil-boom financial aid. Severe welfare cutbacks were mandatory for this funding, and much was made of this 'neo-colonialism' through economics, which even encouraged economic refugees to Canada (Sampath 1989).

10. According to the in-flight magazine of Trinidad's national airline other, albeit smaller, Trinidad-style carnivals also occur in Accra, Melbourne, Atlanta, Long Beach, Orlando, Oakland, San Francisco, Boston, Chicago, Galveston, Washington DC, Jacksonville, Miami, Houston, Baltimore, Montreal, Ottawa, Huddersfield, Leicester, and Liverpool.

11. It should be noted that there were exceptions and interesting permutations to this construction of a West Indian festival. It was neither entirely congenial nor apolitical. See Cohen's (1993) review of the London carnival and its history.

12. The 'Cable News Network' from Atlanta, Georgia is rebroadcast on normal Trinidad television, making it accessible to everyone.

13. See also Rodman (1971: 172–3).

14. The USENET group was soc.culture.caribbean. Out of professional courtesy I have not revealed the name of the anthropologist (not cited elsewhere in this paper), since this was obviously tangential research being undertaken.

15. In January 1995, Trinidad did not have full Internet access.

16. Most of this investment has taken place since the mid-1980s after

the oil-price collapse, and after the election of a national government that had strong grass-roots support in Tobago. Prior to this, with oil-money flowing from Trinidad and the government party's political base on the bigger island, there was no 'need' to develop Tobago tourism.

17. See Brittan (1989), who defines 'masculinism' as the ideology, supported by men and women throughout society, that justifies male domination and makes it seem natural and desirable.

18. When Trinidadians are aware that something is broadcast elsewhere they can be extremely critical. In 1988, portions of Trinidad carnival were simultaneously broadcast to Britain. Middle-class Trinidadians hated the fact that the presenter of these international sequences, Darcus Howe, used a lower-class area to present ostensibly 'authentic' behind-the-scenes interviews.

References

Besson, J. (1993). Reputation and Respectability Reconsidered: a New Perspective on Afro-Caribbean Peasant Women. In Momsen (1993).

Brereton, B. (1993). Social Organisation and Class, Racial and Cultural Conflict in 19th Century Trinidad. In Yelvington (1993).

Brittan, A. (1989). *Masculinity and Power*. Oxford: Basil Blackwell.

Clarke, C. (1986). East Indians in a West Indian Town: San Fernando, Trinidad, 1930–70. London: Allen and Unwin.

Cohen, A. (1993). *Masquerade Politics: Explorations in the Structure of Urban Cultural Movements*. Berg: Oxford.

Crowley, D. (1988 [1956]). The Traditional Masques of Carnival. In Johnson (1988).

De Kadt, E. (1979). *Tourism: Passport to Development? Perspectives on The Social Effects of Tourism in Developing Countries*. Oxford: Oxford University Press.

Douglass, L. (1992). *The Power of Sentiment: Love, Hierarchy, and the Jamaican Family Élite*. Oxford: Westview Press.

Eriksen, T. H. (1992). *Us and Them in Modern Societies: Ethnicity and Nationalism in Trinidad, Mauritius and Beyond*. Oslo: Scandinavian University Press.

Green, G. L. (1995). That's Not My Culture: Blasphemy, Sacrilege, and Moral Degradation in The Trinidad Carnival. Paper presented at American Anthropological Association Annual Conference, Washington DC, December.

Johnson, K. (ed.) (1988). *Trinidad Carnival*. Trinidad: Paria Press [a republication of a 1956 issue of *Caribbean Quarterly* 4(3&4): 42–90].

Joseph, E. L. (1970 [1838]). *The History of Trinidad*. London: Frank Cass.

Littlewood, R. (1993). *Pathology and Identity: The Work of Mother Earth in Trinidad*. Cambridge: Cambridge University Press.

Momsen, J. H. (ed.) (1993). *Women and Change in the Caribbean: A Pan-Caribbean Perspective.* London: James Currey.

Patullo, P. (1996). *Last Resorts: The Cost of Tourism in the Caribbean.* London: Cassell.

Powrie, B. E. (1988 [1956]). The Changing Attitude of the Coloured Middle Class towards Carnival. In Johnson (1988).

Rodman, H. (1971). *Lower Class Families: The Culture of Poverty in Negro Trinidad.* New York: Oxford University Press.

Ryan, S. D. (ed.) (1988). *Trinidad and Tobago: the Independence Experience 1962–1987.* St. Augustine, Trinidad: Institute of Social and Economic Research, University of the West Indies.

Ryan, S. D. (1989). *The Disillusioned Electorate: The Politics of Succession in Trinidad and Tobago.* Trinidad: Inprint Caribbean.

Sampath, N. M. (1989). 'De Country Gone Through': Trinidad East Indian Refugees to Canada. Unpublished paper presented at American Anthropological Association Annual Conference, Washington DC, November.

Sampath, N. M. (1993). An evaluation of the 'Creolisation' of Trinidad East Indian Adolescent Masculinity. In Yelvington (1993).

Segal, A. and K. C. Earnhardt (1969). *Politics and Population in the Caribbean.* Rio Piedras, PR: University of Puerto Rico.

Segal, D. (1987). Nationalism in a Colonial State: A Study of Trinidad and Tobago. Unpublished Ph.D. dissertation, University of Chicago.

Taylor, J. (1991). *Trinidad and Tobago: An Introduction and Guide.* London: Macmillan Caribbean.

Trotman, D. V. (1989). *Crime in Trinidad: Conflict and Control in a Plantation Society, 1838–1900.* Knoxville: University of Tennessee Press.

Weller, J. A. (1968). *The East Indian Indenture in Trinidad.* Puerto Rico: Institute of Caribbean Studies.

Wilson, P. J. (1969). Reputation and Respectability: A Suggestion for Caribbean Ethnography. *Man* (N.S.) 4: 70–84.

Wilson, P. J. (1973). *Crab Antics.* New Haven: Yale University Press.

Wood, D. (1968). *Trinidad in Transition: The Years after Slavery.* London: Oxford University Press.

Yelvington, K. A. (1996). Flirting in the Factory. *Journal of the Royal Anthropological Institute* 2: 313–33.

Yelvington, K.A. (ed.) (1993a). *Trinidad Ethnicity.* London: Macmillan Caribbean.

Yelvington, K.A. (1993b). Introduction: Trinidad Ethnicity. In Yelvington (1993a).

9

Representations of Nepal

Ken Teague

'. . . the tourist experience [is] a voyage through many different "dreamlands"'
(Horne 1984: 1)

A Nepalese proverb says that a good dream should not be disclosed to anyone (Sakya and Griffith 1980: 59), but glossy tourist literature promotes Nepal as the dreamland of 'Shangri La'.

The representation of any culture is necessarily selective. The process involves the appropriation, analysis and re-presentation of that culture, and runs the inherent risk of creating cultural stereotypes. The representation of cultures is also a suggestive activity that raises the problem of the authenticity and typicality of the resources used, whether these are objects, information or people. The difference between 'collectors' art' and 'tourist art' is therefore of central concern.

All three of the activities tourism, anthropology and museums are 'journeys' intended to change perceived images and symbols,[1] sharing a common 'gaze' (Urry 1990: 1, 3) in varying forms, towards a focal subject: 'culture'. All three are engaged in the consumption[2] of the exotic, whether foreign or historic.

'Culture' has been the subject of exhaustive and divergent attempts at definition in anthropology and other disciplines (Williams 1985: 87–93). Kroeber and Kluckhohn (1952) provide one of the better-known definitions: 'Culture . . . is an historical product including ideas, patterns and values; it is selective, is learned, is based on symbols and is an abstraction from and a product of behaviour.' Whether one accepts this definition or not it serves a useful purpose in indicating that culture is an assemblage of activities, including the production, distribution and use of material artefacts and sets of meanings and symbols that may be more or less integrated in different parts of the overall pattern. Culture is usually manipulated and changed by people as they adapt to their various physical,

173

social and cultural environments. Appropriation is thus an inevitable part of socio-cultural processes.

I outline Nepalese 'reality' to question the feasibility of its representation, and follow this by a review of the available sources of information: anthropological literature, tourist literature and objects, and existing museum collections. Tourist art is then examined against Graburn's (1976) scheme and is found to be representative of contemporary changes in the society and culture of Nepal, thus having ethnographic or anthropological authenticity.

Nepalese Reality

A number of questions immediately arise, apart from methodological problems, when one attempts to outline Nepalese 'reality'. What are the facts and figures? How to describe briefly the cosmologies that are so important in Nepalese life? What is the social construction of Nepalese reality, and what images of Nepal do the Nepalese and others present? I start from the apparent safety of positivism.

Nepal is a country situated in the central Himalayan mountain chain between India and Tibet. About 500 miles long by 90 miles wide, it is divided into four main ecological zones: the Terai, a continuation of the north Indian plain in the south; the Siwalik Hills and Inner Terai; the Middle Hills; and the Himalayan peaks, with some continuation beyond on to the Tibetan plateau. The ecological variation of these zones is matched by the ethnic diversity of the population, which is over 18 million (1991 Census), speaking some 40 languages, with Nepali as the lingua franca.

Nepal has been unified as a kingdom since the late eighteenth century, with the capital at Kathmandu. Before this the term 'Nepal' was reserved for the Kathmandu Valley only, as it still is occasionally today. Nepal was never colonised by British India, although it was rendered dependent on India, a condition which still persists, and the rulers were successful in restricting large-scale European entry until 1951. Society is stratified, with an élite and peasantry. The growing urban population is about 6 per cent, whilst over 90 per cent of the population work in agriculture. Nepal is a Hindu kingdom. In 1981 Hindus formed 89.5 per cent of the population; other religions present included: Buddhists 5.3 per cent, Muslims 2.7 per cent, Others 2.29 per cent and Christians 0.21 per cent (Robinson 1989: 45). Both Indian and Tibetan presence and investment are now marked.

Nepal has been noted throughout its history, from at least the 4th century

AD onwards, for the production of textiles and metalwares. Other ancient crafts include painting, embroidery and woodcarving. Whilst craft skills of differing sorts are found among various social groups throughout the country, it is generally agreed that the finest craftsmen of Nepal have always been drawn from the Newar people of the Kathmandu Valley. The Newars combine Hindu and Buddhist beliefs in a syncretic manner. The Sakya caste group, which is particularly involved in the manufacture of religious figures, descends in part from Buddhist monks who renounced celibacy and the monastic life from the Middle Ages onwards. Nepalese metalworking has marked elements of continuity. The working of non-ferrous metals by beating and lost wax casting has been a feature from the earliest historical period to the present. This 'constant' factor in non-ferrous production has persisted despite major changes in the social organisation and distribution of Newar society.

Although caste has been formally abolished, Nepalese social organisation remains based on caste principles. The occupational monopoly exercised by groups within a caste system often has a limiting effect on responses to social change, yet in Nepal modern production involves these 'traditional' metalworkers, and other caste and tribal groups, and continues to expand to meet market demands for local tourists and for export.

Ferrous working and correlated social forms show different patterns of development in Nepal. These include the diffusion of iron ploughs and weapons from India in the twelfth century, firearms in the eighteenth century, and the production and spread of factory-made wares in this century. Ferrous technology thus shows more changes when compared with non-ferrous, yet retains the production of 'traditional' implements such as hoes and *kukris*, which are still appropriate to this environment and economy.

Despite the antiquity and range of craft skills, in terms of '. . . comparative development studies [Nepal] is . . . referred to as techno-logically primitive' (Dutt and Geib 1987: 217), and is among the five poorest countries in the world. The population is rising. Agricultural productivity is constrained by various factors, and is further hampered by deforestation, soil erosion and flooding. Craft production is seen as one of the major avenues of economic development, whilst tourism now provides the second biggest source of foreign earnings.

The development of tourism in the Kathmandu valley is immediately apparent to the visitor. Shops and street stalls or pitches, since many are laid out on the street surfaces themselves, cluster around a variety of large-scale monuments – temples and palaces. The contrast between old and new elements of material culture and in social relations is marked. A common feature, however, is the considerable use of metals: to furnish the materials for a range of tourist goods or souvenirs, as well as to provide for architectural decoration. This preponderance of metal usage is repeated in domestic utensils (although plastic is increasingly in use), which are used both in this rapidly changing urban environment and in the differing context of rural environments. Reaction to the impressive quality and quantity of metalwares is as evident in seventh-century accounts of Nepal as in those of the twentieth. The relationship between technology and the social order, especially with regard to the use of a particular type of material or commodity, metal, is close-knit.

The 'realities' of Nepal are obviously numerous, varied and partial or sectional. A contemporary Nepali scholar observes 'To the world outside, Nepal still remains something of a mystery, or at best invokes such cliches as "the land of fierce fighters" or "the land of mysterious religions and quaint ornate craftsmanship". Even in the midst of the recent plethora of literature on Nepal, the heritage, identity and culture remains . . . at best ambiguously defined. The ambiguity of Nepalese culture is not an apparent one . . . [it] is real and genuine . . .' and is entrenched in Nepali historiography, which largely deals with dynastic history. 'The people of Nepal are left out . . .' (Malla 1979: 225).

Given the range, variety and partiality in the evidence and sources about Nepal, one must question the feasibility of trying to represent Nepal or any other complex society as a whole. If the ethnographic ideal – total representation – is impossible, and is therefore abandoned, which 'reality' should take priority in representation, the physical environment, the peoples, their cultures, or social changes, including tourism? The interests and purposes of those making representations must then come into question.

A further question here is how far one medium of communication, such as a museum display or a monograph, a film or popular literature, can claim or expect to represent the reality of another culture in its entirety? Although anthropology claims to deal with all human societies and cultures, in practice the attempt is made in much more restricted ways. Museum ethnography makes similar claims to universality, yet also must have a pragmatic approach in terms of available collections and resources.[3] From this viewpoint, I now survey representations of Nepal provided in anthropological and tourist literature and artefacts, and in museum collections and displays.

Anthropology of Nepal

The social anthropology of Nepal consists of an increasingly substantial body of work by Nepali and Western scholars. Numerous monographs and papers deal with aspects of the life of various tribal groups or peoples, usually on a village or locality basis. Thematic studies on linguistics, demography, religion, trade and inter-caste relations also form part of this corpus. There is as yet no full-scale synthesising study of Nepal as a whole,[4] such as Mandelbaum (1970) has undertaken for India.

As is common in modern social anthropology, the discussion of material culture is either absent or relatively marginal in most monographs, though with notable exceptions, such as Jest (1974), Macfarlane (1976), Macdougal (1979) and Fisher (1987), who do relate material culture to its social context.

Studies of Nepalese material culture usually focus on religious figurative art, which is discussed in terms of art history and technology.[5] Exceptions to this include Birmingham (1975) on pottery and Dunsmore (1993) on textiles. With the exception of Gajurel and Vaidya's (1984) book on the *Traditional Arts and Crafts of Nepal*, the entire range of craft production in society at large has not been systematically dealt with (Gurung 1989: 240n8), yet Nepalese craftsmen and their products have played a significant role for centuries in trade and the transmission of cultural traits between India and Tibet and further central Asia – notably in the diffusion of Buddhism by means of the production of metal figurative art and religious apparatus. Today, although the form of the icons remains much the same, their functions have changed, as they are produced for, and diffused by both modern pilgrims and tourists. This body of literature thus provides some partial representations of Nepalese realities.

Tourism in Nepal

'The Lost Horizons have been found and put in [my] brochure', George Bales, *The Evening Standard*, London, Friday, 23 November 1984.

'The Nepalese people are honest, attractive, resourceful and good-humoured. Although it may sound romantic, it is true that they sing while they work . . . They have lived for a long time in repression and ignorance, but, with modern communications and the ever-increasing presence of tourists from the West, they are becoming more and more aware of the potentialities of life.'

(Bernstein 1970: 95)

Mass tourism, since its main development after the Second World War, is one of the growth industries of contemporary society, and may already be the largest industry in the world. Nepal has been part of this process, with its associated social changes, during the last few decades. The closure of Nepal to Europeans over the last two centuries was largely successful. During the period 1881–1925 there were only 153 European visitors to Nepal. Mostly British, these visitors were government officials and representatives of commercial interests rather than tourists (Landon 1928: 298–305). Although opened to the West in 1951, and accepting tourism as part of Western plans to develop the country, tourism had a zero growth rate even in 1955. In 1957 the first group tours entered the country. In 1988, 265,943 tourists visited Nepal (Smith 1981; CBS 1990: 143). This figure does not include Indian nationals, the largest group of visitors who cross the open border between the two countries to make pilgrimage, to shop, to gamble at the casino, and as tourists. In 1988, 72,000 Indian nationals entered Nepal by air, but much larger numbers entered by road (Gurung 1989: 153). In 1992/3, as the number of non-South Asian tourists to Nepal fell by 12.2 per cent, the number of Indian tourist arrivals rose (*Image Nepal*, Supp. vi, 10 Feb. 1994).

Tourism in Nepal is of various types: *cultural*, primarily of architectural sites within the Kathmandu Valley; *ethnic*, encounters with the people in both their daily life and at festivals; *adventure*, including trekking, rafting and mountaineering; and *environmental*, including wildlife and floral observation. The promotion of tourism in Nepal is fraught with conflicts and difficulties: a drive to welcome more tourists coincides with increases in airport tax and visa fees; new trekking areas are opened up, with, again, increased fees for trekking permits and internal flights, which are already on two price scales: for Nepalis and foreigners. The infrastructure of roads, food and accommodation is patchy. External factors also play their part. Consumer demand is difficult to forecast in view of world events and disasters such as terrorism, Chernobyl-type accidents and war in the Gulf. This last had less deleterious effect on Nepalese tourism than one might have anticipated, although it did result in some reduction in numbers. More seriously, increasing pollution in Kathmandu now (1994) appears to be a major factor in this decline.

The tourist industry is a rich source of 'representations' of Nepal, providing souvenir art, literature from travel agents, guidebooks and other books dealing with various aspects of Nepalese life. The 'development and success of tourism depends heavily on images. Culture is commoditized and packaged, advertised and promoted, according to an image of anticipated visitor experience' (Smith 1981).

A survey of five tourist pamphlets published in 1991 by the Department of Tourism and the Royal Nepal Airlines Corporation (RNAC) indicates the attempt to illustrate the diverse nature of Nepal's tourist attractions. Of a total of 120 photographs, 65 depict various religious scenes and activities, 30 show a variety of environments, 18 show secular architecture and 7 show portraits of people. Metalwares appear prominently in all these categories, and include jewellery, religious apparatus, architectural features and figures. The 'living history' aspect of Nepal is stressed: 'In Kathmandu . . . to cross a street is to travel across centuries. Shrines, temples, palaces [and] . . . ageless sculptures . . . make living museums of the Kathmandu Valley' (*Nepal Visitor's Guide*, Dept. of Tourism: 2–3). Pokhara is 'a corner of real paradise . . . blessed by the gods' (His Majesty's Government of Nepal 1979).

Nepal also plays its 'Tibet card' as hard as possible. 'Tibet' as a term or connotation is added wherever possible, for example to hotels and guest houses, etc.:

> . . . if Tibet's charm lay in its remoteness, Nepal's lay in its availability; a veteran of the mystic market, it knew exactly how to sell itself as a wholesale, secondhand Tibet. Thus the magic title of the Forbidden Land found its way into every single brand name: local stores were stocked not just with handicrafts, but with Tibetan handicrafts, Tibetan paintings, Tibetan bells, Tibetan scarves, Tibetan pizzas (Iyer 1988: 100).

I would add 'Tibetan' singing bowls to this list. These metal bowls, which are played by rubbing a wooden beater around the rim, for therapeutic purposes and as aids to meditation, are allegedly made in Tibet; but enquiry in Nepal (1991) evokes a variety of responses: they are made in the Kathmandu Valley, they used to be made in the Kathmandu Valley, they are made in the Terai, in northern India, in Assam, in Pakistan, etc. Wherever they are made, their numbers on the Kathmandu market have increased dramatically during the last few years.

Guidebooks to Nepal range from modest to substantial publications, with some containing contributions by leading anthropologists, both Nepalese and foreign, long-term resident expatriates and experienced travellers. Guidebooks are usually well-illustrated: Nepalese people and their country's sights are extremely photogenic, with information on how to get there, where to go, what to see, history and culture, what to buy, where to stay, how to behave and so on. The tourist industry has only developed on a mass basis in Nepal over the last twenty years or so, and it is to its credit that it has become so well organised so quickly, if on a loose basis, with most reliance placed on the private sector.

The laudatory note and the emphasis on the exotic found in tourist literature is also evident in some travel literature: 'Nepal, the kingdom of the Gods' (Toutain 1986: 10); *The Wildest Dreams of Kew* (Bernstein 1970); *Into Thin Air* (Pilkington 1985); *Kingdom in the Sky* (Cunningham 1975); as well as in leading studies of Nepalese art history: *Nepal, Where the Gods are Young* (Pal 1975). The difficulty, for those with a more sober approach, is that Nepal more than justifies such appellations.

Nepal has thus had some share in the tourist pie, but remains part of a regional rather than a whole trip package except for trekkers and mountaineers (Acharya 1991: 3; Singh 1991: 30). In this sense the representations provided by tourist publicity have only partially succeeded: hence the employment of Touche Ross, who are currently preparing a development programme for Nepal's Ministry of Tourism (*Leisure Opportunities* 24.1.90).

Tourist literature generally deals with screened reality – the olfactory aspects of a village path are ignored in favour of the incense in the temples. Museums do the same by tending to omit the waste products of a society from display. The consumption of culture is a problem, not simply for the material consequences it has on the environment, for example, the large quantities of toilet paper and rubbish on the Everest trail, but also for the cumulative effect it has on the culture of tourism itself. If too many people admire a mountain or a temple, it tends to become unfashionable. The tourist 'gaze' becomes saturated, succinctly expressed in the saying, 'been there, seen that, done that', to the detriment of the host society and its economy.

The negative effects of contact with the West are seen in the large-scale and continuing theft of antique items of material culture; figures are literally hacked away from their settings and shrines are removed wholesale by gangs of men. Metal figures may also be used to smuggle drugs from the country.

Material Representations of Nepal

There are two possibilities to represent Nepal in the museum context: to display existing collections in museums, and to make further collections. The assumption that the former category of material is 'collectors' art', which is more 'authentic' and more typical of Nepalese culture than contemporary material, is open to question, whilst the latter course, given that Nepal has antiquities laws, leads directly into consideration of the acquisition of tourist art.

Since I wish to concentrate on discussion of contemporary material, I will keep my remarks about existing museum collections brief. As in many Western museums, Nepalese museums largely contain and display fine art, weapons and memorabilia rather than ethnographic material. There are relatively small quantities of Nepalese material displayed in museums in the UK, although more material is held in store.[6] In general these collections comprise two categories of material that have ill-defined boundaries: art or antique materials, and ethnographic material or items of daily life. The distinction between these two categories merely reflects Western art-historical bias. Most Nepalese ethnographic collections are historical in nature: that is, they have been acquired piecemeal over time, and are limited in scope. Weapons, figurative religious art, mostly Buddhist, and jewellery form the main categories of material. Questions about the typicality and authenticity of existing museum collections thus arise. There is or was, presumably, a core of 'traditional' Nepalese material culture, although, like culture itself, this is not necessarily so easy to define in such a complex and multiethnic society.

Authenticity

The basic activity of ethnographic museums is to educate people by representing cultures. The nature of representations is that they are suggestions of, and inevitably at some stage of removal from, reality, which 'underlies appearances' (COD).

A major concern during the development of museums over the last century and more, and still a current issue, is the authenticity[7] of their collections. The '"Authenticity" [of particular objects] is the special magic of museums' (Horne 1984: 16). '[The] public are interested in original objects in the permanent exhibitions, not in models, copies or dioramas.' However, the Ethnography Department of the British Museum does 'now collect – sparingly – what is loosely termed "airport art": objects made for tourists by traditional methods but adapted by the craftsmen to the taste, as they conceive it, of European or American purchasers. This may sound frivolous, but it is a real expression of the contact between cultures and demonstrates how a commercial approach affects traditional values – a worthy subject for comment at a time of racial tension and economic contact' (Wilson 1989: 31, 119).

Authentic museum collections are increasingly challenged by the production of so-called tourist art in the countries from which ethno-graphic material is acquired. As modernisation and market forces reduce the production of traditional ethnographic material, and make its desirability as 'art' more costly, tourist art when contrasted with 'collectors' art' raises the problems of authenticity and of the suitability of tourist art for collection by museums.

In some senses this is a redundant dilemma. Many specimens in ethnographic collections in Britain and elsewhere were manufactured as tourist art, but are now treasured and displayed as collectors' art. Chinese export porcelain, dolls, paintings and fakes, argillite carvings from the North-West Coast of America, embroidered artefacts from both America and China, and the products of art schools in India are obvious examples in a list which could be considerably extended, and should perhaps include Kashmir shawls and examples of Chinoiserie and Japonism.

Given the rate of change in 'other cultures' during the last two centuries it is interesting to note that most ethnographic collections have been made during this period: for example, half of the Museum of Mankind's collection derives from the twentieth century. In other words, existing collections are already 'compromised' to some extent, before one turns to collecting and displaying modern material and turistica. This tends to disprove the argument that 'the museum curator esteems . . . inwardly directed artefacts . . . items made by peoples for themselves by their own techniques and to their own standards', whilst the developer 'is concerned with . . . externally directed artefacts . . . made for an external often dominant world and . . . essential for trade. They may be identical in form to the first category, and thus be regarded as retaining authenticity. Most frequently they are adaptations, and as products of societies in a process of change induced by contact with alien cultures, they are "arts of acculturation". Tourist art clearly falls into this latter category' (Graburn 1976; Hill, pers. comm., 1991).

However, in some countries, including Nepal, tourism plays such a major role in some parts of culture and society that its products cannot be dismissed so easily if we remain committed to a holistic, ethnographic approach in representing the reality of Nepal.[8] If one held solely to a purist's view of collecting and displaying only 'authentic' material, one would tend to represent reality by de-contextualised 'art' objects rather than trying to represent the reality of everyday life in context over time.

Even so, and despite such difficulties, societies and cultures are often distinctively expressed, or are identifiable by the use of particular materials shaped into particular forms: the use of bamboo in China is an obvious example. This means that we can provenance items of material culture and say: 'this is an Indonesian textile; this is South African beadwork; this is Nepalese metalwork', and so on. The usage of a particular material may ramify throughout a socio-cultural system. Museum representations follow such provenancing of individual objects and sets of objects, and tourist art is often seen as a recent deviation from such 'authentic' material.

Nepalese Tourist Art

In Nepal, as in India, some artefacts, that is, the same artefacts, are produced for domestic use, for the pilgrimage market, and for foreign markets such as tourist and export markets. Tourist art is not necessarily easy to define and separate. For centuries Nepalese craftsmen and artists have produced and sold tokens and souvenirs to foreign pilgrims who were visiting sacred places (Naqvi 1968: 269). Pilgrimage was organised and commercialised to such a degree that Fisher (1991: 41) is led to conclude '. . . there is nothing new about tourism in India and Nepal'.

There is a generally held view that, following the unification of Nepal, and even more so during the Rana regime (1846–1950/1, the period during which most UK museum collections were made) there was a decline in the amount and quality of craft production (Gimlette 1886, 1890–1; Palikhe 1986: 4), although some fine products from this period exist in private collections, and were shown for example in London in 1851 and in 1886 at the Colonial and Indian Exhibition. This view is also belied by several modern craftsmen, who state: 'Things were better for craftsmen under the Ranas' (G. Sakya, pers. comm.). During this period the Newars were still manufacturing a range of items, including turistica, as Gimlette's accounts (1886, 1890/1) indicate, and Nepal was exporting large numbers of utensils to India and manufacturing religious art for the Tibetan market. Nepalese craftsmen have lived and worked in Tibet, Ladakh and China for several centuries, and in Darjeeling and other parts of India and Bhutan from the early nineteenth century. It is probable that a significant amount of the material provenanced to Tibetan and Indian collections in UK ethnographic museums was 'made in Nepal', or by expatriate Nepalese. It is also probable that a significant amount of this material is what we would now term 'tourist art'. For example Darjeeling, where Newar craftsmen were resident, has attracted European visitors for over a century, even if no tourists were allowed to visit Nepal itself.

Versions of many apparently typical Nepalese items in UK museum collections – weapons, religious artefacts (mostly metalwares), and jewellery – are all to be found on sale today in the cities of the Kathmandu Valley. Tourism has stimulated the production of artefacts for the local tourist and export markets. Since the tourist boom these material representations have been joined by an increasing variety of artefacts that were not part of the traditional corpus: 'freaky' clothes – relics of the

Hippy Era and Tibetan rugs – products of the Tibetan diaspora, as well as goods from India, Taiwan, Hong Kong and China, Pakistan, Bali, Bhutan and Kashmir. All find their place on the Kathmandu market, as goods from some of these countries have done throughout Nepal's history.[9] Which are true, typical representations of Nepalese material culture today? What can we collect and display, for which audience,[10] and how can we develop theories of the object and the museum (Ames 1986: 28)?

Graburn (1976: 5–8) provides a basic framework for theorising about objects by correlating tourist art and cultural processes. His concepts, which include syncretisation, extinction, alteration, reduction, commercialisation, assimilation, etc., may be applied more broadly to Nepalese material culture, given that the ethnographic view does not isolate 'art' from material culture as a whole.[11]

'Extinction' occurs where an indigenous art form declines or disappears as a result of external forces. Whilst some ferrous tools such as hoes and *kukris* have remained as a constant factor in forms and functions, although the raw materials may now be imported, non-ferrous domestic utensils show increasing signs of 'extinction'. Water containers and plates, formerly hand-made in copper, brass and bronze, are increasingly factory-made in stainless steel, aluminium and plastic. Silver jewellery, formerly hand-made, is increasingly replaced by machine-made jewellery from India and elsewhere.

Examples of 'alteration', where traditional art persists for local consumption, but shows changes in materials, techniques or forms, or acquires external symbols, are less evident in Nepal. However, 'commercialisation', where traditional art items are made for sale yet adhere to culturally embedded aesthetic and formal standards, and retain a place in their own culture, is particularly apparent. I note two representations as examples of this process: metal religious figures and painting.

In general terms Nepalese scroll paintings are simpler in content and less detailed than Tibetan scroll paintings, with a different colour range, and were traditionally produced by Newar craftsmen. Today the tourist shops of Kathmandu are stocked to overflowing with finely painted 'Tibetan' scroll paintings produced on a workshop basis both by Newars and by Tamangs, a hill tribe with no artistic tradition. The form and style persist, but the craftsmen have changed.

Metal religious images, produced for domestic use and for foreigners in Nepal such as Tibetan pilgrims as well as abroad in Tibet and China, have been collected by museums and private collectors as among the finest representations of Nepalese art. One should note in passing that representations of deities are essentially effigies or stereotypes such as the 'universal monarch' and the goddess, with the latter especially presenting problems of attribution for this reason (Kar 1952: 12–13, 15; Pal 1975, 1985). Production was and is by professional craftsmen, who manufacture images for a range of different religions and secular markets. Today the same images are made as art objects for the tourist market in Nepal, for foreign pilgrims (for example from Tibet), and for export to collectors in a number of countries in Europe and America, and are exported for religious purposes to Asian countries such as Japan, Taiwan, and Mongolia. Although some distaste was expressed at selling images formerly reserved for religious purposes to tourists, the general view (with reservations) among craftsmen was that 'business is business'. 'Commercialisation' and 'tradition' are obviously intertwined in Nepalese culture.

Formerly, figures were often, but not always, made by an individual craftsman, with the help of his immediate family. Whilst this method is still prevalent, figures are now also made on an assembly-line basis by men and women. The scale of production is enormous. The price of wax (for casting figures) has risen considerably owing to the demand created by tourism, and domestic supplies are now supplemented by imported wax from China (Gajurel and Vaidya 1984: 280–1).

Tourism is often seen as causing a decline in the quality of artefacts, although I wonder if fine-quality artefacts ever were produced for popular markets. In the Nepalese case one might ask: has the development of tourism resulted in the 'reduction' of Nepalese art to accommodate the profit motive, or is the new social complexity of Nepal as a host society correlated with sophistication and specialisation in the production of material culture?

The expansion of the tourist market has meant that some 'reduction' has occurred. 'Reduction' is where the profit motive overrides the aesthetic standards of the producer culture, and the alien consumer becomes dominant. Objects are produced in cheaper or different materials to standardised designs by simplified techniques. Nepalese tourist art provides a variety of examples of reduction, including painted papier-mâché masks, twisted copper and brass bracelets, mass-produced, resin-bonded imported figures from Hong Kong that are coyly sold as 'ivory', and poorly-finished, simply-cast metal figures. Copies of older pieces are available, and the antiquing of figures and other items of tourist art is not uncommon; *thankas* and masks are 'smoked', and metal figures treated with bootblack in this process (Lo Bue 1981: 84–5).

I am more uncertain whether the production of bone medallions or pendants, inset with motifs of Yin–Yang and stars in sheet brass, falls within this category. Wearing bone is anathema to high-caste Hindus, and I could not find out where the original notion to make these artefacts came from: perhaps it derives from 'hippy' inspiration. The two craftsmen making these in quantity in a Kathmandu suburb are both hill men, with no artistic background and a determinedly commercial attitude towards production. In the hills, Tamangs and Sherpas now commission blacksmiths, Kamis, to produce non-ferrous wares for the Valley markets.

Reduction does not occur across the board, however. Both poor-quality and fine-quality figures are currently produced, and a general impression in 1991 was that the overall quality of figures had improved during the course of the previous ten years. In both cases, of improvement and reduction, the tourist industry has stimulated the production of metalcrafts and helped economic development in a country where opportunities for small-scale industry are scarce (Michaels 1988: 16–17).

'Syncretisation' is where arts derive from culture contact and are adapted and developed by the receiving culture to produce a new art form that is accepted and valued by it. In this category one perhaps could cite the puppets and 'freaky' clothes, which are totally non-traditional to Nepal but are sold in quantity on the tourist market.

Finally 'assimilation', where alien art forms are accepted by a culture and local artists compete with the aliens at their own game, yields a rich crop of examples, including batik, prints, wool embroidery and Western-style paintings and sculpture by Nepalese artists.

From the basis of Graburn's scheme I would argue that although all of the items of material culture mentioned above are classifiable as tourist art, nevertheless they are appropriate artefacts to represent the social and cultural changes occurring in Nepal in recent times. They thus have 'authenticity' as ethnographic museum objects.

Representations and Appropriation

Anthropology, and ethnographic collections by extension, are in origin 'children of the Enlightenment', or the 'bastards of Colonialism', depending on your preferred terminology. They are the products of post-Renaissance world views and European expansion and imperialism.[12]

By their very nature ethnographic collections are attempts to fulfil a global, encyclopaedic concept. Within this framework, the ethnographer holds to an ideal of representing cultures or societies in a holistic manner, in context. The holistic ideal is also held in anthropology, but more in the breach than in practice: instead a problem-solving approach is predominant. In neither discipline, nor in tourist literature and products, is a holistic representation of a culture possible in practice. Tourism, anthropology and museums are all partial activities undertaken and received by audiences that themselves are partial and heterogeneous in composition.[13]

My problem, then, is to use existing, partial collections to represent the complex range of Nepalese reality, or, given the resources, to extend these collections and thus the possible representations, in order to educate and entertain the public.[14]

The inherent conflict or tension between these two activities is apparent. Should I entertain my public, and adopt the role of one voice among several in the process of representation (Jones 1992: 27; Peirson Jones 1992: 32–3), or try to educate them with more didactic representations, showing them something different and perhaps difficult to comprehend? As a museum ethnographer interpreting 'other cultures', which are by definition 'foreign' to my public in many aspects, despite television and the presence of local multicultural communities, I am obliged towards didactic, educational representations, rather than simply entertaining displays, to avoid or correct stereotyping as much as possible. Obviously a (variable) balance has to be struck. There is no single solution to problems of representation.[15]

Representation, ethnographic or otherwise, inevitably produces stereotypes: hence the need, I think, for 'gatekeepers' or interpreters – that is, informed curators to select display material and to interpret other cultures. Have dialogue and a multiplicity of voices by all means; but the curator's voice cannot be only one among many. This would be an abdication of responsibility, which is even more dangerous in a culture that tends not to support the study of and interaction with other cultures,[16] and where aggressive stereotyping readily and repeatedly arises.

Stereotypical representations are inherent in the dynamism of the cultural process, in the social construction of reality and culture.[17] All methods of communication use implicit or explicit conventions to depict or represent limited or partial views of reality. (For example, most post-cards are rectangular in shape.) Museum displays have an inherent danger of forming stereotypes: 'unduly fixed mental impressions', owing to their static nature and relative permanence.[18] Stereotypes and typologies impart symmetry and regularity to behaviour, even though they may only crudely approximate to reality. The sociological aim is to recognise stereotypes, step back from them, and read them so that they are better understood.

Stereotyping is no new thing, nor is it one-sided nor confined to Europeans. The Nepalese tend to see all foreigners as wealthy,[19] despite the previous invasion by hippies. In relative terms this is true (Armington 1982: 18–22; Reed 1990: 25–8). Such stereotypes were formed quite soon after Nepal was opened. An American Peace Corps report in 1963 gave Nepalese impressions of Americans: 'A fairly large number of Nepalese have had some form of contact with Americans . . . [as] tourists or . . . [in] the official mission. The general stereotype which has arisen from this acquaintance depicts [Americans] as good-hearted, generous and friendly but basically simple people of somewhat limited perception' (Bernstein 1970: 81).

For tourists, souvenirs represent the places and peoples they have seen. In some cases these objects may be of fine, 'traditional' quality, in others not. Their collectors may perceive them as genuine or authentic, or less so, largely depending on the circumstances of acquisition. In either case, souvenirs symbolise or represent the culture in which they were acquired. Their acquisition, whatever their quality or nature, is the appropriation of culture.[20]

The notion of 'the appropriation of culture' is currently popular, usually in a derogatory or critical sense, and may be applied to tourism, anthropology and museums, which all engage in this activity in their various ways. On the other hand 'appropriation' in the sense of the 'taking of culture to oneself' is what any person does during the process of becoming educated in the broadest sense.

Associated with the idea of cultural appropriation there is a concern about the necessity for wider consultation with the culture or community being represented. Whilst agreeing with this view, I have some reservations, since the question then becomes, 'Who represents Nepal?' If the answer is the Nepalese, then which Nepalese represent whom or what? The élite who, during Rana rule, imported European artefacts on a large scale, whilst keeping Europeans out and kept the country as their private estate? (Cole 1972: 94). Tamangs who style themselves 'Sherpas' in order to gain employment as trekking guides? The Nepalese government, which terms Newar craft products and Tibetan carpets 'Nepalese'? The examples could be multiplied.

Syncretisation and assimilation, and the cultural appropriation which these entail, are deliberate governmental policy as means to develop craft production in Nepal. Handicraft Promotion Centres on Industrial Estates foster craft development through research, design and training. In Patan, the second largest city in the Kathmandu Valley, Promotion Centre staff produce new designs of items such as jewellery, cloth and woodcarving, which are then displayed to local craftsmen as a stimulus to their own production. At times such new items gain wider sales for export.[21] A few individual craftsmen take their products abroad to craft fairs and for display, and are mentioned as named craftsmen in museum catalogues and journals, whilst exhibitions are also held in Kathmandu on a fairly frequent basis. Art books and magazines also serve as inspiration for Nepalese craftsmen. These processes of appropriation also require to be represented as part of the current reality of this culture. The appropriation of culture is what many people do most of the time.

I have argued that the process of representing culture necessarily involves a selection of information and material that is at some remove from reality, and that tourist products and so-called collectors' art are both valid, authentic means to representation. These facts in turn raise the problems of the typicality of material and the dangers of reinforcing or creating cultural stereotypes. Although the holistic approach must remain as an ideal, these limitations and obstacles to understanding must also be recognised and worked with in the process of appropriation that necessarily occurs within and between cultures, and on the inevitably partial representations of culture that we produce.

Notes

1. I would argue that tourism in the Western European sense is a secularisation of pilgrimage. Both pilgrimage and tourism are part of a spectrum of socio-cultural activities, rather than being discrete.
2. A 'consumer' is the 'user of an article; a purchaser of goods and services'; whilst 'consumption' is 'the purchase and use of goods; to use up' (COD). Both terms may be applied to tourism, anthropology and museums in various ways, and the notion of 'using up' begs for further research. In terms of social relationships, forms of the patron–client relationship are common to all three activities. Tourism may be seen as a one-off or intermittent relationship of an exploitative nature, not always one-sided, rather than an ongoing structured relationship. In the south and central Asian context, the commercial aspects of travel, whether as 'pilgrim' or 'tourist' are a major element in this activity: for example, for Tibetans 'pilgrimage is trade' and vice versa. Commerce was similarly a significant impulse in Western post-Renaissance exploration. Museums developed out of this secular pilgrimage, and early collections of exotica were made, not only as a result of political colonisation, but from exploratory commercial activities and cultural interests.
3. Tourism, anthropology and museums are all involved in the representation business, but have differing or varying aims, intentions and methods. Their audiences are similarly differing, if

overlapping. The tourist industry largely has commercial interests – to attract anyone with money to spend, both in the interests of the commercial firms operating the resources (transport, board and subsistence), and to aid the economic development of the host country. Tourism is promoted through published literature and graphics, films and television and word of mouth to a general audience largely composed of actual and potential tourists. Museums use artefacts, either in display or demonstration, with the aim of providing education and entertainment to a variety of audiences: children, the general, multicultural home population, specialists from home and abroad, and tourists. Anthropology aims to provide education to an audience of peers, students and a specialist general public. All three activities have an audience of peoples of the countries in which they carry out their various performances, and try to 'bring culture back alive' for their home audiences by seeking experience, information and, in some cases, material artefacts: souvenirs or museum collections. The participants in all three activities are thus involved in power relationships of some kind. Tourists are consumers and distributors of money, a fluid form of Foreign Aid. Anthropologists and museums act as mediators or translators of culture, as gatekeepers. They may or may not give something in exchange for access to the host society.

4. Bista (1987) describes the peoples of Nepal as separate units, rather than the pattern of relationships between them on a national basis. However, the anthropological bibliography of Nepal is large and increasing.

5. Alsop and Charlton (1973), Labriffe (1973), Pal (1975, 1985), Slusser (1982), etc.; although other publications are in process: Dunsmore on textiles (1993), Teague on metalworking (1996).

6. I have made a survey of some of these collections (Teague 1996), and given a more detailed account of the Horniman collection (1988). These are the existing collections, of which future field collecting and display should take some account.

7. See for example the debates about the use of replicas in the early days of the Museums Association, and the concern of modern Education Officers in museums who are antipathetic towards replicas, particularly in so-called 'handling collections', and are concerned to have real artefacts for teaching. The National Curriculum also currently calls for students to deal with real materials. The corollary of 'authenticity' is 'typicality'. Authentic artefacts typify a culture: this *kukri* typifies Nepalese culture. The corollary of typicality is

stereotypicality: all *kukris* are Nepalese, or, all Nepalese use *kukris*. Neither of the last two statements is true.

8. The most recent and still growing tip of Westernisation is the development of mass tourism during the last few decades. Tourism has produced an apparently new form of social system: the 'host' society. In some cases the scale of tourism and the economic dependence of these societies on income from tourism mean that tourists are now an essential part of their social system. Nepal provides a notable example of a 'host' society. Closed to Europeans until 1950/1, Nepal has since accommodated a massive influx of tourists, whose numbers continue to rise and provide a major source of foreign earnings. At the same time industrial development in Nepal remains 'in an infantile state' (Palikhe 1986: i) and over 90% of the population are employed in agriculture. The dependency on income from tourism means that the tourist population is now an essential part of the Nepalese social system, rather than being simply an aspect of the Nepalese economy. A question concerning the nature of Nepal as a 'host' society now occurs. One could argue that it always has been so, accommodating pilgrims, refugees and tourists in an ongoing process.

9. The role of technology and materials in south Asia, both in maintaining and changing social systems, has been considerable. The introduction of commodities such as Lancashire cottons, tea and opium during the colonial period had far-reaching effects on traditional social systems, including caste and craft organisation. More recent examples include tape cassettes and videos. Despite such innovations south Asian material culture also has persisting features. Nepal provides an example of an 'interface' society between the Great Traditions of Hinduism and Buddhism.

10. There are few Nepalese resident in the UK, but many British men have served with Gurkha soldiers and British tourists form the third largest group of visitors to Nepal: between ten and twenty thousand every year.

11. Figurative art is regarded as fine art in Buddhist and European studies, whilst utensils are regarded as decorative art. In Islamic studies, by contrast, utensils are classified as 'fine art' by Islamic and Western scholars.

12. One should note the existence of historical collections from various times and places: Mesopotamia and classical Greece, Rome, Japan, China and various parts of the Islamic world, which

preceded the European Renaissance and subsequent expansion.

13. The typical tourist in Nepal, as on a worldwide basis, is male, aged between 16 and 45 years (Feifer 1985: 223; Kyastha 1985: 24–5). Museum visitors are from heterogeneous backgrounds and personality types, with widely varying levels of literacy, visual–spatial understanding, mental activity, perception and motivation (Thompson *et al.* 1984: 377).

14. Wilson (1984: 58) argues that the primary aim of museum display is experiential, not didactic: '. . . objects . . . must speak for themselves'. Museum education officers (Goodhew, pers. comm.) prefer a didactic approach. Obviously consultation is a necessary, and currently fashionable, approach to the representation of 'other' cultures. At the same time, museum ethnographer/curators cannot ultimately abdicate from the position of the 'voice of authority', since that is the reason for their employment.

15. This dilemma is paralleled in the debate about collecting in a multicultural society: should one collect and show local communities their own material? This ignores the universal brief of ethnographic museums in favour of selective collecting for a limited number of cultures, and would tend to write countries such as Nepal and Tibet out of existence. There are few Nepalis and Tibetans resident in the UK. Or should one collect universally as circumstances allow, and show all communities the similarities and differences between societies? Again, there should surely be provision for both approaches rather than only one.

16. One should note here the reduction or lack of funding by the UK for institutions such as UNESCO, the ODA, the British Council and anthropological research.

17. '. . . culture is created, changed and re-created. It can be used, discarded, segmented and homogenised. Culture is a variegated, ad hoc assemblage of sets of practices, objects, meanings and symbols, some more closely related than others, but not a monolithic, homogenous, bounded entity which can be acted upon by outside forces and either fortified or undermined, commoditized or degraded – it is dynamic and adaptive' (V. King, pers. comm., 1991).

The social construction of reality is one of the major insights of social science. One of my personal reservations, however, is concerned with the limits of this perception when it fails to deal with physical 'reality'. Whilst the boot and knife are social action enough, not all reality is social in nature; and hunger and disease have a singular disregard for social mores, even if heavily influenced by social factors – people, like societies, die. The Ancient Mariner's approach is generally not favoured in tourism, anthropology or museums however. In all three activities there is a marked preference for presenting some kind of 'screened reality'.

18. What is experienced in 'given reality' versus 'experienced reality', especially with regard to photographic images (and museum displays?) needs to be analysed as a means to study stereotypes.

19. 'There is a sense in which the material expectations of tourism (of financial gain by locals) resemble latter day cargo cults' (F. Hughes-Freeland, pers. comm., 1991).

20. Some tourists also appropriate culture by means of ethnic encounters or gaining primary social relations with guides or 'the people', whilst other tourists are content to remain in impersonal, categoric social relationships. This need appears to cut across the difference between package and individual tourists, between lowlanders, trekkers and mountaineers. The repetitive nature of much turistica or many token souvenirs is in conflict with the desire for uniqueness in the tourist experience.

21. In the early 1980s it was estimated that 60 per cent of metalware production in the Kathmandu Valley was for sale on the local tourist market. Of this amount 10–15 per cent was bought by Nepalese buyers for re-sale. In 1991, informed opinion was that export orders for metalwares now earned more than sales on the local tourist market.

References

Acharya, N. (1991). Government and the Tourist Industry. *Image Nepal*, Jan.–Feb. Lalitpur: Monah Press.

Alsop, I. (1989). Highlights of the Newark Museum's Nepalese Collection. *Arts of Asia*, Sep.–Oct.

Alsop, I. and J. Charlton (1973). Image Casting in Oku Bahal. *Journal of Institute of Nepal and Asian Studies* 1(1): 22–49.

Ames, M. M. (1986). *Museums, the Public and Anthropology*. New Delhi: Concept Publishing Co.

Armington, S. (1982). *Trekking in the Himalayas*. South Yarra, Victoria: Lonely Planet Publications.

Bernstein, J. (1970). *The Wildest Dreams of Kew*. London: Allen and Unwin.

Birmingham, J. (1975). Traditional Potters of the Kathmandu Valley: An Ethno-archaeological Study. *Man* 10(3): 370–86.

Bista, D. B. (1987). *People of Nepal*. Kathmandu: Ratna Pustak Bhandar.

CBS (Central Bureau of Statistics) (1990). *Statistical Pocket Book, Nepal*. Kathmandu: His Majesty's Government of Nepal.

Cole, J. P. (1972). *Geography of World Affairs*. London: Penguin Books.

Concise Oxford Dictionary, 7th edn (1982). Oxford: Clarendon Press.

Cunningham, J. (1975). *Kingdom in the Sky*. London: Souvenir Press.

Dunsmore, S. (1993). *Nepalese Textiles*. London: British Museum Press.

Dutt, A. K. and M. M. Geib (1987). *Atlas of South Asia*. London: Westview Press.

Feifer, M. (1985). *Going Places*. London: Macmillan.

Fisher, J. F. (1987). *Trans-Himalayan Traders*. Delhi: Motilal Banarsidass.

Fisher, J. F. (1991). Has Success Spoiled the Sherpas? *Natural History* 91(2): 39–45.

Gajurel, C. L. and K. K. Vaidya (1984). *The Traditional Arts and Crafts of Nepal*. New Delhi: S. Chand.

Gimlette, G. H. D. (1886). *Nepal*. Colonial and Indian Exhibition Catalogue. London: HMSO.

Gimlette, G. H. D. (1890–1). The Art Industries of Nepal. *Journal of Indian Art* 3. London.

Graburn, N. H. H. (ed.) (1976). *Ethnic and Tourist Arts*. London: University of California Press.

Gurung, H. (1989). *Nepal. Dimensions of Development*. Kathmandu: Awarta Press.

Horne, D. (1984). *The Great Museum*. London: Pluto Press.

Iyer, P. (1989). *Video Night in Kathmandu*. London: Black Swan.

Jest, C. (1974). *Tarap, une vallée dans l'himalaya*. Paris: Seuil.

Jones, D. (1992). Dealing with the Past. *Museums Journal* Jan. 1992: 24–7.

Kar, C. (1952). *Indian Metal Sculpture*. London: Tiranti.

Kar, C. (1956). *Classical Indian Sculpture*. London: Tiranti.

Kroeber, A. L. and C. Kluckhohn (1952). Culture: A Critical Review of Concepts and Definitions. *Papers of the Peabody Museum of American Archaeology and Ethnology* vol. 47, no. 1, Cambridge, Mass.: Harvard University.

Kyastha, N. (1985). *Development of Tourism in Nepal for South Asia Regional Co-operation*. Kathmandu: Centre for Economic Development and Administration, Tribhuvan University.

Labriffe, M.-L. de (1973). Etude de la fabrication d'une statue au Nepal. *Kailash* 1(3): 185–92.

Landon, P. (1928). *Nepal*. London: Constable.

Leisure Opportunities 24.1.90 (London).

Lo Bue, E. (1981). Statuary Metals in Tibet and the Himalayas: History, Tradition and Modern Use. In W. A. Oddy and W. Zwalf (eds), *Aspects of Tibetan Metallurgy*. London: British Museum Publications.

Macdougal, C. (1979). *The Kulunge Rai*. Kathmandu: Bibliotheca Himalayica.

Macfarlane, A. (1976). *Resources and Population, A Study of the Gurungs of Nepal*. Cambridge: Cambridge University Press.

Malla, K. P. (1979). *The Road to Nowhere*. Kathmandu: Sajha Prakashan.

Mandelbaum, D. G. (1970). *Society in India*. Berkeley: University of California Press.

Michaels, A. (1988). *The Making of a Statue. Lost Wax Casting in Nepal*. Stuttgart: Franz Steiner Verlag Wiesbaden GMBH.

Naqvi, H. K. (1968). *Urban Centres and Industries in Upper India 1556–1803*. London: Asia Publishing House.

Pal, P. (1975). *Nepal, Where the Gods are Young*. New York: The Asia Society.

Pal, P. (1985). *Art of Nepal*. Los Angeles: University of California Press.

Palikhe, K. P. (1986). *Cottage Industries in Nepal*. Kathmandu: Sankalpa Press.

Peirson Jones, J. (1992). Multiculturalism Incarnate. *Museums Journal* Jan.: 32–3.

Pilkington, J. (1985). *Into Thin Air*. London: Allen and Unwin.

Reed, D. (1990). *Nepal. The Rough Guide*. London: Harrap–Columbus.

Robinson, F. (ed.) (1989). *The Cambridge Encyclopaedia of India, Pakistan, Bangladesh, Sri Lanka, Nepal, Bhutan and the Maldives*. Cambridge: Cambridge University Press.

Sakya, K. and L. Griffith (1980). *Tales of Kathmandu*. Brisbane: Kathmandu.

Singh, B. R. (1991). *Glimpses of Tourism, Airlines and Management in Nepal*. New Delhi: Nirala.

Slusser, M. S. (1982). *Nepal Mandala*. Princeton: Princeton University Press.

Smith, V. L. (1981). Controlled vs Uncontrolled Tourism. RAIN 46 (Oct.): 4–6.

Teague, K. (1988). The Nepalese Collections at the Horniman Museum. *Museum Ethnographers Newsletter* 22. Hull: Centre for South East Asian Studies, University of Hull.

Teague, K. (1996). The Museum Ethnographers' Group Survey of Ethnographic Collections in the United Kingdom: Suggestions for Further Developments. *Journal of Museum Ethnography* 5: 49–56.

Thompson, J. M. A. *et al.* (eds) (1984). *Manual of Curatorship: A Guide to Museum Practice*. London: Butterworth.

Toutain, P. (1986). *Nepal*. London: Merehurst Press.

Urry, J. (1990). *The Tourist Gaze, Leisure and Travel in Contemporary Societies*. London: Sage.

Williams, R. (1985). *Keywords*. London: Fontana.

Wilson, D. M. (1984). *National Museums*. In J. M. A. Thompson, *et al.* (eds), *Manual of Curatorship*. London: Butterworth.

10

The South–east Asian 'Living Museum' and its Antecedents

Michael Hitchcock, Nick Stanley and Siu, King Chung

Post-colonial consciousness has made anthropological representation a vexed issue in Europe and North America. In South-east Asia, however, it has found a new home and rationale, particularly in cultural village museums. Modelled on earlier European folk village museums, these Asian ethnographic displays provide space for tangible and symbolic expressions of modernisation. Elements of the past are portrayed as an integral part of the future in a rapidly changing socio-political climate. Visited by both foreign and domestic tourists, these museums provide venues for national constructions of identity derived from an exemplary past.

Open-air museums dedicated to the popular anthropological topics can be visited in many Asia–Pacific countries. Some of these museums deal with the lives of ordinary people, whereas others concentrate on high cultural traditions, such as Asian court culture. Most follow the cultural village format, and these museums usually comprise a collection of traditional buildings. The buildings are often used to display arts and crafts and serve as venues for music and dance performances. Many employ actors to help re-create old traditions in a living environment. Two of the most impressive of these open-air museums are located in Indonesia (Taman Mini) and South China (Shenzhen).

China Folk Culture Villages

In Shenzhen in Guandong Province in China a tourist development complex has sprung up on the shores of Shenzhen Bay, just over the border from Hong Kong. It is located in the Special Economic Zone, which is financed with Hong Kong capital. Beside the Shenzhen Bay Hotel are three separate but interrelated displays. The first, Splendid China, opened in October 1989, as the 'world's largest miniature scenic spot' of over 30 hectares. It offers the visitor China's scenic attractions, historical sites and folk customs and dwellings all in a single visit. The second display, China Folk Culture Villages (FCV) opened next door in October 1991. In the FCV there are 24 life-size 'villages' (usually comprising two or more buildings large enough to accommodate at least a dozen performers and a continually moving audience of 100 or more), providing a setting for 21 selected minority nationalities. To complete the complex, The World's Windows is under construction. It is designed to work in the same way as the Folk Culture Villages, but brings the rest of the world to China in the form of roughly 50 of the world's great natural and humanly-made wonders, including the Eiffel Tower (already completed), Mount Fuji and the Pyramids.

In January 1992 Deng Xiaoping visited Shenzhen, emphasising official support for the economic experiment that not only created the Shenzhen stock exchange but laid the plans for greyhound racing and other tourist facilities. The most significant and widely reported aspect of Deng's visit to Shenzhen was his tour of the Folk Culture Villages, where he was photographed in a US-made Cushman courtesy carriage. As can be seen by the following extract from one Westerner's comments, the folk culture displays are sometimes seen simply as a theme park 'Here are . . . replicas of non-Chinese "minority villages" to be compulsively photographed and at night a stunning show of stilt walkers, acrobats with kids on their shoulders and a wedding procession with gongs and other attractions.' The journalist continues: 'The show ends in an approved Western theme park spectacular style with multicoloured lasers playing rhythmically on the pulsating waters of a computer-controlled fountain' (Gittins 1992). Whilst this description is accurate enough as far as it goes (except that non-Han minorities are definitely not seen as non-Chinese), it fails to grasp two fundamentally important aspects of the Folk Culture Villages, which distinguish them radically from the normal Western theme park.

The Folk Culture Villages project is designed to fill a number of functions: 'to carry forward Chinese culture in a more vigorous way, to let the world have a better understanding of China, to help boost Chinese tourism and to promote friendship between the Chinese people and people of other nations' (Chinese Folk Cultural Villages official brochure). Only one of its central purposes is then to represent

China; yet the programme evolved may at first appear somewhat paradoxical. By explicit design the Han majority scarcely receives a mention. Instead, as the international publicity announces

> In the Folk Culture Villages there are 24 sets of buildings including mountain villages, residential compounds, streets and markets. Each of them has its characteristic feature forming a relatively independent 'small community'. Among the 86 building units are 65 civilian residencies and 21 supplementary structures, occupying an area of 21,000 square metres. In addition there are 8 fairly large open-air singing and dancing grounds. Performances of folk songs and dances of different nationalities are to be given in 16 villages (China Travel Services 1992: 18).

Through the construction of a museum the exemplary display provides a kaleidoscope of pluralism held together with the cement of nationalist rhetoric.

It is tempting to see the FCV as merely the window-dressing of a centralised state displaying a liberality in ethnological matters. The Folk Culture Villages cannot be dismissed merely as a Disneyland of fables drawn from a mythical past dressed up as an advertiser's confection. It bears marked similarities with another thirty-year-old ethnic tourist display, the Polynesian Cultural Centre in Hawaii (Webb 1994: 59–86). The display at Shenzhen is not stripped of historical or cultural references, but responds to and reflects aspects of the history of China's policy for minority peoples. The exhibition attempts some revisionist readings and implicitly claims that, if proper care is taken, all cultures and their artistic products can be accorded equal respect and attention. The significance in the Shenzhen Folk Culture Villages lies in the strategies adopted to interpret and evaluate this range of material and symbolic worlds.

What Gittins' report on Shenzhen fails to note are these two features: first, the museum display provides a new arena for the development of a more complex nationalism, which no longer stresses an evolutionary model of cultural development from primitive to modern (i.e. industrialised and urban). Second, Gittins' attention to the more obvious technical and marketing innovations prevents him from recognising some highly traditional features that persist in the midst of novelty. Both of these aspects are considered here.

The Folk Culture Villages are built on the site of a former amusement park in Shenzhen Bay. The contents of the amusement park were sold on to an operation in Sichuan for HK$30,000,000. A most ambitious programme has been realised with Hong Kong finance and local planning and construction in a remarkably short time. The twenty-four life-size 'villages' are set in a V-shaped site on the shore of Shenzhen Bay. The two-kilometre-long lake of Cuihu provides a central focus, stretching up the middle of both arms of the display. This watercourse provides the Folk Culture Villages with the opportunity to create some twelve different bridges in stone, hardwood and bamboo. The bridges also echo architectural features in the village buildings. These buildings have had a great amount of attention paid to correct architectural representation and construction techniques. But, interestingly, they also offer evidence of 'reform of practice' philosophy, a feature of China's government minorities policy. For example, the Bouyi, Dai and Zhuang houses follow reformed design principles, separating humans from livestock in the *ganlan* structure, rather than, as tradition would dictate, with animals on the ground floor and humans on the first floor above the animal pen.

The FCV can be seen as an example of a more general movement, and in Kunming, Yunnan Province, a similar project has been mounted:

> Covering an area of 2.7 hectares the village has, in addition to the White Pagoda, five residential houses, two Dai-style buildings and other constructions including a Burmese-style temple and a so-called Wind and Rain Bridge. The first residents were fifty Dai people. Next to the Dai village, a 6.7 hectare Bai village has begun to take shape . . . local officials say that Yunnan Province has 26 ethnic groups and each has its own colourful customs and practices. Thus 26 different ethnic villages will be built beside Lake Dianchi to form a unique cultural scenic group.

The same process also operates at a more local level. Xijiang village in Guizhou, for example, has been developed as a 'natural museum of traditional Miao [Hmong] lifestyle'. The FCV should also be seen as part of a contemporary architectural trend in China, the 'Old Town' idiom, widely employed to provide a conscious copy of antique building in the design of streets and neighbours. But 'antique-modern' schemes offer the most significant opportunity to preserve antiquities:

> Many of the 'traditional' Dong structures remained in disrepair and locals could not afford to put on extravagant rituals which the tourists could observe. They had not the wealth, in other words, to reconstruct a tradition for tourist consumption. Far from threatening a traditional landscape, modernization was awaited as the impetus for rebuilding what outsiders expected to be there (Oates 1992: 11).

FCV does not only display physical evidence of a more widespread official tourist strategy. Much of the Folk Culture Villages concept builds upon the work of the State Nationalities Affairs Commission, particularly with reference to culture, language, education and economic development. The themes of the Folk Culture Villages echo directly elements of the minorities policy. 'Habits and customs', a term employed in the policy to express the essential rights of minority peoples, provides the theme under which all the exhibits are organised. These rights concern both religious and special cultural requirements. For example, the policies on national minorities lay emphasis upon respecting the religious sensibilities of Muslim nationalities: these are partially satisfied with special dietary arrangements. The policies also stress minority rights with regard to special forms of dress and costume. Indeed, so important is the issue of dress that one of the fifteen departments of the Folk Culture Villages is devoted entirely to costume. Costume designers modify original designs to create new ones appropriate for performers. The department also commissions ethnic costume manufacturers in regions like Yunnan, Mongolia and Xinjiang to complete large orders. Costumes provide the emblematic marker and identifier throughout the Villages. Costumes are like uniforms in terms of their narrowness in design variation. The constant reiterating of a common design solution – each nationality is provided with both male and female costumes – creates some special challenges for the costume department. In common with many minority peoples worldwide, the same tendency for males to forsake ethnic dress earlier than females is encountered in China. The Bai men's costume worn in the Bai Village offers a male version of the female garb rather than a contemporary model, which would be the standard form of trousers worn elsewhere in China. This is only one of many issues that the Villages have had to face in making decisions over what 'reality' to present. There is an added irony, no doubt familiar to all performers and viewers in the Folk Culture Villages, that from the Cultural Revolution until 1978 the wearing of ethnic dress was problematic and often discouraged, though, as the official record states 'some areas did infringe the above policy' (Information China 1989: 1283). The renewed promotion of ethnic dress can either be viewed as a proper restoration of previous practices and official policies on minority nationalities, or, alternatively, it can be judged more as a cynical marketing of exotic non-Han designs and costumes worn indifferently by the performers and guides. Of course, both views may be held simultaneously. In this case the significance of costume may be unstable, and likely to shift according to context.

Context in the Folk Culture Villages is provided initially through architecture, a rather difficult medium in which to give actions significant meaning. Although the villages are designed to offer a form of authenticity (the Zhuang bedroom, for example has a hand-crafted bed and chest of drawers as well as a set of 'ethnic' clothes hung on the wall and a bright new electric fan), they remain exhibits, and suggest little if any sense of being lived in. There are few if any marks of personal investment. This highlights, perhaps, Graburn's contention that the content of tourist arts 'consists of signs rather than symbols' (Graburn 1976: 17), signs that point but do not provide context. The only areas that provide any sense of communication are the small sales areas in some of the villages (like the Bai). The way that architecture and costume are brought together is through the festival. In line with the official minorities policy the Folk Culture Villages celebrate minority nationality festivals and holidays. The official programme lists twelve such festivals throughout the year. Interestingly, five of these are specifically Han (the lantern festival, the dragon boat, the birthday of the goddess of the sea, the mid-autumn and the kite festival). No doubt this arrangement reflects the pattern of holidays for visitors as much as for performers. Festivals are further broken down into performances of elements of festivals. For this purpose a song and dance routine has been arranged by the Folk Culture Villages' department of performance management. Such performances usually take place either in the environment of the village during the day or in the central theatre for the 'evening party' or show. There are nine folk and dance performances per hour during the day by the respective nationalities, as well as lunch-time and evening performances at the central theatre. The visitor is therefore bound to see at least three or four performances during her or his visit. This certainly is further increased by many of the performances turning into processions along the lake. The department of ethnological arts researches minority arts and customs and makes proposals to the ethnic affairs committee for execution. Thus the aspects of festival that permeate the display serve to unite architecture, folk customs, dress and performance into a single entity. The Folk Culture Villages have also incorporated the food and drink associated with festivals into many of the displays, which have associated food counters.

The Villages plan was conceptualised under two headings: the 'hardware' consists of the physical construction and layout of the site, the physical environment. The software is the human element – the seven thousand employees working in the Folk Culture Villages. The personnel undergo a fairly rigorous programme of training that lays considerable stress on the political context in terms of the Communist Party and official policy as well as the particular circumstances of the Shenzhen Special Economic Zone. The 1991 training programmes were created to:

> make clear the principle of 'training for the practical'; the training programme should aim at the uniqueness of the minority performers and their craftsmen, and to pay special attention to the trainees' actual cultural disposition as well as their abilities in order to raise the average level of performance as a whole. Through a short training programme the trainee's psychological (political) readiness will be reinforced for the various performances in the Folk Culture Villages.[1]

Whilst the programme may be 'short-term' it is certainly not short. In the original plan there is a total of 294 training hours, devoted to ten areas of learning and training. The list is instructive. The first three elements provide a short context: item one covers the Party's basic direction and the initial stages of socialism (8 hours); item two, the party open-door reforms and the development and construction of the Special Economic Zone (4 hours); item three, the development of the Overseas Chinese Town and its legal regulations (4 hours). The next two units introduce the Folk Culture Villages Philosophy. Item four deals with basic knowledge of tourist culture (4 hours), whilst five provides an introduction to a theory of public relations (12 hours). The sixth element deals with basic knowledge of folklore and ethnology (22 hours). Language acquisition (item seven) is accorded a large segment of the training programme (96 hours for Mandarin, Cantonese and English). The remaining three items receive equal weighting (48 hours each). These cover basic principles of music (score reading, music theory and audio-visual practice), training in personal presentation, and finally, performance training.

This programme was later slimmed down to 161 hours, but still remains a substantial undertaking. The objectives of the training programme are threefold: firstly, to adapt to these changing working conditions of the reformed environment in the Special Economic Zone and to become attuned to the changed working conditions and lifestyles. Secondly, the training is designed to 'understand the value and importance of Chinese ethnicities and their arts, customs and cultures' and to develop a knowledge of and pride in the Folk Culture Villages.

The third objective is to increase levels of aesthetic awareness and to develop personal skills in performance, language, presentation and interpersonal skills in the context of the tourist industry. The training programme in the summer of 1992 was augmented by a six-week formal programme at Guangzhou Chinese Tutorial Institute of 160 hours. The ten courses offered cover much the same territory as the earlier programme. The only significant changes were in the reduction of the language component, the withdrawal of performance training (probably because the facilities were not available in Guangzhou) and the introduction of a new item 'developing spiritual civilisation and general knowledge in legal matters'.

A discernible shift in management style has occurred at the end of the first two-year cycle. Some performers have stayed on (most of the Yi, for example). Performers from other venues are now recruited on six-month contracts to engender a new competitive attitude amongst the performance groups. With the increasing popularity of the ethnic village market in China there is now an ever-expanding pool of potential performers for the management of the FCV to draw upon.

The training programme has to take into account the special circumstances concerning recruitment, namely that the performers have come directly from their home territories into the Special Economic Zone, without stopping, so to speak, in the more ordinary conditions in the rest of China. It is this fact, of course, that provides a major incentive for the performers to volunteer to work in the Folk Culture Villages in the first place. Not only are they able to earn money that they are able to remit home for the purchase of durables like electrical appliances, but they are also located in the most advanced economic sector of China.[2] The minority nationality performers thus leapfrog from some of the least developed regions of China directly into the most economically advanced. This achievement is only possible, however, through the paradox of displaying elements of traditional culture in a new way in a highly innovative and rapidly changing world.

These special circumstances inevitably produce the possibility of stress and conflict. As the Folk Culture Village March 1991 training programme notes:

> In dealing with minority trainees, it is necessary to put in more emotional investment, to promote understanding and constant communication; building on such premises the following four relations should be dealt with appropriately:

1. the relation between modern civilisation and the minorities' life style,
2. the relation between the minority religions and corresponding policies,
3. the positive relations among different minority groups,
4. the equal and respectful relations between the Han nationality and the other minorities.

As the Director of the Folk Culture Villages noted at the time:

> The group of minority employees is composed of teenagers aged between 17 and 20. Most of them are naive and have not left home long. Especially as they have to receive long training and adapt to different living habits they could become homesick and run away. This could occur at any time. Therefore I propose that a high-standing policy officer with considerable patience, a middle-aged female, should be appointed as a political counsellor to look after the extra-curricular arrangements and the trainees' behaviour.

Evidently, the Folk Culture Villages provide potential for social and managerial headaches. In our interview with the Director of the Villages Mr Ma explained that in the work contract intimate relations between different minorities were not encouraged, 'otherwise the people working in the Folk Culture Villages would be Hannised themselves'. On the other hand, working together provided individuals with the opportunity to interact and learn from each other. Similarly, Village employees might be tempted to marry local people to obtain residency in either Shenzhen or Hong Kong. To prevent this a 'Beyond the Eight Hours of Work Consultation Committee' has been established.

There is in the very concept of the Folk Culture Villages a tension that inevitably affects the representatives of minority cultures. The performers are caught, as it were, in a contradiction between the apparently stable environment of their home minority region and the impetus that attracts them to the Villages, offering a modern and plural environment open to international influences.

Performing in the Folk Culture Villages must create tension between the two polar alternatives: on the one side, homesickness and the desire to return, and on the other, the unfolding vision of another world with markedly different career perspectives. This would argue for a rapid turnover of personnel in the Villages, which would underscore the importance of a continually evolving training programme. Inevitably, this raises in turn the question of the selection of cultures deemed appropriate for incorporation and malleable to the Folk Culture Villages philosophy and management ethos.

The Selection of Cultures

The name 'China Folk Culture Villages' (Zhongguo Minsu Wenhua Cun) specifically avoids employing the term 'ethnic minorities' (shao shu minzu) in favour of a homophonic neologism 'people's customs' (minsu). This new term was chosen by the experts 'after long deliberation, to show the harmony of the races'. A decision was made to bypass the sensitive argument about the basis of selection, and more significantly, for exclusion. The Folk Culture Villages only represent a choice of 'people's customs', not necessarily total 'ethnic nationalities'. The display attempts to incorporate as many nationalities as possible within the limitations of space. If a nationality is not represented directly in its own village, aspects of the culture might yet be offered, for example, in the song and dance of the theatrical display. The brochure for the Folk Culture Village neatly avoids the issue:

> For a faithful reflection of the folk customs and practices, hundreds of artists and service workers belonging to 21 nationalities have been recruited for performances and service work in the villages from urban and rural areas in ten provinces and autonomous regions where most national minorities are living. Carnivals of national arts, song and dance performances by professional artists and folk festive celebrations have been organised and an exhibition hall of folk customs has been built, all ready to welcome visitors who wish to have a taste of the colourful cultures of China's 56 nationalities.

Nevertheless, some fairly hard decisions have had to be taken. Twenty-one nationalities are represented in the Folk Culture Villages. This means, of course, that thirty-three are not. The selection is not a representative sample based on the demographic or geographic distribution of China's ethnic minority populations. Indeed, the contrast is instructive. All the nationalities having a population of over a million are represented, even if, sometimes, as in the case of the Hui, their presence is restricted to representation only in the performances. The basis of selection for the smaller ethnic groups is less easy to establish. The formal principle 'originating from real life but rising above it, and discarding dross and selecting the essential' is evoked in the official brochure, which also reminds the reader that the Folk Culture Villages are not an exact reproduction of real life. The argument appears to be that there is a kind of distillation of ideal characteristics that the creators of the Villages were looking for. The Mosou people, part of the Naxi ethnic group of Yunnan, is represented simply because it is a matrilineal society. As such, this people is, in Chinese terms, unique in its social structure. On the other hand, despite a population in excess of seven million, the Hui are not represented because, it is suggested, their culture is so similar to that of the Uygur from Xinjiang. They are therefore eliminated on the grounds of duplication. Another reason for disqualification is smallness of population. If there are only a few hundred people in an ethnic group then it is not deemed necessary to include them. Nevertheless, the smallest 'nationality', the Gaoshan (1,500) from Fujian are well represented – possibly because these people also live in Taiwan, from where many visitors are expected to come. Taiwan has its own 'cultural parks' for minority peoples, which are also popular tourist attractions.

Other considerations of a more display-oriented nature enter into the selection criteria. The Mosou are selected not only for cultural reasons but also because their architecture is unique. Gender ratios are also considered important. The policy is to hire a ratio of seven women to three men. The Director of the Folk Culture villages explained that beautiful female performers are more attractive to visitors, especially to male visitors from Hong Kong. This decision is further justified on the basis of display. In traditional Chinese society, the Director maintains, more women are engaged in handicrafts than men. It is also impossible within the confines of the Folk Culture Village environment to show men engaged in typical occupations like farming or hunting. Men, however, have their uses. In the Hani display – a society where smoking is very widespread – men are employed to smoke all day rather than women, as such a spectacle involving women would be unacceptable to the visitors.

There is, nevertheless, a cultural agenda discernible in the architecture of the Folk Culture Villages. At first sight the prominence of the Tibetan exhibits is puzzling. Not only is there a large Tibetan stone watch-tower, peopled with a good complement of performers, but also a large separate building on a small hill constructed as a Tibetan Lamasery. The interior of this latter building has large frescos that advance a political message: the scene represents 'the marriage ceremony of King Zongzan Ganbu of Tibet and Princess Wencheng, the adopted daughter of the Tang Emperor Li Shiming'.[3] The Chinese government continues to validate its disputed claim to Tibet with reference to this dynastic marriage. The grandeur of the Lamasery and the detailing of the site and interior give it and the watch-tower a pre-eminence out of proportion to the population's size. Perhaps the status of Tibetan culture in the Folk Culture Villages reflects the attention that the nationality has received in Chinese academic study of late. The 1990/1 *People's Republic of China Yearbook* emphasises how much research work on Tibetan studies has taken place in the last two years, particularly the 'King Gesar' international academic seminar held in Chengdu.

If the Tibetan exhibits underscore the significance of that culture, the mosque provides a contrary puzzle. The exhibition is significantly named 'Moslem architecture'. This approach – purely architectural – contrasts very markedly with all the other displays. In this display there are none of the normal Skansen-like 'living pictures': there are no interiors, no culture or performances. Most significantly, there are no nationalities mentioned. Yet ten of the fifty-five minority nationalities are Muslim, and four of them, Hui, Uygur, Kazak and Dong, are represented in the Villages. Yet none of these displays makes significant reference to Islamic social or religious features. What there is in the newly opened mosque is merely a bazaar for the sale of Uygur products; textiles, carpets and a wall of highly variegated paintings. The display suggests that Islam has to be seen to be addressed – perhaps for architectural purposes, as there are Buddhist and Taoist structures represented in the Villages. But the practice of Islam seems quite unassimilable to the general design of the set; no bridge is offered to link the religion to its adherents.

Visitors to the Folk-Culture Villages

The organisation of the Folk Culture Villages is, as some of the observations on selection criteria above suggest, market-oriented. There are three quite different audiences that are catered for in the display. Each of these is constantly present, and to some extent interactive with the other two. The declared objective is to bring in an audience from outside China. In the first instance Hong Kong provides both a channel for an international audience and also a conduit for Hong Kong residents. Twenty per cent of the visitors come from Macao, Taiwan, Hong Kong and elsewhere. This audience represents a significant proportion of the total. Another small but highly significant section are officials from China, for whom the Folk Culture Villages represent an element of the modern Shenzhen experience alongside the other elements of the new economic policy. Most of the nation's leaders, such as Li Peng, Yang Shang Kun, Jiang Zemin and Wan Li, have visited the Villages and, like Deng Xiaoping, have been publicly photographed for the press there. Such official interest at the highest level no doubt prompts others less exalted to undertake reconnaissance visits for themselves.

Finally, nearly 80 per cent of the visitors are members of the Chinese public, mainly from Guangdong and neighbouring provinces. These come as part of their new 'developmental experience', and as part of a new phenomenon, Chinese tourists, intent on combining an exploration of this internationally-oriented display with a feature which should not be overlooked, pure enjoyment. Whilst the Villages offer astonishing features like the artificial waterfall 'like white ribbons fluttering in mid-air and pearls rebounding in all directions', they still retain aspects of the traditional fair – such as entertainers with performing monkeys. Indeed the visitors to the Villages are provided with photo opportunities, such as sitting in the Tibetan house at a table, toasting the camera with the Tibetan beakers conveniently provided. The Lahu big wheel similarly provides an ethnically inflected fairground attraction. It would be wrong, however, to overemphasise this aspect of the Villages.

The ethnographic and educational mission of the enterprise remains constantly visible. Indeed, the third audience for the Folk Culture Villages is the minority national visitor. As the director of the Villages remarks:

> they are concerned about their ethnic dignity. They are curious as to how they are being represented in terms of their architecture, dance, handicraft and food. They come to see whether they are accurately represented. Even minority leaders come to visit their performances. Officials from Tibet, Xinjiang, Mongolia and Korean nationalities have seen the Folk Culture Villages and found it well done and very satisfying.

The Director argued that these leaders felt that the Folk Culture Villages provided a channel to let the rest of the world understand their cultures. Indeed, the Chairman of the State Nationalities Affairs Commission in Beijing, Ismael Asmat, is reported as speaking very highly of the Villages.

All three audiences have ample opportunity not only to see the exhibits but to observe each other. The throughput of visitors is very high. In the first six months of existence three million visitors have been entertained. The highest record for a day stands at 40,000. This puts Shenzhen in the major league of tourist attractions, and on par with such spectacles as Disney World.

Taman Mini

It remains unclear precisely when the cultural village concept was introduced to South-east Asia; though the modern open-air museums owe much to local inspiration, they did not develop in isolation. The idea for these seems to have taken root in the early decades of the twentieth century in the countries that were under colonial rule, and their development may be linked to the growth in tourism.

The Dutch, for example, introduced tourism in Bali shortly after the pacification of the island between 1906 and 1908. This was not only an economic measure, since it was also designed to restore the Netherlands' international image, which had been tarnished by the bloody campaigns needed to subdue the island. To the colonial authorities, tourism appeared to be an effective means of restoring respectability to a regime blighted by turmoil. The authorities decided to revive what they perceived to be the 'real' way of life of the islanders and turn Bali into a 'living museum'. The Balinese were deemed to be the custodians of a Hindu culture that had flourished before the collapse of the kingdom of Majapahit and the triumph of Islam in Java (Picard 1993: 74).

One of the first museums in Asia to make use of traditional buildings and open-air display areas was the Bali Museum in Denpasar in the Netherlands East Indies (now Indonesia). The museum, which had serious educational objectives, was developed in conjunction with the rise in tourism in Bali in the inter-war years. Western painters, musicologists and anthropologists witnessed the rejuvenation of Balinese arts and performances, which arose partly in response to tourism in the 1920s. This development continued in the 1930s, despite the worldwide recession (Boon 1977). Walter Spies, the German-Russian painter, became the Curator of the Bali Museum, a museum that combined the two principal architectural edifices in Bali, the temple and the palace. In his capacity as Curator, Spies was responsible for organising the cultural programme for the visit of the Viceroy of the Netherlands East Indies. Spies had the task of welcoming the distinguished visitor and showing him the Balinese treasures that he had collected and therefore saved from the souvenir hunters (Rhodius and Darling 1980: 41). It was museums such as the Bali Museum that later served as local models for the development of cultural village museums in the post-war era in South-east Asia. There is, however, some evidence that the developers of the major open-air museums looked further afield, especially to Europe and North America, when designing cultural village-type museums.

The Dutch were responsible for introducing the museum concept to what was to become Indonesia; but it was not until well after the formation of Suharto's 'New Order' government that museum building on a monumental scale began in earnest. The first major development, *Taman Mini,* commenced at the behest of the second president's wife, Mrs Tien Suharto, at an estimated cost of US$26 million (May 1978: 277). In late August, 1971, Mrs Suharto attributed her decision to build the complex to the sudden inspiration that occurred during a recent visit to Disneyland: 'I was inspired to build a Project of that sort in Indonesia, only more complete [lengkap] and more perfect, adapted to fit the situation and developments in Indonesia, both "materially" [materiil] and "spiritually" [spirituil]' (Pemberton 1989: 215). Mrs Suharto announced the scheme in November 1971 amid polite protests and small student demonstrations, though it was widely condemned in private as a waste of national resources.

The plan was to build an open-air museum devoted to Indonesian architecture, arts and crafts on a site measuring approximately 1,350 by 580 metres near Jakarta. In a lavish brochure, Mrs Tien Suharto placed emphasis on her desire to 'develop and deepen the love of the Indonesian people for their fatherland', though the first promotional point mentioned was the attraction of tourists (May 1978: 277).

The museum was to be called *Taman Mini Indonesia Indan (taman,* 'garden'; *mini,* 'miniature'; *indah,* 'beautiful') and was designed to display the enormous diversity of Indonesia's population. The centre-piece was to be a miniature version of the Indonesian Archipelago, set in a lake, which included a 'tall and dignified monument' to reflect the national philosophy of *pancasila* (five principles put forward by the state for political and social rule) (May 1978: 277). The museum was created to celebrate the national motto of *bhinneka tunggal ika* 'unity in diversity', and to draw attention to Indonesia's exemplary traditional culture.

In order to appreciate why *Taman Mini* should serve as a showpiece for Indonesian identity, it is necessary to consider briefly how the nation came into being. It is important to note that Indonesia's political space was created as a result of many centuries of Dutch colonial interference. Dutch expansion in South-east Asia came to a halt during the first two decades of the twentieth century, thus laying down the borders of what was to become the Indonesian motherland (Hubinger 1992: 14). The inhabitants of this vast region, regardless of their ethnic or religious affiliation, shared Dutch overlordship, and this introduced a kind of negatively defined consciousness of an entity known as 'Indonesia'. According to Hubinger, Indonesian nationalism is a created reality, which is derived from the Herderian brand of nationalism, in which the nation's founders are its people, the 'folk' (1992: 4).

In 1975 a 174-hectare site was cleared near Jakarta, and 27 pavilions were erected, representing the provinces of Indonesia. The 300 families whose houses and gardens were razed to make way for the site complained that the compensation, fixed by the sponsors at 100 Rupiahs per square metre, was insufficient (May 1978: 278). Adnan Bujung Nasution's legal aid/public defence institute became involved in defending the householders, but did not pursue the matter. At the height of the dispute, powerless though the home-owners were, Mrs Suharto claimed that she would go on fighting for her project as long as she lived (May 1978: 278).

It is possible that the expenditure of $26 million on a tourist project at a time when Indonesia badly needed other kinds of investment (industrial infrastructure, schools, etc.) was justified in the long run. Critics have, however, noted that the land was purchased and the plans made public in advance of any sound evaluation of the scheme. Despite reassurances from the government that the museum would be examined in terms of profitability, and its benefits compared to those of other forms of development, the project went ahead. By 1990, when tourism in Indonesia had moved into fourth place as an earner of foreign exchange, outstripping rubber and coffee, these objections had largely been forgotten.

The Skansen Movement

Museums such as the Bali Museum, though devoted to Asian ethnography, belong to the wider tradition of European open-air museums. The forerunner of the cultural village museum made its appearance at the turn of the century, though there is some dispute regarding its origins. Skansen near Stockholm is widely regarded as the first of its kind, though this is disputed by the Norwegians. What is significant as far as this chapter is concerned is that a strong sense of nationalism, particularly ethnonationalism, can be detected in the work of the founder of Skansen, Arthur Hazelius.

When Hazelius travelled in Sweden's rural hinterland in the 1850s and 1860s he noticed that the traditional forms of village life were disappearing as a result of the growth of industries and modern communications. Hazelius was convinced that if future generations were to be able to understand what Sweden had been like, then collections had to be formed before the material disappeared. The museum was to provide a vital link between the ancient and the modern. Hazelius started acquiring objects in the 1870s, and eventually mounted a small exhibition in Stockholm. In 1878 Hazelius broke new ground by displaying scenes from country life using models dressed in Swedish costume set against reconstructions of peasant rooms; he called them 'living pictures'. Hazelius was motivated not just by social science, but by nationalism, and wanted, among other things, to purify the Swedish language of foreign loanwords (Hudson 1987: 120).

Hazelius arranged for the purchase of the site known as Skansen in 1891, the original displays comprising two wooden and stone cottages, as well as a Saami camp and two charcoal burners' huts. Development continued with the purchase and re-erection of buildings from all over Sweden. Houses, farms, workshops and mills were reassembled at Skansen, and in 1911 an open-air theatre was added. Folk dancing was also introduced, and a special area was set aside for performances in the 1930s. The world's first cultural village museum was undoubtedly popular, and by 1938 was attracting two million visitors per annum (Hudson 1987: 122).

From the outset the museum aimed to provide relaxation as well as education. The first café opened in 1892; in 1952 a restaurant was added, with seating for 800 people inside, and an additional 1,000 outside on the terraces in summer (Hudson 1987: 122). By the time that he died in 1901, Hazelius had the satisfaction of knowing that his concept of an open-air museum was not only being copied elsewhere, but was also extremely popular.

Hazelius' approach was undoubtedly highly original, but he was not working in an academic vacuum. Hazelius' approach was in keeping with the intellectual climate of the time. For example, at the same time that Hazelius was formulating his ideas, the German scholar, Ferdinand Tönnies, was working on his book *Gemeinschaft und Gesellschaft* (1887). Tönnies was born into a North German rural family and had an abiding interest in the development of rural life. Like Hazelius, Tonnies was interested in describing the way of life of ordinary people in North Germany and the changes that were taking place in response to increasing urbanisation and industrialisation.

In retrospect, Hazelius' ideas seem somewhat romantic, if not a little naïve, and there is a certain 'folksiness' about Skansen that has more to do with European ethnonationalism than serious Swedish ethnography. To a certain extent Skansen reflects how Hazelius and his nationalist-oriented folklorist movement wanted us to see Sweden, though one cannot dismiss the quality of some of the underlying ethnographic research. Hazelius' concept spread rapidly, and the early twentieth century saw the introduction of Skansen-type museums across the length and breadth of Europe. Open-air museums dedicated to the lives of ordinary people were, for example, opened in the Netherlands (Arnhem) in 1911; in Wales (St Fagans) in 1949 and in Ulster (Cultra) in 1958 (Hudson 1987: 125–7). Open-air museums inspired by the example of Skansen, but not necessarily the folklife principles advocated by Hazelius, were also set up in North America. Perhaps the most striking similarities between Skansen and one of its descendants are encountered in Romania.

The opening of the Village Museum in Bucharest in 1936 repre-sented the culmination of ten years of research under the leadership of Professor Dimitrie Gusti. Mixed-disciplinary teams of sociologists, ethnographers and students recorded the customs and culture, and particularly the material culture, of the inhabitants of forty Romanian villages, under the supervision of Victor Ion Popa and H. H. Stahl. Traditional houses were taken down and reassembled in the museum by craftsmen from their villages of origin, and the research teams also made collections in each of the villages, supported by careful documentation and photography. The researchers set themselves the task of recording Romanian popular culture by showing the daily activities of a '. . . householder's family from each village' (Negota 1986: 21). Like Skansen, the Village Museum was built beside a lake near a major urban conurbation that had a poor, rural hinterland. The parallels with Shenzhen and Taman Mini are striking.

Despite their success, the village museums were not without their critics. Hudson, for example, asks whether or not dancing and farm animals can really bring to life the world of nineteenth-century Sweden? The cultural context of Skansen has changed, and the society that visitors see in the museum today is more remote from their experience than it was from the first urban tourists who went there. Modern Skansen is more exotic than it was at the time of its foun-dation, and a greater effort is required on the part of the visitor to imagine what life must have been like in reality (Hudson 1987: 124). As G. B. Thompson has noted, there are two in-built weaknesses in folk village movements. First, the transfer of materials to the museum may romanticise them, especially when they are restored and kept in good repair. When the buildings are cleaned up, many of the unpleasant associations that they had for the people who once lived in them are removed. Second, only a special kind of society is represented – rural society. Hazelius felt that it was the rural way of life that was disappearing, and townspeople tended not to be represented. There were also practical considerations, since it was usually only rural buildings that could be transported, because they were wooden (Hudson 1987: 125). In practice, attention is devoted to the material culture of the pre-industrial age, and what we are left with is a collection of attractive buildings.

The Asia—Pacific Cultural Village

In the case of Taman Mini and Shenzhen, what is interesting is that they both portray nations that are simultaneously ethnically diverse, but unified. In the case of Shenzhen it is the non-Han minority cultures that are represented, whereas Taman Mini promotes the national philosophy of 'Unity in Diversity' and, in theory, embraces all the nation's ethnic groups. For Indonesians, the creation of a united nation-state involved either shedding 'ethnic' identities (seen as symbols of backwardness within the process of modernisation) or reconceptualising them as part of the nation's past, its 'folk culture' and hitherto 'living traditions'. In the development of Taman Mini these traditions were to be displayed and admired by both the local and international public. This represents a continuation of the earlier European practice of celebrating the nation's brilliant present and admirable past through exhibitions (Hubinger 1992: 7). Both Taman Mini and Shenzhen present varying aspects of nationhood and, through their exemplary displays, show a kaleidoscope of peoples held together by nationalistic rhetoric. Although the outward appearance of these museums closely resembles that of their European prototypes, their underlying philosophies differ greatly.

Museums have been set up in the Asia–Pacific region with the development of national culture very much in mind. The ethnographic exhibition has become a popular medium in Asia, where the tourist's curiosity has been harnessed to the needs of nationalist politics. Audiences, as yet, seem to be unconcerned with issues such as ethnographic accuracy and authenticity, and the displays are often quite eclectic. Genuine ethnographic artefacts may be combined with objects devised by on-site design departments, and folk dance displays may be dreamed up by trained choreographers. The buildings displayed in the museum may be more elaborate and even larger than the originals on which they are based, and, therefore, convey an idealised view of culture.

The rising wealth of Asian populations and new opportunities to travel have provided political leaders with opportunities to promote their views in ways that could never before have been contemplated. The cultural village museums are designed to fulfil a number of functions, ranging from the need to promote international friendship through an understanding of culture to the desire to boost both domestic and foreign tourism. It would be tempting to dismiss these museums as Disney-like theme parks that rely on a mythological past dreamed up by advertisers; but there are good reasons for considering alternative explanatory frameworks. The museums clearly draw on the ethnographic traditions devised by Hazelius, and are not devoid of serious cultural and historical references. Taman Mini tries to make sense of a heterogeneous nation that was brought together by colonial intervention; Shenzhen reflects China's attitudes to its minority peoples. The essential elements of tradition persist in combination with other elements that are changing. Tradition, an essential element of identity, is constantly being created and recreated in response to new needs.

When considering the relationship between museums and national culture, one also needs to bear in mind the use made of tourism by governments seeking to reinforce their legitimacy. According to Picard, tourism was seized on as one of the means of restoring Indonesia's troubled image after the bloodbath of the 1965 alleged coup and counter-coup. The spectacle of thousands of holiday-makers queuing to visit Indonesia, especially Bali, enabled the 'New Order' to claim that it had earned the confidence and respect of the rest of the world. To a certain extent, the regime's methods were not unlike those of the Dutch earlier in the century; in both cases tourism was seen as an effective means of restoring respectability in regions blighted by strife. In Suharto's Indonesia the culture of Bali has become a resource, one of the 'cultural peaks' in the emerging national identity, whose function is to facilitate the growth of tourism and foster national pride (Picard 1993). Especially significant within this context appear to have been the ideas of Dewantara, who actively promoted the development of many regional cultures that would subsequently contribute to the emerging national culture. Together these cultural peaks, *puncak-puncak dan sari-sari kebudayaan*, would lay the rich foundations of a unique national culture (Nugroho-Heins 1995:

16–17). The rough edges that characterised real social relations between the different ethnic groups had to be smoothed over so as not to obscure the objectives of national unity. The individual cultures of Indonesia were re-evaluated, especially those being marketed as tourist destinations. Diversity in this new set of orderings had to be expressed aesthetically: hence the importance accorded to expressions of identity in an artistic manner. 'Balinese culture', like the other 'high cultures', is perceived as holding a similar position with regard to both tourism and Indonesian identity; its culture serves the needs of international tourism in Indonesia and the development of Indonesian national culture (Picard 1993: 94). Bali has been remoulded so that it conforms to the national philosophy of 'unity in diversity', and can therefore take its place in the national cultural village.

Tourism and Display Theory

The Folk Culture Villages exhibition draws on two strengths for its marketing success. Firstly, it continues a long tradition of representing folk culture in China, most notably in the genre of peasant painting. Joan Lebold Cohen describes this tradition as working in two basic styles (Cohen 1987: 145). The first is for propaganda, portraying local heroes and deep space. Some of the publicity for the Folk Culture Villages works in this way. This can be seen, for example, in the official catalogue, where a Naxi youth is depicted as 'a bright and brave ethnic youth'. The other style is 'decorative with strong geometric organisation and repeated patterns. These scenes are populated with happy peasants at work. The designs were inspired by textiles, embroidery, paper cut-outs and cartoons.' Such representations have not been confined to art publications, but were to be seen in the 1980s in such public places as Beijing International Airport, where Yuan Yunsheng's 'Water Festival, Song of Life' mural was drawn directly from the Dai Water Festival. Subsequently, other public commissions have employed specific minority references to emphasise a visual pluralism in contemporary art as a determined policy to incorporate non-Han culture. The incorporation always remains, however, either at an abstract or symbolic or, alternatively, at a resolutely practical level. The relationship between different groups or, perhaps more importantly, with majority Han culture never finds expression in the Folk Culture Village displays. The symbolic unity is portrayed as deriving from the physical proximity of different cultures on a single site. The real significance of the display is not to be found in the historical and political rhetoric. It draws from a quite new and a very different source.

Following the great success of its topographical predecessor and neighbour the 'Splendid China' exhibition, the Folk Culture Villages exhibition was designed to offer a kind of 'integration between tourism and cultures to suit the tourists' psychological needs'. If 'Splendid China' permits the visitor to see all the sights of China in one visit, then the Folk Culture Villages let one meet 'all of the people' in a similar whirlwind tour. People are psychologically curious, the Director of the Villages maintains, to see exotic things. This psychological propensity provides the basis for 'Chinese-Style Tourism', which actively seeks to reduce the trend towards Westernisation, particularly prevalent among the youth in contemporary China. The exhibition provides a focus for diffused nationalist sentiment with a determinedly non-Han focus. As the official catalogue concludes, the purpose of the display is to attempt a reflection of China's culture, as well as fostering its tourism, with distinctive national features.

Nevertheless, certain features of the Folk Culture Villages cannot be explained entirely by recourse to ideas of nationalist sentiment. The laser folk music fountain that plays a significant part in the evening entertainment provides pure tourist spectacle. The justification offered for its incorporation is somewhat unconvincing – that it signifies the advance of Chinese culture in a technological sense, and shows that Chinese civilisation is not a stagnant entity and that it can keep pace with the modern world. Furthermore, it is argued, all music played is genuine folk music, in line with the policy of 'Chinese-style tourism', which stipulates that every element in the display should consistently exclude foreign and non-folk influences (no foreign handicrafts, no MacDonald's hamburgers). The laser fountain, however, does not seem to obey the directive to avoid 'borrowing from others the idea of those mechanical amusements to try and attract foreign visitors'. We argue that the visitors to Shenzhen in general, and the Folk Culture Village in particular, approach the experience specifically as tourists. Obviously, the overseas and Hong Kong visitors fit the category. The other 80 per cent buy into this mode of experiencing as travellers partaking of the modern-style tourist attractions. The Villages provide a new kind of fusion between the tradition of the spectacle of the fairground, with its stress on exoticism and novelty, and the opportunity for visitors to become 'ethnographic subjects' – self-conscious consumers and evaluators of the spectacle and ethnic evidence before them. Visitors can still expect to be served by the performers (taking sedan-chair rides or making detailed interrogations of performers on aspects of the village life displayed), but they can also 'disappear' by hiring ethnic costume or joining in the dance performances. Telling a visitor from the authentic requires a good eye for shoes and hairstyles. The Folk Culture Villages are advertised both within China and extensively through the China Travel Service (Hong Kong) in the rest of the world. Other promotional activities, including overseas visits and performances, take the Villages out into the international tourist market. It is further reported that the personnel from the Folk Culture Villages are involved in consultancy exercises with thirty or more other countries to help establish similar Chinese folk villages in these countries. There is, so the Director of the Villages maintains, a vogue for building cultural villages. Two are planned in Japan and others elsewhere. The Hong Kong Institute for the Promotion of Chinese Culture is launching a series of programmes with Hong Kong schools to visit the Villages. The Institute is also forming a research committee and hoping to provide a means of integrating education on nationality into the Hong Kong civics curriculum.

The import–export potential of the Folk Culture Villages in Shenzhen is considerable. As Kirshenblatt-Gimblett notes, 'events staged specifically for visitors are well suited for export because they have already been designed for foreign audiences on tight schedules'. The Folk Culture Villages provide a highly visible index of political and cultural vision. At one level, it could be argued by those unconvinced by the spectacle, the Villages offer but a surface appearance not consistent with the texture of life within these minority communities. The performances and paraphernalia of costume are driven by the exigencies of the tourist show. They provide what Kirshenblatt-Gimblett calls 'the illusion of cultural transparency in the face of undeciphered complexity and the image of a society always on holiday'. Yet, at another level, it could be argued that the display represents an attempt – either in terms of domestic consumption or of a cultural export potential – to show China working through elements of a policy on multiethnic cohabitation, which, as the promoters are quick to point out, contrasts markedly with reality in other parts of the world. Whilst some of the display and philosophy may appear relatively unsophisticated to the world-travelled tourist, nevertheless, the Shenzhen Folk Culture Villages provide a site both physical and metaphorical for the pursuit of modernisation while at the same time aiming to preserve elements of tradition. It can be claimed with some confidence that the modernising element is well advanced in the development of the Folk Culture Villages. What remains to be seen, in the short and medium term, rather than the long, is whether the liveliness of the youthful minority displays can be sustained over time and under the pressure of mass tourism. Inevitably, political considerations will play a not insignificant part in the development of the Villages. The danger that they must face is that the actors cease to represent a credible present and become merely mechanical performers of a nationally prescribed culture.

Acknowledgements

We gratefully acknowledge the assistance received in preparing this chapter from Mr Ma Chi Man, Director of the Chinese Folk Culture Villages, Shenzhen, and Mr Van Lau, Chairman of the Hong Kong Institute for Promoting Chinese Culture, as well as to our colleagues in Hong Kong Polytechnic who have contributed both in interviews and discussion of ideas, Lydia Ngai, Matthew Turner and Phoebe Wong. We are also grateful for the researches of Kenichi Ohashi of Fukushima Women's College, Japan. Our thanks are also due to the British Academy, the Economic and Social Research Council and the Indonesian Institute of Sciences (LIPI). Earlier versions of this paper were published as two separate papers in the *Journal of Museum Ethnography*. We would also like to thank Stella Rhind and the Centre for South-East Asian Studies, University of Hull, for their generous help.

Notes

1. Internal documents on the preparation of the Folk Culture Villages' Employees Training Programme, March 1991.
2. Wang, Zhe, Chuang Shijie De Minzu cun Ziaojie. *Shenzhen Qing Niang*, October 1992: 14–16.
3. Chinese Folk Culture Villages Official Catalogue (1991). Shenzhen: 27.

References

Boon, J. A. (1977). *The Anthropological Romance of Bali, 1597–1972: Dynamic Perspectives in Marriage and Caste, Politics and Religion.* Cambridge: Cambridge University Press.
China Travel Services (Hong Kong) Ltd (1992). *Enjoyable Trip to China* (Travel Brochure).

Cohen, J. L. (1987). *The New Chinese Painting 1949–1986*. New York: Abrams.

Gittins, John (1992). Mudpaths Paved with Gold. *Weekend Guardian*, 1 August.

Graburn, N. (1976). *Ethnic and Tourist Arts: Cultural Expressions From the Fourth World*. Cambridge: Cambridge University Press.

Hubinger, Vaclav (1992). The Creation of Indonesian National Identity. *Prague Occasional Papers in Ethnology* 1: 1–35.

Hudson, K. (1987). *Museums of Influence*. Cambridge: Cambridge University Press.

May, B. (1978). *The Indonesian Tragedy*. London: Routledge & Kegan Paul.

Negota, J. (1986). *The Village and Folk Art Museum. Bucharest – Romania*. Bucharest.

Nugroho-Heins, M. I. (1995). Regional Culture and National Identity: Javanese Influence on the Development of a National Indonesian Culture. Unpublished conference paper, EUROSEAS, Leiden 1995.

Oates, T. S. (1992). Cultural Geography and Chinese Ethnic Tourism. *Journal of Cultural Geography* 12: 2.

Pemberton, John (1989). An Appearance of Order: A Politics of Culture in Colonial and Postcolonial Java. Ph.D. thesis, Cornell University.

Picard, Michel (1993). 'Cultural Tourism' in Bali: National Integration and Regional Differentiation. In M. Hitchcock, V. T. King and M. J. G. Parnwell (eds), *Tourism in South-East Asia*, pp. 71–98. London: Routledge.

Rhodius, H. and J. Darling (1980). *Walter Spies and Balinese Art*. Amsterdam: Terra, Zutphen.

Webb, T. D. (1994). Highly Structured Tourist Art – Form and Meaning of the Polynesian Cultural Centre. *Contemporary Pacific* (6)1: 59–86.

11

Packaging the Wild: Tourism Development in Alaska

Mark Nuttall

Introduction

It is a commonplace remark that tourism contributes to social change and the destruction of the very things that the industry both promotes and depends upon. Sociological and anthropological approaches that focus on the negative aspects of tourism have been concerned with, among other things, tourism as an extension of capitalist economic interests that involves the commoditisation of culture (e.g. Greenwood 1989), tourism as a form of imperialism (Nash 1989) and the impact of tourism on the environment (Budowski 1976; Parnwell 1993). Furthermore, it has also been noted that tourists themselves are often embarrassed by each other's presence (Jedrej and Nuttall 1996), and alternative travel destinations are sought out by those disillusioned with the development of mass tourism in previously remote and 'untouched' areas such as the Himalayas and South-east Asia. However, it appears that even relatively inaccessible parts of the world, such as the Arctic and high mountain regions, are not immune to the inexorable spread of global tourism. This has the effect of making the adventurous traveller in remote areas acutely aware of both the area's inaccessibility and its vulnerability, and this emerges as a dominant theme in much contemporary travel writing.

In many parts of the world, as more tour companies offer 'cultural' and 'anthropological' holidays, there are fears that this form of tourism will erode traditions and ways of life, and will come into conflict with local culture, as tourists typically do not share the values and ways of life of local residents. Furthermore, when tourism involves the exploitation of local resources, such as fish, wildlife and even the landscape

223

(when it is appropriated as scenery), there is often a direct threat posed to local residents who depend upon those resources. And when local culture is appropriated by outsiders and then exploited as a resource for economic gain (especially if income from tourism goes outside the local area), for some local people tourism development and the presence of tourists can only nurture a sense of alienation and imminent social change.

Despite recognising that local cultures can be and are disturbed and affected by tourism, not all sociologists and anthropologists involved in researching tourism subscribe to the view that it is necessarily negative for all host communities. Rather, tourism can benefit an area by bringing prosperity and employment, especially when industry and agriculture or fishing is in decline (e.g. Villepontoux 1981). Tourism is also considered to play an important role in strategies for both sustainable development and environmental conservation, while Lanfant (1995: 6), refusing to see tourism as simply as an exogenous force, has argued that some communities are not always passive but 'often seize upon tourism as a means of communication to display their existence and to establish their own power'. In this way, local communities can use tourism to develop strategies for self-determination and cultural survival.

This chapter discusses the development of tourism in Alaska, and considers indigenous involvement in the tourism industry. The Alaskan tourism industry depends on images of wild nature and its frontier history, while the emergence of locally-owned and controlled tour companies has given many Alaskan Native communities opportunities to develop cash-earning enterprises and at the same time gain control of an industry that outsiders have otherwise dominated. Alaskan Native leaders argue that tourism will form part of diversified local economies as traditional subsistence activities become more marginalised, while at the same time local control allows communities to regulate the numbers of visitors to Native lands. Native-owned tourism is also linked to the politics of community empowerment, with some companies arguing that cultural preservation is only possible through cultural presentation and by educating visitors about indigenous ways of life.

While claiming to reject the marketing of Alaska as a land of super-latives and extremes, Native tour companies none the less also play on the idea of Alaska as a 'wilderness' and 'last frontier' to attract tourists who are looking to experience both an Arctic landscape and authentic and traditional Native culture. By doing so, they construct indigenous views of the environment and represent indigenous culture for touristic consumption. In the process local rituals and events, which are often private, become public cultural performances. Above all, by marketing themselves as a tourist attraction, indigenous communities in Alaska attempt to empower themselves and constantly reconstruct and renegotiate cultural identity.

Tourism in Alaska: In Search of the Last Frontier

Currently Alaska's major growth industry, travel and tourism generates $1.4 billion in revenues each year, with over $50 million of direct revenues going to the State of Alaska (Alaska Division of Tourism 1995). And with a workforce of 20,000 people (including seasonal employees), the visitor industry (as tourism is officially known in Alaska) is one of the state's main sources of employment. Although tourism in Alaska accounts for only about 1 per cent of gross state product, it contributes more to the state's economy than the timber industry (Alaska Division of Economic Development 1994). Anticipating the national White House Conference on Travel and Tourism, called by President Bill Clinton and held in Washington DC in October 1995, the Alaska Division of Tourism sponsored a state summit on tourism and travel in Alaska in April 1995, which underlined the state government's commitment to expanding further the visitor industry.[1]

Tourists have been travelling to and in Alaska for over a century, ever since it became a possession of the United States in 1867. John Muir, the Scots-born naturalist who was almost a zealot in his worship of the natural world, was one of the first travellers to popularise south-east Alaska in his written accounts of his journeys. By the mid-1880s, the Pacific Coast Steamship Company was operating regular trips through south-east Alaska's Inside Passage, carrying as many as 5,000 passengers in a summer season. Annual shiploads of tourists to south-east Alaska helped to generate a local industry of Native crafts and curios by the beginning of the twentieth century (Lee 1991). Following the Gold Rush of 1889, more tourists (including among their number many vacationing gold prospectors) ventured to the Far North, while Eskimos from the coasts of Seward Peninsula and the Bering Strait were attracted to new settlements of pioneers and seasonal visitors, where they found a ready market for ivory carvings. And as more steamer services became available on the Yukon River, as well as more extensive coastal routes, tourists were able to visit parts of Alaska, such as Nome, the Aleutian Islands, and the interior, that had previously been accessible only to explorers, scientists, the military and government officials.

Tourism increased steadily during and after the First World War, and the building of roads and the completion of the Alaska Railroad enhanced the possibilities of travel within Alaska, enabling more tourists to catch a glimpse of Mt McKinley, North America's highest mountain and the very symbol of Alaska's wild nature. During the Second World War, the Alaska Highway was constructed to provide, through Canada, a land link for the military between Alaska and the rest of the United States. Following the war, and since the 1960s especially, it has become an adventure in itself to drive the Alaska Highway – and some 13 per cent of summer visitors enter Alaska by road from Canada. Alaska has steadily become a popular tourist destination for both independent travellers and those who visit on a package tour. Since the mid-1980s the number of tourists has increased by 50 per cent to over one million a year. And it is now possible to visit virtually any part of the state. For example, day trips to Barrow, the most northerly town in the United States, offer the tourists a chance to walk on tundra and dip their toes in the frigid waters of the Arctic Ocean, while for the more adventurous Alaska offers opportunities for cross-country skiing, dog mushing, climbing and wildlife watching. Many areas, such as remoter parts of the Brooks Range in northern Alaska, are being opened up to tourism for the first time as popular destinations such as Denali National Park become overcrowded and people have to make reservations for accommodation several months in advance.

As in the early days of Alaskan tourism, Alaska continues to be marketed as a land of superlatives and extremes, where nature can still be experienced as raw and untouched. Tour brochures (as tour brochures are apt to do: see for example Selwyn 1993) reproduce predictable stereotypical descriptions and images of pristine wilderness, fascinating Native culture and abundant wildlife, so that a trip to Alaska will be an unforgettable encounter with majestic scenery, gold rush history, indigenous people, and a once-in-a-lifetime opportunity to see whales, spawning salmon, bears and other animals. And while tourism is confined primarily to the months between mid-May and mid-September, there is also a modest number of winter visitors. Japanese tourists are attracted to interior Alaska, especially the area around Fairbanks, in the coldest, darkest months to view (and to consummate their marriages under) the *aurora borealis*. The demand is such that a specialist Japanese-owned tour operator, Japan–Alaska Tours (which is based in the small town of North Pole, a place renowned in Alaska for both its Santa Claus House and its religious fundamentalism – neither of which is apparently linked to the other) caters exclusively to intrepid Japanese. But tourism industry officials wish to develop Alaska as a winter destination for people from other countries as well, and are beginning to encourage investment in winter sports as well as marketing annual dog-sledding races such as the Iditarod and the Yukon Quest as international events.

While the wildness of nature is packaged as something to be experienced, Alaska is perhaps more famously marketed as 'the last frontier', and several writers have commented that the image of Alaska as the last frontier has long been a potent one for many Alaskans and for people living elsewhere in the United States. For example, Nash (1982: 272) has written that Alaska has long been valued 'as a permanent frontier where Americans could visit their past both in person and as an "idea"'. The image of life on the last frontier is fundamental to the construction of Alaskan cultural identity. At opposite ends of the social and cultural spectrum of the state are categories of 'Native Alaskans', who are usually and for official purposes defined as the indigenous peoples (such as Eskimos, Athabascans and Aleuts), and 'non-Alaskans', who are either recent arrivals or transient residents (known as Cheechakos), and tourists and visitors. In between there are categories of 'genuine Alaskans', people of long-term residence born in Alaska of Euro-American or other parentage, and often called 'sourdoughs'. The history of Alaska is also one of migration and residential mobility, and newcomers have in common the fact that they are migrants to the last frontier, and this contributes to the defining and working out of a sense of identity amongst them (Cuba 1987).

Synonymous with the idea of the frontier is the history of gold-mining, and tourism development in towns such as Skagway, Nome and Fairbanks has capitalised on nostalgia associated with the gold rush and the social character of the pioneer. Although abandoned mining machinery litters many hiking trails, gold-mining is still an active industry in Alaska, and tours of active gold dredges are available during the summer months of operation. Panning for gold in Alaskan rivers and streams is often mentioned in tour brochures as one of the many activities available to the tourist. In Fairbanks, visitors can attend turn-of-the-century dance-hall revues in Alaskaland and listen to daily readings of the poetry of Robert Service in rustic bars such as the 'Malemute Saloon'. Jarvenpa (1994: 29) has argued that the imagery and mythology of the gold rush, in particular the lore associated with the heroic pioneer, has contributed to a process of cultural commoditisation, which he calls 'Klondikephilia'. Although writing on tourism in Canada's Yukon Territory, Jarvenpa (1994: 42) has remarked how 'there is a pilgrimage-like quality to Klondike tourism as thousands of Americans journey to the remote locale each summer, in essence, to witness a re-enactment of a chapter of their own history'.

But the Alaskan frontier is also a modern industrial frontier, and the 800-mile Trans-Alaska Pipeline, once at the very centre of debate about the future of Alaska (Coates 1993), is now marketed as a tourist attraction, while several companies offer one-day tours from Anchorage and Fairbanks of the oil-production complex of Prudhoe Bay on the Arctic coast of the North Slope. Just as visitors consume the image of the lone pioneer who endured isolation in a harsh environment, while imagining themselves to be modern-day pioneers as they travel Alaska's roads in their camper vans and recreation vehicles, they can also see for themselves the power of late-twentieth-century technology that harnesses resources vital for the economy of the nation. The Dalton Highway, a rough dirt road linking Prudhoe Bay with roads just north of Fairbanks, which was constructed for the exclusive use of pipeline and oil-industry-related vehicles, has recently become part of the state highway system and has been opened to the public, making it possible for anyone with the time, inclination and money to drive to the North Slope of Alaska from virtually anywhere in the United States. Yet, while responding to the call of the Arctic wild, it seems that tourists driving the Dalton Highway wish to be reminded that they are still in the United States of America. During summer 1995, a local Alaskan newspaper, the *Fairbanks Daily News-Miner* published articles reporting on tourists using the road, many of whom complained about the lack of facilities and outhouses. One article related how 'Wisconsites Emil and Dorothy Pedersen, on their way back to Fairbanks, described sleepless nights in the omniprescent sunlight and sightings of grizzly bears, musk oxen herds, countless caribou and moose . . . As for the facilities at the north end, Emil Pedersen said, "There isn't any. You want to buy a quart of milk, you can't buy a quart of milk," he said.'[2] Public access to the Dalton Highway continues to inform heated debate between developers, who see wilderness as a resource to be exploited in return for more tourist dollars, and environmentalists, who fear the day when hamburger restaurants will open to cater for tourist demand along the road.

In Search of Native Culture

Increasing numbers of tourists to Alaska now cite indigenous culture as the main attraction of the state after scenery and wildlife. Some visit Alaska with the sole aim of having an ethnographic experience. One tourist to Alaska, a London investment banker who travelled to Fairbanks, Barrow and Nome during summer 1995, said quite simply of his reason for visiting Alaska, 'I want to break bread with the Inuit.' Having experienced an organised tour to a Native community and having visited Denali National Park, through local contacts he was able to travel to Inupiaq Eskimo villages on the Bering Strait coast, often in the company of local people. Along the way he was able to learn something of the social and political situation of Alaska's indigenous people – and he fulfilled his ambition of meeting people in their homes. As has been well documented by anthropologists, this kind of ethnographic tourism is increasingly popular. Linked to the continuing preoccupation amongst tourists from Europe and North America with visiting non-Western countries (Zurick 1995: 113), there is a growing market eager to consume images of indigenous peoples and to understand something of their relationship with the environment. As Zurick puts it, 'If contemporary Western society no longer holds a valid myth . . . then that may be why people search other cultures – to discover that which may be lost in their own' (1995: 133).

The peripherality of Alaskan villages (many of which are only accessible by air) and traditional Native culture is attractive to tourists in search of authenticity. Recognising this, tourism development agencies in Alaska and other parts of the circumpolar north, such as Yukon Territory and the Northwest Territories, have long used images of indigenous culture as a marketing strategy, and tourist brochures stress the ancient relationship between people and the land. And tourism in the Arctic has been given a boost over the last decade by not only the ease of travel, but by the popular writings of people such as Barry Lopez (1986).

In contrast to the experiences of the investment banker mentioned above, it is very difficult for travellers to visit Native villages independently. The Alaska Native Claims Settlement Act of 1971 made many villages and their lands in effect private reserves, making it necessary for visitors to have permits before entering a community. Concerned with alcohol and illegal drugs entering communities, village elders often meet aircraft that land and check people's baggage. Together with a suspicion and distrust of strangers (perhaps because many visitors to Alaskan villages are representatives of state and federal agencies), tourists can encounter hostility if arriving unannounced and with no local contacts. As well as the expense of flying to a village there is often a scarcity, if not a complete absence, of visitor accommodation, and tourists can place strain on local stores, which have limited supplies and are used to supplying local demand only. The easiest and safest way is to travel on an organised tour.

From the end of the Second World War the development of organised tourism in rural Alaska, where tourists could 'experience' Eskimo culture, was started by non-Natives. Many local people were also uninterested in being involved in it as a business, and remained exotic attractions rather than entrepreneurs (Smith 1989). Smith (ibid.: 63–4) has commented on some of the insidious aspects of tourism in rural Alaska when, in the mid-1960s, tourists visiting Kotzebue offended Eskimos with endless, repetitive questions and disturbed local people in their daily work. Smith noted how 'Eskimo women began to refuse photographers, then erected barricades to shield their work from tourist eyes, and some finally resorted to hiring a taxi to haul seals and other game to the privacy of their homes for processing' (ibid.). Tour companies are sensitive to the intrusive activities of tourists and, before landing in Kotzebue today, Alaska Airlines requests that people on its tours to the village refrain from taking photographs of the Native tour guide as they disembark from the aircraft.

Taking photographs of the locals is only one of many exploitative touristic pursuits, however. Residents of many Alaskan communities express concern over the increasing numbers of visitors who use Native-owned lands for recreation and sports hunting. Subsistence and sports fishing often come into conflict, for example. On Alaska's Kenai Peninsula south of Anchorage, the runs of king salmon in June and July each year bring several thousand fishermen to the Kenai River, making it the most heavily fished river in Alaska. In a practice known in Alaska as 'combat fishing', fishermen jostle for elbow room on the riverbanks while speedboats crowd the water. Fish that are caught are weighed and then thrown back into the water, only to run the risk of being caught as they make their way up-river to spawn by several more fishermen. The sports fishermen come from many parts of North America as well as from Alaska's growing and sprawling metropolitan area of Anchorage, and they disrupt the traditional subsistence fishery of the Kenaitze, a Dena'ina Athabascan tribe. The Kenaitze argue that the practice of catching, weighing and then throwing back the fish does not respect the spirit of the fish, which may then refuse to be taken by Native fishermen who fish primarily for food.

The appearance of tourists in Alaskan villages is also seasonal. When tourists do arrive in the summer months, tourism may involve a high proportion of local people in servicing directly, and indirectly, the needs and demands of tourists, rather than indigenously generated needs. In this way tourism produces dependency relationships; and local people may also become dependent on outsiders for seasonal or long-term employment when primary industries, such as fishing, decline. Tourism often develops in areas at the same time as they are experiencing rapid social change, and while it contributes to social and economic transition, as Gilligan (1987) has observed, the success of tourism can become necessary for the economic survival of some areas. As one man from the Alutiiq community of Old Harbour on Kodiak Island put it to the author, 'In fifty years there will be no subsistence or fishing. We have to think of alternative ways of making a living and tourism is one of them.' Yet, Alaskan tourism creates low-wage seasonal jobs, and much of the tourism industry does not benefit local communities: the earnings go outside the state.[3]

Alaskan Native communities are beset by severe social and economic problems. But tourists visiting Alaska are looking to experience authentic and traditional Native culture, and do not want to be presented with lectures on social problems and how Alaskan villages are ravaged by unemployment, alcoholism and substance abuse. Some things are worthy of the attention of the tourist, while there are other things that they cannot see, such as 'hidden behind the ceremonies and the masks, the poverty and the suffering that would dismay them' (Zurick 1995: 158). Similarly, evidence of modernity and change is either hidden or played down. Locals dress in traditional clothing to meet tourists and to perform for them, men hold demonstrations of how to make hunting and fishing equipment, and banquets of traditional foods are laid on by women, who also sell their homemade crafts while visitors munch on dried salmon.

Following Greenwood's (1989) influential anthropological perspective on tourism as cultural commoditisation, Alaskan Native culture is appropriated as a commodity by tour companies, who then package it and sell it. Greenwood's argument, based on his own work in a Basque village, is that the cultural meanings of local rituals and events that have religious significance and importance for community identity become commoditised, depriving local people of the meanings of vital societal events. Local rituals and events, which are often private, become public cultural performances subject to the agendas and demands of tourists, tour companies and tourist boards. This perspective sees local 'colourful' and 'ethnic' rituals as being exploited by the tourism industry for profit, and for consumption by tourists. And the sense that cultural events become colourful displays is heightened by the fact that tourists themselves are also deprived of understanding cultural meanings. For example, organised tours to Barrow include a display of Inupiaq Eskimo dancing and a blanket toss on the beach, where a person, usually a child, is thrown in the air by a group of people holding a large bearded seal skin or walrus skin. Tourists are invited to participate, by holding the skin and helping to throw the child in the air. On the occasions this was witnessed by the author, the tour guide did not explain the significance of the blanket toss: that it was practised traditionally so that a person might glimpse bowhead whales beyond the pack ice, and thus herald the beginning of the spring whaling season.

In a sense tourists induce tradition, and their appearance provokes a search by the host community for those aspects of culture that visitors value as traditional (cf. Jedrej and Nuttall 1996), with the particularities of local history, subsistence lifestyles and indigenous environmental knowledge underpinning the cultural production of authenticity. In this way, tourism contributes to an indigenous representation of Alaskan Native culture, such as dancing, singing, storytelling, mask-making, the sewing of skins, basketry and ivory-carving, as for ever traditional. Above all, the people themselves are portrayed as remaining in harmony with their environment, in complete contrast to those for whom they are performing.

Local Involvement in Environmental Tourism

Capitalising on tradition as a resource and determined that communities should benefit directly from tourism, several Native-owned tour companies have emerged in Alaska over the last few years. This development of a Native-owned tourism industry is linked both to the emergence of specialist adventure tourism and eco-tourism and to the politics of community empowerment. The tour companies are owned by village corporations, which were established as profit-making enterprises by the Alaska Native Claims Settlement Act of 1971. Native communities see in tourism an opportunity for developing cash-earning enterprises based on the desire of other people to experience wilderness and visit non-Western societies, and at the same time for gaining control of an industry that outsiders have otherwise dominated. There is an indigenous political movement, not only in Alaska but throughout the circumpolar north, that emphasises the importance of indigenous knowledge for sustainable development; and locally-controlled cultural tourism also represents an opportunity for Alaskan Native communities to educate visitors about indigenous ways of life and about human–environment relationships. Alaskan Native leaders see the local control of tourism as an industry that can form part of a highly-diversified local economy and at the same time regulate the numbers of visitors to Native lands.

As a promotional leaflet of the Alaska Native Tourism Council puts it, the Native peoples of Alaska 'welcome visitors with a smile' and the tourist to Alaska is invited to visit Alaska's Native peoples 'for a few hours or for a few days'.[4] Native-owned tour companies produce leaflets and brochures that emphasise the environmentally-friendly and educational nature of the tours they offer, in contrast to the mass tourism in other parts of Alaska close to urban centres and linked to the state highway system. The casual visitor to Alaska, with money enough to spare, can choose from a number of 'cultural experiences' that range from one-day visits to Inupiaq Eskimo villages such as Barrow (marketed as the 'Top of the World') and Kotzebue, where they are greeted by traditional dancers and can learn about whaling and the local subsistence culture, to journeys of several days along the Koyukon River, in the company of Athabascan hunters and fishermen. None of these tours are cheap, and on top of the cost of reaching Alaska in the first place tourists can expect to pay over $500 for a one-day tour to Barrow from Anchorage. Tourists making an excursion from Anchorage to Nome or Kotzebue would pay almost $500, and once there have a choice of extending their itinerary (and parting with a further $300 or so) to include sightseeing in surrounding villages only accessible by air, but where they will 'learn about the subsistence lifestyle' of their 'friendly hosts'.

Visitors with little time and money can also attempt to gain insight into Native culture by visiting villages close to Anchorage (such as the Dena'ina Athabascan Eklutna Village Historical Park), Fairbanks (which is connected to several Athabascan villages by road and also has a Native village in Alaskaland, the local theme park), and other villages in south and south-east Alaska accessible by road or coastal ferry. Most Native communities are able to provide regular guided tours. For example, half-hour tours of Eklutna Village Historical Park begin every thirty minutes, and in Sitka in south-east Alaska the Sitka Tribe of Alaska operate bus tours that give visitors the history of Sitka from the perspective of the indigenous Tlingit tribes. Yet tourists can only hope to glimpse a little of what their tour companies have selected to show them. Yukon River Tours, for example, which is owned by the Athabascan people of Stevens Village, take tourists on a one and a half hour-long trip on the Yukon River to visit, not the village itself, but a fishcamp and the Stevens Village Cultural Centre, a considerable distance downriver. Yukon River Tours describes itself in its brochures as 'dedicated to offering environmentally responsible and educational tours for all to enjoy and appreciate' and the emphasis of its tours is on hardship, survival and tradition in a remote region 'where the air is clean and the land is blessed with an abundance of wildlife and natural beauty'. Tourists are told that they are to 'embark on a journey that others have only read about' and that they will be 'encouraged to peek inside the smokehouse' and will be able to 'participate in the traditional ritual of Salmon harvesting or just relax and enjoy the peaceful majestic beauty of this truly unique last frontier'. They are lectured on Athabascan culture and customs, and the exhibitions at the Stevens Village Cultural Centre focus on life on the Yukon River in the 1930s and 1940s.

Another Athabascan tour company is Arctic Village Tours, owned by the Gwich'in people of Arctic Village in north-east Alaska. Residents of Arctic Village already require visitors to have a permit to visit the community, and Arctic Village Tours offers one day cultural tours from Fairbanks, as well as overnight 'wilderness' excursions. In this way, Arctic Village residents can control how many people visit their community and how they get there, and ensure that they spend money. In 1995, a one-day tour from Fairbanks cost $250, while an overnight wilderness excursion cost $150 per person per day, plus a return air fare of $260.

The Arctic Village Tours brochure describes the Gwich'in as 'a people anxious to share their village and the simple pleasures of life in this far-north locale with visitors from southern climes'. A visitor to Arctic Village will have already read promotional tour leaflets produced by Arctic Village Tours, from which they will learn that the village is the northernmost Indian community in the world, that the Gwich'in are 'a people dependent physically, culturally, and spiritually on a way of life that includes a large measure of hunting, fishing, berry gathering and other subsistence skills. A people deeply committed to the care of the land that sustains and nourishes them'. Furthermore, the residents of Arctic Village are marketing themselves as 'the Last Indians on the Last Frontier', and Arctic Village Tours informs its potential clients that

> you will set foot on the Last Frontier where you will experience the traditional Native culture. This is not a commercialized attraction, but a chance to experience life on the VERY LAST FRONTIER as it exists today. It is one of the very last areas in North America to be touched by Western Culture which has had both negative and positive impact. CULTURAL PRESERVATION through CULTURAL PRESENTATION, while educating the public about our traditional way of life is the aim of our tourism program.

A one-day visit to Arctic Village from Fairbanks (from 9 a.m. to 4 p.m.) includes a guided tour of the village by local residents (contrast this turn of events with Smith (1989), who noted that guides in the past were non-Natives with little experience or knowledge of the Arctic), a lunch consisting of traditional food, and presentations of songs and dances. Overnight journeys have wildlife-watching focus, sports fishing, and hiking. In a similar vein, Athabasca Cultural Journeys offers a wilderness experience of several days' duration on the Koyukuk River. As their brochure enticingly puts it

Come, share our culture with us. Let us teach you to read animal signs, set a fish net, and learn traditional Athabascan crafts. Or listen as we share ancient myths and folklore of our ancestors. Our Native culture is alive and well, not something to experience in a museum. We invite you to become part of our culture and experience the spirit of this great land called Alaska.

Such indigenous representation plays on the image of Alaska as the last frontier and a remote wilderness, and contributes to the perpetuation of the myth of the Arctic environment as hostile, wild, untamed, and pristine. In the imagination of the tourist, primitive Native culture still survives in remote Alaska, and Native-owned tour companies try their best not to disappoint. This is in stark contrast to the political reaction to the Arctic's being labelled a 'frontier' or 'wilderness' from indigenous leaders, who have called instead for international recognition of Arctic lands as *homelands* (Nuttall 1992). In both international and regional contexts the Arctic's indigenous peoples construct for themselves an identity as custodians of the Arctic environment; but one consequence of the politicisation of Arctic peoples has been the emergence of an indigenous environmentalism that appeals to and emphasises enduring spiritual values and traditional culture. That this should underpin indigenous representation for tourists is entirely consistent with current indigenous discourse.

Concluding Remarks

A currently fashionable argument in social science tourist literature is that, done well, tourism can empower local communities by 'giving them a pride in their communities' development' (Whelan 1991: 4). In Alaska, Native communities are participating in environmental and cultural tourism projects at both planning and implementation stages, as well as benefiting from the outcome. Yet whatever labels Native tour companies use for their tourism (sustainable, environmentally responsible, etc.), and while an aim may be cultural preservation or cultural conservation, they are still involved in commercial ventures that need to make a profit and may not be entirely compatible with traditional values (see for example Hinch 1995). Anders and Anders (1987), for instance, have written on the conflict between individualism and the profit motivations of Alaskan Native corporate organisational culture established by the Alaska Native Claims Settlement Act, and the communal, kinship-based values of Alaskan Native villages. More research on specific case studies is needed before it is clear whether tourism development is generating Native prosperity at the cost of further erosion of local culture.

Alaskan Native communities, through the activities and marketing skills of both outsiders and Native peoples themselves, have become tourism marketplaces where visitors can consume images of aboriginal people and the wilderness in which they live, purchase traditional handicrafts, and view staged culture. In controlling the level and extent of tourism development Native communities are seemingly enjoying a degree of empowerment consistent with other aspects of political and economic development made possible by land claims settlements. But host communities may not necessarily be able to exercise total control over what their guests can and cannot do. As environmental, cultural and other forms of alternative tourism continue to grow in popularity and expand into more peripheral regions of the world, local communities may not be able to withstand entirely tourist demands for services – a situation evident in many parts of the world. As environmental, cultural and other forms of alternative tourism in Alaska continue to grow in popularity, Native communities may not be able to withstand entirely demands from tourists that may conflict with local ways of life and divide community opinion over the maintenance of tradition *vis-à-vis* perceived benefits of change. Already, some Alaskan Native communities face demands from tourists, who expect to see authentic, traditional culture. By way of response they construct an identity as a people living in areas largely untouched by modernity and change, and both hosts and guests conspire together in the production of authenticity.

Acknowledgements

This chapter draws on material from research funded by the Economic and Social Research Council. I would also like to thank Asish Dey for his generosity, for being an excellent ethnographic tourist, and for allowing me to observe him on the trail, and Anita Dey-Nuttall for her companionship in Alaska and, as ever, her unfailing criticism.

Notes

1. Since the eighteenth century, Alaska's economy has been characterised by cycles of 'boom' and 'bust'. From its accredited Russian discovery by Vitus Bering in 1741, the development of Alaska, as of other parts of the circumpolar north, has followed the exploitation of its natural resources. From the beginning, when Bering's expedition returned with sea otter furs, Alaska was prominent in both the Russian and British fur trades. Fur seals and sea

otters, together with a number of fur-bearing land mammals, were exploited to near-extinction over a period of 140 years. Whalers from New England hunted the bowhead whale in the waters of Bering Strait from 1847, and, from the 1880s, gold-mining provided the foundation for the expansion of the Alaskan economy. With the discovery of vast reserves of oil and gas at Prudhoe Bay on the Arctic North Slope in 1968, the agenda for Alaska's future economic development was set. However, oil production is now declining, and there are doubts as to whether any other industry or combination of industries can provide a viable alternative. Yet while politicians, economists and industrialists debate what natural resources will underpin the state economy, tourism is considered important for the future.

2. 'Dalton Breaks in the Tourists', *Fairbanks Daily News-Miner*, 27 June 1995.

3. By far the largest numbers of tourists to the state come in the summer months on cruise ships to south-east Alaska. The cruise companies are based outside Alaska, and the short stops that each ship makes in south-east communities are usually only long enough for passengers to buy souvenirs. Similarly, backpackers and other budget travellers spend relatively little on accommodation.

4. Alaska Native Tourism Council 1994, *Alaska Native Journeys* 4.

References

Alaska Division of Economic Development (1994). *Alaska: Economy Performance Report 1994*. Juneau: Department of Commerce and Economic Development.

Alaska Division of Tourism (1995). *Good News Travels*, Spring Issue. Juneau: Department of Commerce and Economic Development.

Alaska Native Tourism Council (1994). *Alaska Native Journeys* 4. Anchorage: The Council.

Anders, G. and K. Anders (1987). Incompatible Goals in Unconventional Organizations: The Politics of Alaska Native Corporations. In T. Lane (ed.), *Developing America's Northern Frontier*. Lanham: University Press of America.

Budowski, G. (1976). Tourism and Environmental Conservation: Conflict, Coexistence, or Symbiosis? *Environmental Conservation* 3: 27–31.

Coates, P. (1993). *The Trans-Alaska Pipeline Controversy*. Fairbanks: University of Alaska Press.

Cuba, L. (1987). *Identity and Community on the Alaskan Frontier*. Philadelphia: Temple University Press.

Gilligan, J. H. (1987). Visitors, Outsiders and Tourists in a Cornish Town. In M. Bouquet and M. Winter (eds), *Who from their Labours Rest? Conflict and Practice in Rural Tourism*. Aldershot: Avebury.

Greenwood, D. (1989). Culture by the Pound: An Anthropological Perspective on Tourism as Cultural Commoditization. In V. L. Smith (ed.), *Hosts and Guests: The Anthropology of Tourism*. Philadelphia: University of Pennslyvania Press.

Hinch, T. D. (1995). Aboriginal People in the Tourism Economy of Canada's Northwest Territories. In C. H. Hall and M. E. Johnson (eds), *Polar Tourism: Tourism in the Arctic and Antarctic Regions*. Chichester: Wiley.

Jarvenpa, R. (1994). Commoditization versus Cultural Integration: Tourism and Image Building in the Klondike. *Arctic Anthropology* 31(1): 26–46.

Jedrej, C. and M. Nuttall (1996). *White Settlers: The Impact of Rural Repopulation in Scotland*. Luxemburg: Harwood Academic Publishers.

Lanfant, M. (1995). Introduction. In M. Lanfant *et al.* (eds), *International Tourism: Identity and Change*. London: Sage.

Lee, M. (1991). Appropriating the Primitive: Turn of the Century Collection and Display of Native Alaskan Art. *Arctic Anthropology* 28(1): 6–15.

Lopez, B. (1986). *Arctic Dreams: Imagination and Desire in a Northern Landscape*. London: Macmillan.

Nash, D. (1989). Tourism as a Form of Imperialism. In V. L. Smith (ed.), *Hosts and Guests: The Anthropology of Tourism*. Philadelphia: University of Pennsylvania Press.

Nash, R. (1982). *Wilderness and the American Mind*. New Haven and London: Yale University Press.

Parnwell, M. (1993). Environmental Issues and Tourism in Thailand. In M. Hitchcock, V. King and M. Parnwell (eds), *Tourism in South-East Asia*. London and New York: Routledge.

Nuttall, M. (1992). *Arctic Homeland: Kinship, Community and Development in Northwest Greenland*. Toronto: University of Toronto Press.

Selwyn, T. (1993). Peter Pan in South-East Asia: Views from the Brochures. In M. Hitchcock, V. King and M. Parnwell (eds), *Tourism in South-East Asia*. London and New York: Routledge.

Smith, V. L. (1989). Eskimo Tourism: Micro-Models and Marginal Men. In V. L. Smith (ed.), *Hosts and Guests: The Anthropology of Tourism*. Philadelphia: University of Pennsylvania Press.

Villepontoux, E. J. (1981). *Tourism and Social Change in a French Alpine Community*. London: UMI.

Whelan, T. (ed.) (1991). *Nature Tourism: Managing for the Environment*. Washington DC: Island Press.

Zurick, D. (1995). *Errant Journeys: Adventure Travel in the Modern Age*. Austin: University of Texas Press.

Index

239